Praise for
A WEAK AMERICAN IN RUSSIA & UKRAINE

"A delightful read for any American who has tried to jump into the Slavic world. Parchomenko is an American with soul (something our Slavic detractors think impossible). He manages to capture many of those fascinating moments of genuine incomprehension between Americans and Slavs and, interestingly, sometimes among Russians and Ukrainians as well. Anyone who can defend Ronald McDonald to Kyivians and Muscovites is anything but a weak American."

-Dr. Blair Ruble, *Director of the Kennan Institute for Advanced Russian Studies, Washington, D.C.*

AWeakAm Books

A Weak American in Russia & Ukraine

Adventures & Misadventures
Living among the Natives

Walter Parchomenko

A WEAK AMERICAN IN RUSSIA & UKRAINE. Copyright © 2012 by Walter Parchomenko. All rights reserved. No part of this book may be reproduced or transmitted in any form or by any means, electronic or mechanical, including photocopying, recording, or by any information storage and retrieval system, without written permission from the publisher.

A WEAK AMERICAN IN RUSSIA & UKRAINE (trade paperback edition) may be purchased for business or promotional use or for special sales. For information, please write to: A Weak American Books, 205 N. Cleveland St., Arlington, VA 22201.

Visit us on the web at www.aweakamerican.com

Design & Illustration by Vikki Chu and Guy Parkhomenko

ISBN-13: 978-1478336341
ISBN-10: 147833634X
LCCN: 2012904289

Dedicated to George Carlin, Jerry Seinfeld & Larry David, in appreciation for filling our aching souls with the best medicine, laughter.

"Comedy at its finest is a dark and beautiful art."
-Tony Hendra, "Introduction" to *Last Words*, George Carlin with Tony Hendra (NY: Free Press, 2009)

Contents

1. Coming to America   **1**
2. The Post-Soviet System   **8**
3. The Soulless American   **13**
4. Russian "Holiday of a Lifetime"   **17**
5. Slavic Khamstvo and the Sovok Mentality   **21**
6. Flying Slavic Style   **27**
7. A Smoker's Paradise   **32**
8. The Smiling American   **36**
9. The Generously Proportioned American   **40**
10. Slavic Public Toilets   **45**
11. The Sweaty American   **50**
12. Mayo Heaven   **55**
13. My Khrushchovka   **60**
14. Howling Stray Dogs   **66**
15. My Weak American Cat   **70**
16. Meet My Slavic Neighbors   **74**
17. Fornicating Flies   **80**
18. Slavic Attack Pigeons   **85**
19. Dr. Kovalenko, Master of Sports Medicine   **89**

20. Inside Ukraine's Collapsing Medical System **94**

21. Navigating Slavic Minefields **99**

22. Slavic Bat Radar **103**

23. Slavic Formula-1 Drivers **107**

24. My Slavic Mega-Market **111**

25. School of Defensive Walking **117**

26. Sexpats on the Post-Soviet Playground **122**

27. Khytrist a Key to Understanding Slavic Women **127**

28. Looking for Love in all the Wrong Places **131**

29. My Lovely Russian Rose **135**

30. In Defense of Little Red Sports Cars **139**

31. In Defense of Slavic Women **142**

32. In Defense of Slavic Men **147**

33. Po-nashemu—"It's a Slavic Thing, You Wouldn't Understand" **151**

34. Slavic Go-Slow Lifestyle **157**

35. Vodka & the Weak American **163**

36. My Friend Kolya **167**

37. Slavic Faux VIPs & Elite **173**

38. Slavic Fashion Police **179**

39. Orthopedic Consequences of Foot Candy **184**

40. A Proud Tradition of Stealing & Cheating **188**

41. Your American Cash Is No Good **194**

42. Slavic Bureaucracy & the 7 Circles of Hell **197**

43. Western Union Slavic-Style **202**

44. In Defense of Ronald McDonald **205**

45. Swimming with the Slavs **209**

46. Ukraine's Ticking Time-Bomb **214**

47. Abraham Maslow in Moscow & Kyiv **219**

48. Coldest Winter in 80 Years **224**

49. World Smile Day in Kyiv 2010 **229**

50. Slavic Humor **233**

51. Slavic Superstitions & My Tortured Childhood **237**

52. Slavic Fear of Cold Drinks & Deadly Drafts **241**

53. Moscow Summer 2011 **246**

54. The Cab Driver from Hell **252**

55. You Know You Are in Russia & Ukraine if... **257**

56. Things I Miss about America **262**

57. Things I'll Miss if I Leave Russia & Ukraine **266**

58. A Lecture for Foreign Men Seeking Slavic Brides **270**

59. Coming Home from the Insane Asylum **277**

About the Author **285**

Preface

Over the past 20 years I've spent a great deal of time, mostly summers, in Russia and Ukraine, living and working among the natives. My lifestyle there has differed dramatically and intentionally from that of Americans who work in a perk-filled embassy ghetto, and from the cliques of cheerful American and other Western expats who have their own indulgent ghetto of sorts. Not surprisingly, my accumulated experiences in these foreign countries include more misadventures than adventures.

Why write this book? I've asked myself this question countless times over the past decade. A former colleague of mine at a Washington, DC college first gave me the idea of writing this book. Upon returning to Washington, after spending yet another summer in Russia and Ukraine conducting academic research, I shared some of my misadventures with him—the trials and tribulations of daily living in an alien Slavic culture without American creature comforts.

The stories I shared with him were, from my perspective, sheer horror stories. My colleague's reaction, however, stunned me. He laughed uncontrollably, adding measurably to the pain I felt. When he regained his composure, he made a thoughtful suggestion. Familiar with the genre of travel-humor literature, he suggested that I record my stories of suffering in Russia and Ukraine and share them with a wider audience. Naturally, I was flattered by his suggestion but did not take it seriously at the time. Instead, I continued to devote my energy over the next few years to my heavy teaching and administrative responsibilities. During the same period, I continued my summer trips to Russia and Ukraine and my obsessive habit of scribbling down my observations of daily life among the natives in little notebooks.

I eventually left teaching after many years in the profession but continued to visit Ukraine and Russia. My unmanageable mountain of small notebooks, with their fitful observations of Slavic life, increasingly reminded me of my former colleague's suggestion. Each time, however, I convinced myself that reliving and recording these foreign experiences would be too painful an exercise for me to endure. Each time I put off this exercise. With my college career behind me and more personal time available, I finally undertook this painful exercise in a genre I prefer to call travel horror rather than travel humor.

What audiences am I targeting? What are my objectives? This book is not for readers who want to learn about the privileged and very sheltered existence of Americans and West Europeans living in Russia and Ukraine and working for their respective embassies, international organizations or wealthy foreign investors. In contrast to average Russian and Ukrainian natives, these expats typically live in luxurious, exorbitantly priced apartments overlooking central parks with 24-hour security, a native driver, translator and a maid who also provides childcare. These "lucky Americans" live a lifestyle many of them could only dream of leading in the U.S., yet they often complain in their expat circles about the many hardships they encounter daily—the unavailability of Doritos and other staples of American life.

Nor is this book for readers interested primarily in the exploits of mostly middle-aged American and other expats who come to Russia, and especially Ukraine, to engage in what is commonly termed sex tourism. I don't shy away from addressing the heavy drinking and promiscuity of barely dressed, striking Slavic women and their foreign sponsors but there is much more to Slavic life than a live-for-today infectious lifestyle.

My basic objective is to convey with dark humor what it feels like for an American, who has spent most of his life living in the U.S., to live and work among the natives in an alien and often overly romanticized Slavic culture without American creature comforts, including a car, uncontaminated tap water, hot water (and often any water), central heating (and often any heating); and to describe what it feels like to interact with average Slavic natives, shopkeepers, lowly bureaucrats, medical workers, police and others.

In many respects this is a book about nothing. More specifically, it's about the trivial, banal and yet often fascinating events of daily existence which are aggravated greatly by living in a foreign, largely non-English speaking culture. Here I must agree with H. L. Mencken who aptly observed: "The basic fact about human existence is not that it is a tragedy, but that it is a bore. It is not so much a war as an endless standing in line."

I should also note that I intentionally do not employ the many insightful concepts of anthropology such as polychromic, high-context and monochromic, low-context cultures to shed light on what many Americans view as the alien, and even offensive, culturally-conditioned behavior of many Russians and Ukrainians. To do so would be inappropriate, and even sacrilegious, in a book whose primary purpose is to entertain readers and whose very short chapters with dark humor may likely become restroom reading.

Although this book was written primarily to entertain, it may prove useful for many people whose lives involve contact with average Russians and Ukrainians in their respective countries, or even at home in the U.S. and other western countries. For American men experiencing a mid-life crisis and impulsively thinking about bringing home a very young Slavic bride there is much practical advice that may even save a few of them from bankruptcy, jail or even confinement in an American mental institution.

In short, I've tried to produce a painfully funny collection of travel nightmares—country and culture shocks—without trivializing serious issues, including AIDS, rampant corruption and ecocide. In addition to providing aching souls with a bit of laughter, it is my hope that my stories will help clear up some important culturally based misunderstandings Americans typically have of Slavs and shed light on their psychology and behavior, in particular.

Why focus on Moscow and Kyiv? My stories about Russia and Ukraine, the two most populous and developed republics of the former Soviet Union, focus on their respective capitals, Moscow and Kyiv. I've traveled to many other cities and rural villages in these two countries, but most of my time there over the past 20 years has been spent living and working in these very historic capitals. Significantly, most foreign visitors rarely have time to explore beyond these very large and often exciting cities.

Russia's enormous size is a well known geographical fact. However, it is worth noting here that Ukraine, with a population of less than 46 million in 2012, is the largest country on the European continent—larger than France, Poland or Spain. Kyiv, its lovely capital, is more than 1500 years old.

Lastly, *an important caveat*: I use the term Slav here to refer collectively to Ukrainians and Russians living in their separate countries (Ukraine's population also includes nearly 20 percent ethnic Russians). I do so for convenience and stylistic purposes. Strictly speaking, the term Slav includes the inhabitants of many more countries classified as East or West Slavs. The term expat, of course, refers simply to a person living and often working in a foreign country.

Acknowledgements

Special thanks must go to Jim Major who planted the seed for this book a decade ago, and Bill Sheweli who has nourished my deep interest in comedy over many years by generously providing me with a small library of comedic DVDs, CDs and books. Thank you both for your inspiration and friendship.

Across the Atlantic I would like to thank my friends, Valery in Moscow and Kolya in Kyiv, two streetwise Slavic men with rich Soviet and post-Soviet experience. Thank you both for helping me break the code on many culturally based misunderstandings I've held for many years about Slavic behavior and psychology. Over the years your kind and patient efforts have helped me better understand, cope with, and ultimately enjoy Slavic life.

And on this side of the Atlantic, it has been my great pleasure to work with two very gifted illustrators, Vikki Chu and Guy Parkhomenko. Their conspicuous artistic talent, evident in these pages and cover art, is richly complemented by their keen sense of humor. Collaborating with them has been a rare pleasure, indeed.

Lastly and most importantly, I would like to express many thanks to my loving wife, Hazel Sirett, for her excellent suggestions and help editing. To this day she remains perplexed by my endless fascination with the cultural differences between Slavs and Americans but tolerates it, and has always been supportive in all I do. She also deserves the lion's share of credit for raising our two sons, Adam and Guy. I'm immensely proud of them both and not only because each reached the age of 21 without any arrests.

Coming to America

> *"Suffering is the key to happiness."*
> -Fyodor Dostoevsky

(*Reader alert!* Readers needing a quick dose of travel horror should skip immediately to Chapter 3, "The Soulless American." All others read on.)

Before describing some of my adventures and misadventures living and working among the natives in Russia and Ukraine, I feel it's essential to provide some background about myself and the system that has tenaciously survived the collapse of the Soviet Union. A thumbnail sketch of my childhood and adult life in America will provide readers with an understanding of the formative experiences that have shaped me and will allow them to judge what kind of American I am. My hypothesis, for readers to ultimately confirm or deny, is that I am a weak American living in Russia and Ukraine.

Growing Up in an American Gulag

My parents were poor Ukrainian peasants torn from their simple Ukrainian village when Germany invaded Ukraine in 1941. They were not alone. According to Ukrainian historians, Germany destroyed 27,000 Ukrainian villages and 700 of its cities. As a result, 2,300,000 Ukrainians were driven out of their country into forced labor in Germany. Nine million Ukrainians died during WWII.

Like countless fellow countrymen, my parents were forced to fill the ranks of forced labor in Germany and were known as displaced persons (DPs). Due primarily to the stubborn resistance of my mother they were not repatriated and sent back to Stalin's Soviet Union as countless others were with the end of WWII. Instead, they remained in German refugee camps for several years until they were able to immigrate to America.

I was born in one of those German refugee camps and was just 12 months old when my parents immigrated. Along with my 6-year-old sister, we made what my mother described as a seemingly endless and sickening crossing of the Atlantic and arrived to find Ellis Island reopened for a new batch of boat people.

My parents arrived in America penniless, without a word of English, with little formal education, two small children, and a single footlocker containing all of our worldly possessions. We eventually settled in a Ukrainian-American community in upstate New York.

My father was a kind soul but a typical muzhik, a salt of the earth Slav, who provided for his family by doing back-breaking work in a meatpacking factory. His free time was spent working in the family garden, planting and caring for trees, and raising turtle-neck doves—his passion. He never drank alone but often made up for it on weekends with his closest co-workers.

My father was a prankster with a silly smile and always cheerful. Amazingly, despite having only limited, broken English to the very end, he loved to meet and talk to strangers. He also enjoyed cooking family meals and cleaning.

The heavy burden of surviving and thriving in America fell squarely upon my mother's shoulders. Like many old world Ukrainian women, she was always the towering figure in our family and "she who must be obeyed."

My mother was a very complex person: very kind but tough, bold and fearless in America despite initially speaking virtually no English, and a tireless worker with uncommon stamina and persistence in pursuing important goals.

My mother's unusual strength of spirit and body was the product of several formative experiences. Just 11 years old at the time, she survived Stalin's man-made Great Famine in Ukraine of 1932–33 which took nearly 10 million lives. With the start of WWII she was uprooted from her primitive Ukrainian village, along with other family members, and literally carted off to Germany by the Nazis. With the end of the war she fought tirelessly to resist repatriation to Stalin's Soviet Union and won immigration to America; her mother, brother and sister were not as fortunate.

Next there was the daunting task of establishing a new life in America with no real resources at hand. My mother tackled the challenges squarely and never complained. She experienced many setbacks in pursuing her major goals but never gave up. She was a survivor who thrived under pressure and repeatedly overcame overwhelming obstacles.

The Dark Side

Yes my mother was a kind and loving person who would help any soul in need, but there was also another side to her, the dark side. When it came to raising and educating her children, she was a severe, results-oriented disciplinarian, a dictator and a big fan of corporal punishment. This "school of tough love" was the social norm in my parent's Ukraine and most American private schools while I was growing up.

Famed Russian writer and former political prisoner, Alexander Solzhenitsyn, in his highly acclaimed writings painted in gruesome detail a vast network of Soviet political prisons and camps established by Josef Stalin and known as the *Gulag*. My mother never read Solzhenitsyn and left the Soviet Union when she was just 19 and, yet, she constructed her own repressive Gulag for me in upstate New York.

Objectively speaking, my childhood was very harsh and character building. My mother's Gulag insisted that my left-handedness was evil and needed to be eradicated: the devil I learned resided just behind my left shoulder and an angel behind my right one. At one point, my mother even tied up my left hand to discourage my evil habit. However, I tenaciously resisted and at the age of seven I recall doing my homework behind a large sofa using my left hand. In the end, I proved more stubborn than my mother and prevailed.

In my mother's Gulag I was forced not only to attend three-hour Ukrainian Orthodox services every Sunday and major holy days but also to serve as an altar boy on those occasions, the special masses, that followed and during funerals. This lasted about eight long years.

One day my mother happily announced that she wanted me to become a priest—Ukrainian Orthodox, of course. Her words crushed my dream of ever becoming just an average American boy. *Welcome to America*, I thought. And just what America needs another Ukrainian Orthodox priest!

To add insult to injury, I was forced on Saturday mornings, along with my sister, to attend Ukrainian-language and religious instruction at our church. This lasted for several years. All the while, I was a disinterested, mediocre student and even at this early age believed that I had no need to develop further my Ukrainian-language ability. My strongest recollection of those Saturday mornings was my repeated effort, along with several like-minded boys, to escape during break time. The exits, however, were always carefully guarded.

My mother was a great believer in disciplining children—the "spare the rod, spoil the child" school. Although we were Ukrainian Orthodox, my mother insisted on sending my sister and me to Catholic elementary and high schools primarily because they were stricter than public schools and practiced corporal punishment enthusiastically. I recall vividly the quick reflexes of angry nuns with large wooden rulers, hidden in the sleeves of their black habits; and the disciplinarian in my all-boys Catholic high school who swung a wooden paddle that resembled a large cutting board.

To help defray the cost of my private high school education and keep me out of trouble, my mother repeatedly surprised me by finding employment for me. Beginning with my first year of high school, I worked as a dishwasher and helper in the school cafeteria. I also worked in a nearby bakery before and after my classes.

When it came to the prospect of teen dating, my mother was categorically against it. In her mind, all young women had one thing in mind: They wanted to trick young men, and especially me, into marriage by making them pregnant. Apparently this is what all the young girls in my mother's Ukrainian village did.

At the age of 18 I finally openly dated a girl and on more than one occasion recall my mother following us in her car at a discreet distance, in her opinion like the KGB (Soviet secret police), whenever we went for a stroll. With time I learned not to argue with my mother about such sensitive matters as dating. For me it was always a no-win situation. Instead, I learned to agree with her but then went ahead and did whatever I wanted to do. With time I learned to become as determined and stubborn as my mother.

Yes, my childhood and teen years, objectively speaking, were harsh but they also included much happiness and many secret pleasures outside of my mother's Gulag. My parents worked long, hard hours in the hammering noise of factories leaving me large pockets of unsupervised freedom especially during school holidays and summer vacations. These periods were typically spent playing with a handful of children who also were immigrants.

Like the mischievous characters in the classic TV series, *The Little Rascals*, we roamed city streets, parks, and even the very steep river banks of our city, and had great fun with only pennies in our pockets. Over the years, we became very close friends, shared many secrets and became streetwise. Thus, the many fond memories of my childhood trump the harsh times.

My college years were set against the background of the Vietnam War and Woodstock. Nonconformist behavior was the social norm in America at the time. This increasingly clashed with the conformist, old world demands of my mother. After completing some graduate work in upstate New York, I decided to break free from my mother's Gulag, and its forced Ukrainianization, which was never more than partly successful in my case.

I fled to Washington, D.C. a safe distance of 400 miles from my parents' home. I was out of the Gulag and free at last! I was no longer forced to be Ukrainian and attend related ethnic functions. My closest friends for the next few years would be a small mountain of books.

My low rent, studio apartment was a single room of just 20 square meters (125 square feet) with no kitchen facility or even a small refrigerator. My few possessions included a desk, a large book case, four large old sofa cushions which served as a makeshift bed and sofa, an electric skillet, and an electric kettle. During winter months I was able to store milk on my windowsill.

My transportation for the next few years was a bicycle which I enjoyed immensely and allowed me to move freely, and at no cost, all about the nation's capital. I spent my days as a graduate student at Georgetown University and evenings worked the night shift as a doorman and elevator operator, and security in my predominantly black apartment building just three blocks from the nation's capital. I had very little money and few possessions but remember this time as the happiest period of my life.

All I ever wanted as a child was to be an average American boy. In some ways I was just that. By the time I finished my graduate studies and took my first professional job I developed my mother's deep appreciation and respect for hard work—the essence of our traditional American work ethic. I held a long string of part-time jobs: dishwasher, bakers' assistant, short-order cook, propane factory assembly-line worker and punch press operator, landscaper, truck driver, warehouse worker, bank and gift-shop cleaner, truck loader, bookstore worker, doorman-elevator operator, library assistant, and translator at the U.S. National Archives.

Fond memories, indeed, trump the harsh times of my childhood and teen years in my mother's Gulag. Moreover, the image of my mother that I hold today is that of a role model: an exceptionally kind and giving person devoted to family and friends, who exhibited uncommon persistence and determination in achieving every major goal she set. Through her tireless efforts, she unquestionably achieved the "American Dream." An important part of her dream was to provide her children with an education second to none and thus help them achieve a meaningful and dignified life.

The Post-Soviet System

> *"Culture determines what we perceive, how we react to situations, and how we relate to other people."*
> -Edward T. Hall & Mildred Reed Hall

Twenty years after the collapse of the Soviet Union, important aspects of that system and mentality remain stronger than ever. Anyone planning to live and work in Russia and Ukraine, or even visit, should take to heart the following harsh realities about the deeply entrenched system in these countries.

In the Soviet Union, there existed a traditional system of morality at the family level and a deep respect for culture. Today this system of morality and government support for culture has collapsed. It has been replaced by a system of total corruption evident in government institutions, businesses, schools, hospitals, police, and society, in general.

Stealing is not considered wrong and is, in fact, a social norm. Bribes are the lubricant of Russian and Ukrainian life, and insatiable greed is a pervasive characteristic of political and business life which are virtually inseparable.

Sex is a currency and young Slavic women generally have little money. Desperate ones often allow themselves to be manipulated and exploited in order to survive and advance. Generally speaking, the public is forced to operate and try to survive within this system. Honest citizens do exist within this system but it typically comes with a heavy price tag, poverty.

Russian and Ukrainian politics have a closed, Kama Sutra–like quality: A fixed number of players change positions but do not give up the levers of power, and do not leave the political scene. Professionalism is not respected and is sorely lacking in the political elite; nepotism is commonplace.

There is no rule of law in Russia and Ukraine. Many good laws exist on paper, but there is no enforcement and no real punishment for corruption. The court system is totally corrupt and notorious for providing documents to the highest bidder, resulting in illegal takeovers of businesses, office and apartment buildings. Street crime and burglaries are increasing, along with poverty. Today it is not safe for anyone to be out alone after dark in Moscow or Kyiv.

Europe does not really want Ukraine to integrate: Ukraine's rich steal and don't want their country to be part of Europe because they can't steal there. Russia does not want Europe; it wants Ukraine back in its sphere of influence.

The Soviet economy was never consumer oriented. It was marked by a non-service mentality especially evident in stores and restaurants. The Soviet Union collapsed but this non-service mentality remains deeply rooted in Slavic institutions, despite serious post-Soviet challenges from fast food franchises such as McDonald's.

Post-Soviet Historic Events

I've experienced some historic events while living and working in Russia and Ukraine over the past 20 years. Together they provide an essential background for my chapters on daily life in Russia and Ukraine.

Following the dramatic end of the Soviet Union in December 1991, I witnessed the public impact of the new Russian government's "shock therapy" experiment, an effort to bring the free market quickly to Russia. Instead, it brought too much shock and acute hyperinflation and wiped out the savings of average Russians and citizens throughout the former Soviet Union. I also witnessed firsthand the bold public protests against shock therapy and the growing instability in Russia.

Years later in August 1998, I was in Russia for the country's financial collapse which drastically affected the entire former Soviet Union. This amounted to a second knockout punch for a country and region that was finally recovering from shock therapy. As a result, the Russian ruble was devalued by three-fourths and similar shock waves engulfed Ukraine and other new countries in the former Soviet Union.

In August 1999 I witnessed the nation's horror as three Moscow apartment buildings were destroyed (allegedly by terrorists), resulting in some 300 people losing their lives. In August 2000, I arrived in Moscow the day the Kursk nuclear-powered submarine and its crew of more than 100 sailors came to a tragic end, an event officials refused to disclose for more than a week to anxious Russian citizens. And in September 2001 my scheduled flight from Moscow back to Washington was canceled because of the 9/11 terrorist attacks in the U.S., a tragedy that received 24/7 coverage on Russian television for days.

In Ukraine, I also witnessed firsthand the devastating impact shock therapy and the Russian financial collapse had on Ukrainian citizens. And for several years prior to Ukraine's democratic Orange Revolution of 2004, I interviewed Ukrainian journalists and human rights activists who had been physically assaulted for their writings and participation in public protests. In the years following the Orange Revolution I watched the hopes of Ukrainian citizens for achieving a European standard of living in their lifetime gradually slip away and feelings of a revolution betrayed prevail.

In April 2006 I visited Chornobyl on the 20th anniversary of the world's worst civilian nuclear disaster. That same year I experienced Ukraine's coldest winter in 80 years. During 2008–2009 I witnessed the devastating impact of the international economic crisis on Ukrainian citizens just starting to recover from the 1998 financial collapse. And in 2011, just a year after the election of a new president, I watched Ukraine increasingly slide down an authoritarian path similar to Putin's Russia.

Choose Ukraine over Russia

Interestingly, in recent years there has been a dramatic increase in the number of Americans, Canadians and West Europeans who choose Ukraine over Russia to experience Slavic culture. I'm no exception. The reasons are many and quite compelling.

Topping the list since the Orange Revolution of 2004 is Ukraine's visa-free stay for up to 90 days (out of each 180 day period) for foreign citizens of these countries. Additionally there is Ukraine's stunning and diverse physical beauty, which includes Crimea a very popular summer resort, the Carpathian mountains, more than 300 castles and citadels peppering the very fertile countryside, many historic cities, and Kyiv which admiring Russians call the "green city" and the "Miami of the former Soviet Union," with its population of 3 million compared to Moscow's 10 million.

Another attraction, one noted by many foreign men, is the fact that many Ukrainian women are very striking in appearance. Ukrainian men point with pride to the selection of a Ukrainian femme fatale to play the lead in a recent James Bond film as cogent evidence, and to Ukrainian-born Hollywood actress Milla Jovovich.

Foreigners who only speak Russian also find Ukraine an ideal country since years of Sovietization have left it, and other former Soviet republics, bilingual. Ukrainian and Russian are routinely spoken in a single conversation between two speakers on its city streets.

Russia, on the other hand, is a very different story when it comes to rolling out the welcome mat for foreign visitors. Its visa regime remains firmly intact and requires AIDS test results for visitors staying more than 30 days. Interestingly, a tourist visa application for Americans wishing to visit Russia in 2011 even required phone numbers for major educational institutions attended in the past, the names of past employers and phone numbers for past supervisors—information that could be 20 or 30 years old.

Moreover, the xenophobic policies of today's Russian leaders, and Vladimir Putin, in particular, in recent years are especially discouraging to many potential foreign visitors. These include the restoration of Soviet symbols and the effective rehabilitation of Josef Stalin (2007–2009); Russia's quasi-isolationism and espionage hysteria (2005–2007); its controlled confrontation with the U.S. (2007); Russia's proclamation of the post-Soviet region as the zone of Russia's privileged interests (2008); and its continued efforts to reintegrate Ukraine into its sphere of influence (2010–present). Add to this picture, expat and even Russian descriptions of Moscow as a typically inhospitable and intimidating city, and Kyiv as friendly and with more of a Western feel.

A Weak American

One might logically expect that someone with my upbringing in a Ukrainian-American community, my interpersonal skills gained from numerous diverse part-time jobs, my Ukrainian and Russian language ability, my academic and professional background in Russian and Eurasian affairs, and extended time spent living and conducting research in London, Amsterdam, Munich, New York City, and Washington, D.C. could make a soft landing in Russian and Ukrainian society, or even be a fish in water. How presumptuous of me to ever think so.

Equipped with insights into my personal background and the deeply-entrenched system in Russia and Ukraine, I think my readers will now better appreciate the adventures, misadventures, tips for living in Russia and Ukraine, and even bringing a Slavic bride back to the U.S., to be found in the very short chapters that follow. As mentioned earlier, my hypothesis for readers ultimately to confirm or deny is that I am a weak American living in Russia and Ukraine.

The Soulless American

> "The Russian nature [soul], with favorable conditions, is like forest and steppe in summer, full of peace and grace and charm…But it also has the strength and terror of steppe and forest."
> -Edna Dean Proctor

(August 1992)
The days and nights were unbearably hot and humid. Two weeks had passed since I arrived in Moscow. To escape the heat my Russian friend, Valery, invited me one evening to his modest but air-conditioned two-room apartment in one of those nine-story buildings in the heart of the city. To make the evening more interesting he also invited several of his close friends, including Natasha, a former classmate, for drinks and conversation. Natasha, like Valery, was in her early thirties and was an accomplished but poorly paid translator of Czech and other languages. Natasha, I learned, had put on a few kilos since her college days but was still quite attractive.

After a few hours of drinks, food, and let's get acquainted conversation around a communal table, I excused myself and stepped out on to the balcony to get a view of the bustling city below. The balcony was tiny, barely enclosed and just large enough for the two folding chairs facing one another. I sat on one of the chairs enjoying a welcome light breeze for just a few minutes before Natasha appeared with a wine glass and bottle in hand and asked whether she would disturb me, if she joined in. I welcomed her company and we sat quietly for a few minutes. Soon Natasha broke the silence and out of the blue became very outspoken.

She startled me by saying, "You Americans have no soul, no spirit. You care nothing about the finer things in life: music, literature, serious discussions and deep friendships. You are philistines!" I didn't have my dictionary handy but this sounded ominous.

This litany continued for more than 30 minutes with interruptions only to fill her wine glass, wet her whistle, and puff on a cigarette. I began to fear that all of this might end badly. The balcony was nine, very high stories above the street and quite flimsy.

Natasha quickly became increasingly loud and excited, and it was not always easy to follow her train of thought. She jumped from one subject to another often stabbing her finger into the air. However, the subtext of Natasha's harangue was unmistakably clear: I was a member of a spiritually impoverished and decadent society, while she and her countrymen were morally rich and virtuous.

To call Natasha loquacious would be a supreme understatement. She was an unstoppable talker, who spoke seemingly at an average rate of 150 words per minute, much of the time talking about herself.

My initial reaction to Natasha's virulent, neurotic attack upon a perfect stranger and his country was shock and insult, especially given my Slavic roots. How dare this stranger who knew virtually nothing about me, attack me so viciously. For all she knew, I might have just returned from a year of missionary work in Africa fighting famine with Mother Teresa. Moreover, without knowing much about Natasha's relatively privileged upbringing in Moscow, my guess was that I had probably suffered much more than she during my childhood years in the Stalinist-like camp erected by my Slavic mother in upstate New York.

But there was no reasoning with Natasha, and I made no effort to add fuel to her fire. Instead, I listened and listened and listened. As to Natasha's assertion that I had not suffered much in my allegedly comfortable American life, I had one immediate thought: another 15 minutes listening to her and I would be eligible for a modern-day equivalent of the old "Hero of the Soviet Union" medal.

The only logical response I could think of to Natasha's tirade was to drink more. By this time our host had brought us another bottle of wine and I quickly filled our glasses. Natasha certainly was not holding back on this front. She immediately emptied her glass and I reluctantly refilled it. By the end of the evening I had the distinct impression that there were only two things Natasha didn't drink: water and kerosene.

Natasha stopped lecturing me briefly but only to light another cigarette. A professional translator of several languages, she then attempted to play her trump card. She began by first criticizing Americans for not speaking foreign languages—and Russian, in particular—and then demurely asked how many languages I spoke. When I replied four languages (English, Russian, Ukrainian and German), she excused herself to use the toilet.

Before long, all the alcohol and cigarettes were gone and so were most of the guests. Valery and I helped Natasha into a cab for safe passage home.

Alone with my friend Valery, I told him how offensive I found most of Natasha's remarks and how surprised I was that, despite her advanced university education, she was very closed-minded and full of Soviet stereotypes about Americans. Valery laughed heartily and said Natasha was just being Natasha and that I shouldn't take her words too seriously. He said that she was just being candid and opening up her Russian soul to me, and that this was classic Russian-conversational style: a typical Russian litany, a rant, and not at all peculiar to Natasha. "This is how we Russians release steam when we are at home with friends. It is a national habit of ours. You should not take it personally."

I then thanked Valery for an unforgettable evening and slowly made my way back to my apartment. His message made sense but did little to relieve the deep sense of personal hurt I felt as a result of Natasha's words. I had gone to Valery's that evening in search of soulful conversation and a glimpse of the caring friendly-Russian soul I had heard so much about while living abroad. Instead, I was repeatedly insulted by a perfect stranger in a nearly two-hour-long monologue and told that I had no soul. Yes, Natasha opened her Russian soul to me but what I saw thrust me into a Slavic circle of hell, left me shell shocked, and feeling like the image in Edvard Munch's classic painting *The Scream*.

The next afternoon I called Valery to again thank him for the previous evening. He told me an incredible fact. He said that Natasha had called him early that morning and said that she had one of the most enjoyable evenings ever, and especially enjoyed chatting with the American. And she hoped Valery could soon arrange another similar evening with the American present. I was speechless.

Russian "Holiday of a Lifetime"

"Our memories are the only paradise no one can cast us out of."

-a Slavic saying

It was the late 1990s and I found myself back in Moscow. A year earlier, Russia's financial collapse dealt a devastating blow to citizens who were still recovering from the economic shock therapy imposed following the collapse of the U.S.S.R. Once again Russians faced acute economic instability and a Klondike environment where the "new rules were no rules" and where "money talks and nobody walks." To survive and help their extended families, desperate *babushkas* (Slavic grannies) were buying a dozen loaves of bread at several bread shops, only to resell outside of metros and other busy spots to tired workers returning home.

It was summertime and the weather was agreeable for a change. Sasha, a young researcher from an institute with the Russian Academy of Sciences, whom I had known for several years, invited me out for a few drinks and catch-up conversation at a café on the Old Arbat, a historic, tourist stretch in the heart of Moscow. I met him after work outside the well-known McDonald's on the Old Arbat and we strolled along this short avenue before retreating to a modest, nearby café.

After an hour or so of casual conversation, Sasha mentioned he had a very interesting friend and former classmate, Lesya, who was a doctor of sports medicine and daughter of a famous Soviet Olympic trainer, and worked nearby. He said Lesya could tell me many interesting things about the state of Russia's educational institutions and sports training, in particular, nearly a decade after the collapse of the Soviet Union, and asked if I would like to meet her. I gladly agreed. Sasha called Lesya who said she was would soon finish work and could meet us in about an hour outside the entrance to the Lenin Library metro station.

We met Lesya, who was very punctual, and again strolled along the Old Arbat. Lesya was in her early thirties, almost six-foot tall, sturdy with attractive features, and a striking contrast to the countless Barbie-doll-looking young women in Moscow. She wore a fashionable Nike sports outfit and was refreshingly unpretentious and quite outspoken. In our first half hour she expressed the view that Americans are a weak, coddled people but tempered this view by saying that she considers American black track athletes the equivalent of Greek gods.

Lesya directed us to her favorite Old Arbat café. The evening grew memorable quickly. Lesya immediately proposed a first toast, a shot of vodka, and then moved on to drinking B-52s. This was my first exposure to the literally fiery drink, one of Lesya's favorites. A young waitress lit the alcoholic concoction in a shot glass at our table and a few seconds later Lesya downed it. This was followed in short order with more B-52s for Lesya; Sasha and I stuck with vodka. After a while Lesya shifted to Campari and orange juice. At this point I began to worry about the future of Russian Sports Medicine.

Around 10 P.M. Lesya proposed that we leave Old Arbat and retreat to her flat for a *prazdnik zhizn'*—holiday of a lifetime. I immediately turned to Sasha hoping that he would offer an excuse for bringing the evening to a close. Instead, he said, "We live but once, life is short," which delighted Lesya. She immediately began to organize the party. We stopped at a tiny 24-hour grocery store near the metro station. Following Lesya's orders we bought two large bottles of Campari, a liter of orange juice, a loaf of bread, sausage, and cheese. Lesya said she had marinated mushrooms, tomatoes and pickles at home. I felt a bit queasy upon hearing what awaited us. Since I was the stereotypical rich American, I insisted on paying for our supplies.

We arrived at Lesya's unusually large two-room flat, obtained while her father was a famous Soviet Olympic trainer, to find a huge surprise. Her two identical rottweilers, each weighing well over 100 pounds, had been left home alone and were very excited to see Lesya and two strangers in their apartment. I only remember the name of one of the dogs, Borya, and it's etched indelibly in my mind.

Lesya quickly made a plate full of open-face sandwiches with slices of sausage and cheese to go along with some marinated treats. When she told me to help myself to the *buterbrody*—Russian for sandwiches—Borya apparently heard his favorite word. As soon as I lifted one of the sandwiches off the plate, 100-plus-pound Borya quickly engulfed my hand and swallowed the buterbrod. I immediately looked to see if all my fingers were still there, and then said a silent prayer of thanks. My hand was covered in a thick slime. *Welcome to Moscow!* Borya clearly had been salivating the entire time the sandwiches were being prepared. Interestingly, Lesya and Sasha didn't even blink an eye at the incident.

The Campari continued to flow and Lesya announced that she was going to treat us to a special dance from the Caucasus region. It was now after 1 A.M. and Lesya, with arms outstretched and feet tapping furiously on the wooden floor of her third floor apartment like a flamingo dancer, loudly sang a Chechen song. I didn't know what to expect next. I was certain this was not the first time Lesya treated her neighbors in the flat below to this dance.

With 2 A.M. approaching, I thanked Lesya for the "holiday of a lifetime" and said it was time for me to leave. The metro was no longer running and it wasn't easy to catch a cab after midnight on the outskirts of Moscow. Lesya insisted on escorting the two of us to the street. I thought we would flag a car and negotiate a price like most locals do. Instead, Lesya boldly stepped into the middle of the small side street when she saw a police car approaching and flagged it down. This was unusual. People in Russia normally run in the opposite direction when they see the police coming, but not Lesya.

She told the two officers that two of her friends, including a visitor from abroad, needed a ride home but no cars were available. They immediately replied, "No problem, this is our district anyway." Before we reached our destination I asked one of the policemen how much I could give them for the kind service they provided, and he said the equivalent of four dollars in rubles.

Years later, after many more evenings spent with Russian and Ukrainian friends, I occasionally reflected upon the evening spent with Lesya and her kind effort to organize a Russian "holiday of a lifetime." It revealed a very Slavic tradition: a desire to seize the moment, show a foreign visitor an enjoyable and unforgettable evening Slavic style, and gather special memories for oneself. And it reminded me of the Slavic saying, "Our memories are the only paradise no one cast us out of."

Slavic Khamstvo & Sovok Mentality

"Good manners cost nothing."
-mothers' advice to children

If there is a single word in both Russian and Ukrainian that best captures the opposite of American civility and politeness to strangers in public, it's *khamstvo*. An understanding of this ubiquitous Slavic phenomenon is essential for any foreigners planning to live and work in Russia and Ukraine, or even just visit.

Unlike simple rudeness, khamstvo is when a person intentionally acts in a rude manner to a perfect stranger in public and expects to get away unpunished; the key distinguishing words are intention, perfect stranger, public, and unpunished. The person who behaves in this manner is called a *kham*. Interestingly, this name is derived from Ham, Noah's irreverent son in the Bible. *Sovok* is slang in Russian and Ukrainian for Soviet man, and also can be used to describe his rude (sovok) public behavior and boorish mentality.

Khamstvo is deeply rooted in 70 years of Soviet experience. However, it received a big boost with the collapse of Soviet Communism 20 years ago and the introduction of wild capitalism and extreme materialism. Since that historic event, Russia and Ukraine have been steadily descending into debauchery, chaos and lawlessness.

During Soviet times, workers would routinely express their hatred of their jobs, supervisors, and the Soviet system, in general, by being rude to fellow citizens, especially if they were in positions of even modest authority. Today this tradition of robbing average citizens of their dignity is stronger than ever and practiced by cold and arrogant police officers, low and mid-level bureaucrats, sales clerks, hospital nurses, hotel staff, security guards in stores, and administrators, in general. This khamstvo is institutionalized and is an important pillar in a culture where the customer is always wrong and is guaranteed non-service and rudeness.

For all of its many shortcomings, the Soviet system at least made an effort to battle khamstvo. The same cannot be said about post-Soviet rulers. During the Soviet era, babushkas were on the front lines in the battle against khamstvo and *sovki* (plural of sovok). They were rugged, no-nonsense national vigilantes, who would sit in groups on benches outside their apartment buildings all day and look out for mischief.

God forbid if you were a Slavic teenager and a babushka caught you smoking in public. She would read you the Riot Act and find your parents if you lived in her building. She would even publicly shame an adult caught chewing gum on the metro with the sarcastic words, "very cultured," and give them the evil eye.

The good old Soviet days are gone. Today Orbit gum is doing a thriving business in Russia and Ukraine, and great progress has been made in introducing hooker-style stilettos and dozens of new brands of vodka—the two new icons of contemporary Slavic life.

These days the traditional babushka has been silenced and

literally is a dying breed. In small courtyards like mine outside Soviet-built apartments, today you can see young teenagers brazenly smoking and drinking beer even during school hours. And if a babushka or two should criticize their behavior, they will quickly tell them where to go with a few choice words.

But to truly understand Slavic khamstvo you need to experience it, which I have far too many times. A telling indicator of the Russian and Ukrainian ruling elite's continued disrespect for their citizens, and their sovok mentality, is the horrendous state of public toilets—very bad in Soviet times and worse today. The ruling elite and their "newly-rich" supporters inhabit a different world, far removed from the public toilets and other essentials of average Slavic citizens.

Moreover, most Slavic restaurants today might as well put up a large sign at their entrance alerting potential customers, "We guarantee you will wait at least 15 minutes for service while our waiters and waitresses see you and stand idly by." Often it seems you actually need to touch staff to activate them. This is a culture where the customer is always wrong and is guaranteed non-service and rudeness. Workers often try to justify their public displays of khamstvo and sovok mentality by saying they feel they are doing a very humiliating job by serving others.

If there was an Olympic event for queue jumping, I think Slavs could win gold. Slavic boarding procedure on international flights leaving Moscow and Kyiv is a good example and a sight to behold. Despite an obvious orderly line at a departure gate, a group of grumpy and arrogant Slavs will routinely march to the front and push through as though they are rescue workers, or passengers who fear someone may take their designated seats. For them the only rules are no rules. A Russian friend put it simply: "They just don't care. That's the problem. In Russia, money is king and allows you to behave in a way that suits you."

I frequently encounter khamstvo on public transport in Moscow and Kyiv. Often someone on a crowded metro will step on my foot without excusing themselves and, not fearing that I will shame them, will look me straight in the eye as though I should apologize to them for stepping on my foot. Standing up to such persons accomplishes little. It creates a scene and has little impact on a veteran kham. Occasionally, I will use a bit of humor as a defense in such situations and with a big smile will say, "Thank you, that's just what I was lacking for total happiness." This is a favorite Slavic saying for many similar situations and there is really no good response to it.

Slavic motorists are especially egregious khams. Most drivers, including the political elite and other newly-rich Slavs, insist on having blacked-out windows on their cars. This allows the sea of reckless and speeding drivers to hide their identities as they threaten and kill pedestrians daily at crosswalks and even on sidewalks. This khamstvo is deeply rooted in today's Russian and Ukrainian culture of driving and is getting worse by the year. Making blacked-out car windows illegal would help save lives but is callously resisted by the political elite in both countries.

Khamstvo is also very evident in Slavic apartment buildings. The doormats outside apartment entrances tell a story of profound sovok disrespect for communal areas and their neighbors. The doormats are all dirty and raggedy. No one in their right mind would touch these filthy mats. This condition virtually ensures they are theft proof.

I've learned that it is very naïve to keep a nice, clean doormat outside your Russian or Ukrainian apartment. Foreigners often make this mistake. Such a mat will immediately draw attention, make neighbors envious, and typically disappear or be desecrated in the course of a single evening. Even on the raggedy mat outside my Kyiv apartment, I often find cigarette butts, Q-tips, beer bottles and other rubbish, and this happens throughout Slavic buildings. The tradition here is to keep a nice, clean doormat just inside one's apartment and to put on household slippers immediately to keep one's "non-communal," personal space clean. Just more evidence that the sovok mentality is alive and well 20 years after the collapse of the U.S.S.R.

I always find it amusing and unconvincing when some Slavs try to defend khamstvo behavior and sovok mentality as "cultural diversity," which should be understood and accepted by foreigners. Some even call it, "honest and unpretentious," in contrast to what they claim is American false politeness. I enjoy telling these individuals that there are many exclusive European resorts and hotels which no longer take reservations from Russians because repeated incidents of serious Russian drinking, fighting and cursing at their establishments quickly destroy their respected image.

Interestingly, Slavic college-age students who have had an opportunity to work or study in the U.S. are amazed that Slavic khamstvo is not a universal condition. They admit they just assumed it was. The core problem fueling khamstvo and the sovok mentality today is the growing moral crisis and decay in Russia and Ukraine. Sorely needed is a moral-spiritual rebirth. None, however, is in sight.

Is the situation hopeless? There's still hope for college-age Slavs today but it should not be overstated. All of them no doubt have been exposed countless times to sovoks and khams, and many even raised by them. It's hard not to get infected under such conditions. A Russian sociologist on Moscow talk radio offered a pessimistic view. He said he believes this is a lost generation and authorities should focus their attention on Russian children 10 years old and younger.

I'm not quite as pessimistic. My Mega-supermarket in Kyiv employs an army of largely college-age men and women. It does so, no doubt, because they are less infected with a sovok mentality, more easily trained, and more satisfied with the meager wage paid to most Slavs. This naturally makes them more attractive employees.

This supermarket has 30 female cashiers working during peak hours. They're all are college-age and normally work 12-hour shifts. I've inevitably interacted with the store's young workforce countless times and must say it's an improvement over many of their sovok parents, but there's still a long way to go. The shelf-stockers, for example, typically will never yield the right of way to shoppers and nearly run you over with their heavy equipment.

The young female cashiers, in keeping with Slavic tradition, sit rather than stand at their registers and many appear comatose. Nine out of ten times (I'm keeping track) after I say, "Good Day!" to a cashier, I will get a reindeer-caught-in-headlights look and a foggy, "What?" response. I always repeat my greeting. At first I was annoyed with this consistent response, but now find it amusing and have even learned to expect and enjoy it.

I haven't given up yet on this new, college-age workforce and my supermarket cashiers, in particular. But I do hope management will wake up soon and program these sedentary, yawning employees to realize that their customers are alive, and doing more than sociological research when they greet them and expect a response other than "What?" Checking their hearing is also advisable.

Flying Slavic Style

> *"The reward of suffering is experience."*
> -Harry S. Truman

Flying Slavic style is truly an adventure and more of it takes place on the ground than in the air. Over the past 20 years I've flown dozens of times across the Atlantic to Russia and Ukraine on major American, Russian, Ukrainian, and European airlines. The experiences, generally, have been more exhausting and nerve-wrecking than exciting.

My most memorable moments were in the early 1990s. Shortly after the collapse of the Soviet Union, I had the occasion—I feel uncomfortable using the word opportunity—to fly several times to Moscow out of JFK airport on Aeroflot, the Russian national airline. Even during this early post-Soviet period, frequent flyers still referred to the airline by its earned nickname, Aeroflop.

I recall my virgin flight on Aeroflop as though it were yesterday. The waiting lounge outside the assigned gate at JFK was packed with Russians and resembled a flea market with its non-stop buzzing activity. Many of the waiting passengers had enormous brown cardboard boxes as part of their carry-on luggage.

When it became time to board it was as though someone pulled a fire alarm and everyone headed for the exit. The scene was not for weak Americans. Babushkas, with several large boxes in hand, sliced through the crowd in an effort to get the best seat, only to be told they must keep their assigned seat.

I recall vividly having been assigned a window seat in a three-passenger row with a gold-toothed babushka in the aisle seat. I felt fortunate to have a free seat separating us until the elderly woman placed two enormous boxes in the seat between us and boxed me in. I was amazed when the Russian stewardess allowed the woman's boxes to remain there during our flight. Exiting my aisle during this long trans-Atlantic flight became a nightmare.

Meanwhile, the natives on board were having a grand time. The alcohol was flowing nonstop and clouds of cigarette smoke filled our cabin. Russians pulled bottles of hard liquor out of carry-on bags and proudly placed them on their food trays to share with fellow travelers. These were the good old days of no rules for Russian travelers.

Conditions in the plane gave the term economy class new meaning. Many of the seats were tattered, some even broken. The bathrooms had a communal cloth towel to bring passengers closer together. The food included cold boney chicken, sardines, rice, and very stale hard rolls. It's still a great mystery to me how Aeroflot was able to provide us with this classic Soviet cuisine on a flight departing from NYC. They obviously went to great effort. Nonetheless, the natives on board ate heartily and each seemed to have a personal bag full of delicacies to supplement the meager airline provisions. That day I learned that the minute you board an Aeroflot flight to Moscow in JFK with a plane full of natives, you are, for all practical purposes, already in Russia.

My next memorable Aeroflot experience, also in the early 1990s, was a Moscow to JFK flight with a refueling stop in Dublin. Passengers were allowed to deplane for the one-hour stop. Despite free-flowing alcohol on our flight, many of the Russian passengers who deplaned insisted on visiting the Irish bar; it would be a "sin" not to, according to Slavic custom.

One of those Russian passengers invited me for a drink and I graciously accepted. Forty-five minutes after entering the airport lounge, our Russian pilot got on the loudspeaker and requested his passengers to immediately return to the plane. At this point, I was surprised that the Russians at the bar and snack area seemed to take no notice. About 15 minutes later our pilot made a second beseeching announcement in Russian, of course.

Rather than move in the direction of the plane, Russians sitting at the bar ordered another round of drinks. I was getting quite anxious at this point but one of the Russians turned to me and said, "Don't worry, I fly this route regularly and the pilot cannot leave without us."

In 1996 I had another taste of flying Slavic style. I was a member of a small unofficial American delegation made up mostly of retired diplomats visiting Kyiv and Moscow. It was wintry weather and we boarded a Transero flight for Moscow after finishing our meetings in Kyiv. Transero was a new private airline at the time and was selected by our tour organizer because it had a better safety and service record than the Ukrainian state airline.

As we taxied down the runway, we heard a loud crunching from our airplane before it came to a bumpy, abrupt stop. For the next half hour or so we sat in the plane without a word from the pilot about our predicament. Finally, he announced that the aircraft had a broken part and passengers would need to contribute to pay for the new part. Fortunately, the plane was packed mostly with Slavs and they refused to even dignify the request.

We deplaned and spent the next nine very long, cold hours in Kyiv's old Boryspil airport waiting area, an enormous glass-walled area with a huge dome. It was unheated, with broken glass at many points, which allowed small birds to enter along with the bitter cold. Airport officials provided our party with no news regarding our flight status for the entire nine hours, and it was only after about six hours that a Transero representative rolled out a tall, metal food rack for stranded passengers containing cold-bony chicken, fatty salami, rice, and stale rolls.

Eventually, without even an audible announcement and gate information, passengers started to board our plane. We finally arrived in Moscow airport at 2 A.M. with a seminar scheduled for 10 A.M. the next morning.

Without a doubt, credit for one of my worst experiences goes to Delta Airlines. It was a Washington–JFK–Moscow flight shortly after the turn of the century. A direct link from JFK to Moscow made this flight highly desirable. As luck would have it, bad weather crippled the east coast leaving me stranded at JFK.

No flights were departing and no hotel rooms were available. I had to fight tooth and nail to get any attention from the numerous Delta attendants I stalked. Eventually I was able to extract a seat on a flight the following evening to Paris with a connection a day later to Moscow. I ended up spending a night sleeping at JFK and the following day waiting for an evening flight to Paris, where I spent a day in a tiny, dingy terminal without adequate seating. I arrived in Moscow around midnight, two days late and with no luggage.

I was told at Moscow airport that my luggage was somewhere in a storage room the size of an average American convenience store. I was shocked when I entered and found suitcases piled 10-feet high. Thoroughly exhausted, I began the search without any assistance. After nearly an hour and no luck I reported this to the airport attendant who informed me that there was a second baggage room. I entered that room to find a few dozen suitcases, including mine.

However, as mentioned earlier, most of the fun flying Slavic style occurs on the ground. The following has been my typical experience upon arriving at passport control at Boryspil international airport in Kyiv.

You depart Amsterdam in a plane mostly full of Ukrainians and land at Boryspil airport. Veteran Ukrainian travelers frantically descend steep stairs to a large lobby in front of a dozen passport control booths. You immediately notice that several planeloads of passengers have simultaneously swarmed into this small area and have formed a huge sea of people. In front of each passport control booth you have at least three or four individuals, mostly Slavs, standing abreast rather than attempting to form any proper line.

You watch large Slavic families divide and strategically place their members in separate flocks of passengers converging on a passport agent, and eventually scramble and regroup at the quickest control booth. You are nudged continuously from all sides as queue jumpers appear. It seems to take an eternity to clear a single passenger. Passport control agents periodically leave their booths and disappear with no word as to when and if they'll return. More than 90 minutes pass and finally it's your turn. You present your documents and receive a standard, "Why did you burn my house down?" look and are made to feel as though INTERPOL is looking for you. You clear customs and see a huge banner:

"WELCOME TO UKRAINE!"

A Smoker's Paradise

> *Two young Russian friends meet and one says to the other, "Your American fiancé doesn't drink or smoke? Is she sick?"*
>
> -a Russian anecdote

The first thing that greets an American upon exiting Moscow or Kyiv international airport is a very dense cloud of cigarette smoke. Smokers are everywhere. This cloud, which varies only in density, follows the visitor until he returns to the airport to depart for home. Contrast this with America, where in recent years one can easily spend several months without ever encountering cigarette smoke.

Cigarette smoking is on the rise among young Slavs. According to a major 2009 World Health Organization (WHO), survey more than 60 percent of Russian men smoke, women are catching up at a current rate of over 20 percent, and more than 50 percent of all adults report regular exposure to secondhand smoke in public places. Viewed in this light, it is not surprising that the average Russian male life expectancy in 2012 was 59 years.

The WHO survey provided more disturbing information. Unlike West European and American trends, smoking among Russian men and women has been increasing steadily since the collapse of the Soviet Union in 1991. It is also growing among Russian boys and girls, with over a third of them currently smoking.

A picture is worth a thousand words: Take, for example, McDonald's young employees in Kyiv and Moscow. I often see two or three college-age male and female employees in full uniform chatting and smoking conspicuously near the entrance door during their authorized breaks. I think Ronald McDonald would be very saddened by this scene.

Widespread smoking among Russian and Ukrainian teenagers is not at all surprising. Cigarettes are very cheap and easily available at countless street kiosks and from grannies selling them on busy street corners. Although meat and dairy prices in Ukraine and Russia in 2012 were as high or higher than in America and Western Europe, brand name cigarettes, such as, Marlboro, Virginia Slims, L&M, Parliament, Gitanes and Gauloises, were little more than a dollar a pack.

Bad role models abound and are a key reason for growing teenage use of cigarettes. Doctors, including cardiologists, nurses, and medical students are the most egregious examples. In Kyiv, for example, on any given work day you can easily spot a handful of young women in high-heels and white-lab coats glamorously sucking on slim cigarettes and chatting outside any one of the city's many health clinics. Nor is it at all unusual for a Russian or Ukrainian cardiologist to be a smoker. This image is even projected positively in many Soviet and post-Soviet films.

Token efforts have been made recently, notably, in Ukraine, to curb smoking in city underpasses. However, a strong tobacco lobby in the country's parliament ensures that cigarettes remain inexpensive and easily available. Even those charged with enforcing a new law that restricts smoking in public provide bad role models. In Kyiv you will often see three policemen patrolling downtown areas and all are smoking. Moreover, they routinely extort free cigarettes from grannies, who sell them on street corners near metros in downtown Moscow and Kyiv, in return for permission to remain there.

Each year an estimated 100,000 Ukrainians (in a 2012 population of less than 46 million) die as a result of smoking-related diseases. An additional 10,000 die annually as a result of passive smoking. Even a straight line projection of this trend is instructive. At the current rate of death due to smoking, four million Ukrainians will die by 2050 and 400,000 more as a result of passive smoking. Certainly things can change and improve this forecast. The fact is, however, cigarette smoking and drinking among Slavs shows little sign of abating.

Cigarette smoke is inescapable even at home. It seeps into my Kyiv apartment from hallway smoking areas, neighbors' apartments below me and soon saturates my tiny living space. To add insult to injury, cigarette ashes cascade down upon me daily and into my balcony from smokers on floors above me.

Early one morning I went into my Kyiv apartment's tiny bathroom and gagged on the smell of cigarette smoke. For a brief moment I was convinced someone had entered my apartment and bathroom during the night. I even checked my apartment door to see if it was locked. Later I realized the unbelievably strong stench must have come through my bathroom vent.

Americans who live and work in Ukraine and Russia among the natives will eventually understand that there is a deep Slavic culture of smoking. The act of smoking, especially for Slavic men, is not a personal act, it is a Slavic ceremony. It is fundamentally a form of communion: a spiritual break and opportunity for a private talk. This cultural norm, and the typically very small apartments, also explains the Slavic tradition of smoking and drinking in stairwells of their apartment buildings.

Over the years I've learned that if a Slavic friend says, "Let's go for a cigarette," you should never refuse to go, even if you quit smoking 20 years ago, are asthmatic, or even on oxygen with a tank in tow. You need not smoke but it is important to go and support him and have an opportunity for special communication and bonding. A refusal to go is viewed by a Slav as rude, insensitive and soulless behavior.

Unlike jogging, smoking and drinking are respectable pastimes for Slavic men. Jogging, however, remains a suspicious activity when done away from stadiums; joggers are thought to be athletes. In Moscow and Kyiv, I'll occasionally spot a native who, while smoking and drinking beer with friends, mocks a jogger by briefly running after him with a cigarette dangling from his lips and a beer in hand.

The outlook for the future isn't very promising. I recall an October 2009 outdoor "Healthy Living Day" celebration in downtown Kyiv with a portion of the main avenue sealed off from automobile traffic. As usual, crowds of young and not-so-young Ukrainians gathered for the free party. It was a very festive occasion with a rock band, balloons, information booths, and free blood pressure and HIV-AIDS testing (though not many takers for the latter). I was disappointed, but not at all surprised, to find a sea of young smokers and beer drinkers celebrating Healthy Living Day. Elderly Slavs like to say, "They are our future."

But there's good news for visiting Americans who are light smokers! Russia and Ukraine are "smoke-free countries" for you. You don't need to buy cigarettes here. You can smoke "gypsy style" as my Slavic friends like to call it (i.e., smoke passively in public areas with many smokers).

Walk down any central street in Moscow or Kyiv and you are surrounded by an army of smokers. Typically you'll walk into cloud after cloud of exhaled smoke from smokers walking in front of you. And after just a week in downtown Moscow or Kyiv you'll feel like you're living in a big ashtray.

My favorite places to get a "free smoke" are in Moscow and Kyiv's long bus lines where natives smoke freely, outside of metro entrances, in underground pedestrian crossings, and most cafes and restaurants. You can even get a buzz on public transportation. Most Slavic bus drivers smoke while at the wheel but crack their windows open a bit as a courtesy to passengers. Just be sure to sit in the front of the bus, and be prepared to be an organ donor if you want to make Slavic friends.

The Smiling American

"A smile is an inexpensive way to improve your looks."
                                        -Andy Rooney

Americans have an international reputation for being a smiling, polite, good-natured people. Just ask any foreigner visiting America. In their hour of need, be it for directions or information about basic amenities, they'll usually get a thoughtful, cheerful response. This is not surprising. After all, we are a nation of immigrants, former foreigners.

However, when we travel abroad our smiling countenances often mark us as oddities. In Russia, I have been told frequently that to walk the streets with a big grin or a smile suggests to strangers that you may have escaped from a mental institution. This view is widely shared in Ukraine. Ride the metro in Moscow or Kyiv and the standard facial expression of natives is a tired "Why did you burn my house down?" look. Make no mistake, these Slavs love to laugh and smile but generally reserve these expressions for close friends and family at home and work.

To stand alone on crowded Moscow public transportation and

smile will immediately draw many worried looks from natives. Just try it. Only very small Slavic children, not yet programmed with the "How did you escape from the insane asylum?" gene, will be amused by your expression and may even return an impish grin.

Public smiles are often the object of Slavic jokes. I have been told by Russian friends that if two men approach one another on a city street and one smiles at the other, it can only mean one of two things. The smiling man is gay, or he has noticed that the approaching man's zipper is open. A word to the wise: It is not advisable for a man to smile at a Slavic man who is a perfect stranger. The typical response will be a gruff, "What's your problem?"

However, there's another compelling and rather sensitive reason why many Slavs do not choose to smile publicly. Despite remarkable advances in Slavic dentistry since the U.S.S.R. collapsed in 1991, many Russians and Ukrainians have missing or very bad teeth. Significantly, dental floss remains an alien substance and dentists in TV commercials, amusingly, still tell listeners to brush their teeth twice a day. Once, in my opinion, would be a welcome start.

And what about those dazzling Soviet-metallic teeth that used to be in vogue 20 years ago. I'm always startled when a middle-aged female, Russian-grocery clerk finally graces me with a smile and I'm blinded by her gold teeth. It's like staring directly into the sun.

Russians and Ukrainians who have a casual opportunity to meet Americans on their own turf typically do not find that the ever present American smile with "big white teeth," as they love to note, is engaging. Rather, they describe it as insincere and even stupid. They also view American politeness peppered with constant use of "Excuse me" and "Thank you" as superficial and insincere. Ruslan's story is illustrative.

Ruslan, a 33-year-old Russian driver for an American family working and living in Moscow in 2002, recounted the following incident to me. Early mornings he would drive the couple's two small boys to their elite international school where he would deposit them with an American instructor waiting for them at the guarded school gate. Each morning Ruslan would hear a glib, "Hi Ruslan, how are you today?" And before Ruslan could take a breath to respond, the smiling American had turned away and carted the children off to the schoolhouse.

This repeated experience made a very negative impression upon Ruslan. One day over coffee at a café, he admitted being bewildered and slighted when this first occurred. He expressed his disappointment with this hollow greeting and "American habit" and said Russians expect an answer, and even a discussion, when such a personal question is asked.

I wanted to tell Ruslan to lighten up but instead I suggested he try to adjust to this non-Slavic habit and be thankful that there is at least a smile on the surface and a polite hello from this American school teacher rather than a condescending look at a Slavic driver. Ruslan's slighted expression remained unchanged.

Ruslan's reaction to the American school teacher becomes more understandable in the light of Slavic history. In Russia and Ukraine the art of conversation is alive and deeply ingrained in Slavic culture. It's a tradition which includes having long, soulful conversations about life's hardships and absurdities around tiny kitchen tables with endless cups of tea and even stronger drinks. There is also a tradition of very close friends calling upon one another at any hour of the night because they need help with a problem, and a mutual understanding that this is acceptable behavior. However, this social norm is being chipped away steadily with the collapse of the Soviet Union and the introduction of wild capitalism.

But not all Slavs share Ruslan's critical reaction to smiling Americans. A Ukrainian psychologist I interviewed during May 2009 described her recent visit to the U.S. to attend a professional conference on a college campus. Between sessions of the conference she found time to stroll the campus grounds. Despite her expert knowledge of American society, she was pleasantly surprised by how nearly every passing student gave her, a perfect stranger, a friendly hello or commented on what a lovely day it was. She said it immediately raised her spirits and brightened her day. She shared this experience with me to illustrate the power of kind words and a smile, and to observe how sorely lacking they are in Ukraine and Russia.

This psychologist's story was reinforced by the comments of two Russian girls who recently spent their final year of high school and college, respectively, in the U.S. under a USAID-funded program.

The girls lived with American families in different, small midwestern cities. The Russian high school student recounted how friendly perfect strangers were in her town and how teachers treated American students with respect and kindness unlike her Slavic experience. The Russian college student echoed these remarks and added that her American professors would encourage student interaction in class and would empathize with their personal problems, very unlike her Slavic professors.

These positive stories about America, and the typically sour expressions people wear in Russia and Ukraine, have made me drop my criticism of what I once believed was a meaningless American expression, "Have a nice day." I now see it as compelling evidence of civility, a virtue sorely lacking in Russia and Ukraine. And the next time I earn this expression in the U.S. from a perfect stranger, I intend to reply, "Thank you, I plan to."

In fairness, I should note that there are an increasing number of young Slavic professionals, especially in the business community, who do believe that a smile is an inexpensive way to improve your looks and a good way to promote interpersonal relations. A Russian friend told me the following illustrative story. A Russian man in his late 20s read Dale Carnegie's classic work, *How to Make Friends and Influence People,* and was determined to apply some of its lessons, especially the need to smile at people.

One day on the way to work, he smiled sincerely at everyone he saw on the street and in the metro. At the office he also smiled at his co-workers all morning long. During lunchtime, his boss came up to him and said, "If you come to work drunk one more time, you're fired!" It seems that smiling in public for no apparent reason remains suspicious and unnatural activity for Slavs.

The Generously Proportioned American

> *"Why can there never be another revolution in America? Because there is not enough time between meals!"*
> -Zadornov, Russian humorist

Growing obesity in America is no secret. Today (2012), nearly 70 percent of Americans are obese: especially disturbing is the steady increase in obesity among elementary school children. Ironically, we consume more fat-free products than any other nation and, yet, the results are obvious.

To put it mildly, we are a nation of great girth, a nation of snackers, victims of a "bigger-is-better" culture, a hand-held food nation where most Americans look exceedingly well nourished. Thus, it is not surprising that some foreign humorists make fun of our size and eating habits.

The brilliant American statesman Thomas Jefferson once said, "We never repent of having eaten too little." Oh, how wrong he was! Even a casual visitor to America's all you can eat "Old Country

Buffet" chain—and there are countless similar chains across the U.S.—will see an army of obese customers ravenously and repeatedly attack multiple main-course and dessert bars. Many, in fact, sit anxiously in mall parking lots waiting daily for the opening bell to such establishments.

Who can honestly say that these loyal "all-you-can-eat-and-more" buffet revelers never regret not having had a third or fourth helping of fried chicken, mashed potatoes swimming in gravy, and banana cream pie, washed down with another liter of coke at an Old Country Buffet the day before? Viewed in this light, it's not surprising that many cultures of the world, including Slavic ones, recognize two basic schools of nutrition: eating healthy and "eating like Americans."

When a generously proportioned (obese) American arrives in Russia or Ukraine, he or she is in for some serious culture shock. Most distressing is the fact dinner plates are the size of dessert plates. Give one of these to an average American and a fist fight is likely to break out.

But there's more bad news. There are no "all-you-can-eat-and-more" American-style buffets restaurants. Slavic dinner portions generally are kids' size by American standards (1950s kids' size, not today's). And before you're able to get to the meat and potatoes you're served a first course of a liquid substance in a bowl called soup—very un-American, indeed.

When young Slavs come to America summers on work permits, they are shocked to learn that we are essentially a soupless nation. They fall asleep nights dreaming of their mother's borscht, a very rich Slavic national stew and staple of their life that must be served with a heaving spoonful of sour cream.

Make no mistake. Slavic food is very rich and filling. Dinners usually include several tasty salads without lettuce and typically held together with a generous amount of mayonnaise. Bread, white and dark, is a must on Slavic dinner tables. It's so essential that Russians and Ukrainians have a saying, "The right hand is for a fork or spoon and the left hand for bread."

The big American, however, will also be disappointed to learn that average Slavs don't share our tradition of "washing down" our meals with enormous tumblers full of soda or iced tea. And if you ask for tea or coffee with your meal, you'll get an odd look and a polite "That's later." In Russia and Ukraine there is the tradition that no meal is complete without tea, and then more tea, as a last course with a few cookies or chocolates.

Slavic family meals typically are simple but always at a table in their typically tiny one or two room apartments, and usually at a small kitchen table. The generously proportioned American will also have to stop finishing his food in record time. Life here is a "go-slow culture" and this is very evident when it comes to meals or just having tea or coffee.

There's more bad news for Americans. In living and working in Russia and Ukraine over the course of 20 years, I've never seen an ice cube in a Slavic home. Here drinks are chilled and that, generally, means lukewarm. Anyone who finds ice cubes here should realize they are probably made with contaminated tap water.

But the visiting, hefty American will also find much good news readily available. Since the Soviet Union collapsed 20 years ago, each city block in Moscow or Kyiv generally has a few kiosks and often a tiny one-room convenience store with all of life's necessities: many types of beer, cigarettes, fatty sausage, potato chips, pastries, chocolates, coffee, tea, water, juices, gum and more.

And there's more good news. The Golden arches of McDonald's, with the forced smiles of young Slavic workers, are easy to find. TGIF ("Thank Goodness It's Friday"), a popular American restaurant, also can be found in Kyiv and Moscow and it advertises famous "American size portions" (but hardly Old Country Buffet fare) in big bold letters. In addition, there are a few very large malls in downtown Kyiv and Moscow, each with very eclectic and busy food courts.

European-style pizza parlors have been springing up with greater frequency in Moscow and Kyiv in recent years. Two noteworthy ones in downtown Kyiv are Lola and Verona Pizza. A few years ago I made the mistake of going with a friend to Lola Pizza, a pretentious, allegedly Italian-style restaurant in a basement with a dozen tiny tables. We arrived late one afternoon and were the only customers there—in hindsight an important clue. We quickly decided on two small, thin crust pizzas and a glass of red wine each. Nearly an hour and another glass of wine later, still no pizzas! At that point I was tempted to go in the kitchen and help the chef.

The pizzas finally arrived and were not worth the wait. To add insult to injury, after we finished eating the waiter had the nerve to ask if everything was OK. I wanted to reply with the Ukrainian expression, "Don't make the chickens laugh" but was polite and simply smiled. Hopefully, Lola has since gone out of business.

Just a few doors down from Lola is one of Verona Pizza's several quick service restaurants. They offer high quality pizza, quick-service and even provide a variety of pizza by the slice. Unlike Lola Pizza, which has difficulty delivering pizza to their tables within an hour, Verona delivers to apartments and businesses in the area within 30 minutes.

In short, if you have money everything is available. However, if you live like a native and earn the average Ukrainian monthly wage of $250 (in 2012), or average pension of $110 a month, you're in for hard times and will need to practice anger management. Many elderly Slavs are forced to survive on a diet of bread, macaroni, soups, cabbage salads, apples, and very little protein.

Over the past two decades I've had an opportunity to interact with many American graduate students who've come to Russia or Ukraine for an academic year on a U.S.-funded academic exchange program. Typically, after a few months they're singing the Slavic blues. Often I would chat with them at big Thanksgiving Day dinners and other social gatherings sponsored by their U.S. parent agency to help lift their homesickness. Many of them were generously-proportioned Americans and their message after just two or three months in this Slavic wonderland was one of country and culture shock.

In Kyiv I often heard them complain about very fatty and greasy Ukrainian food. Most told me the same story: after just a few months in Ukraine, they felt they had consumed more mayo and sour cream with the dinners their Slavic host families had provided them than in their entire lifetime back home. Many were curious why preparation of every Ukrainian meal seemed to start with frying onions, and said they often suffered as a result. They also grimaced when they told me about their failed efforts to acquire a taste for Ukrainian *salo* (pork-fat slices), a national treat, and jokingly called Ukrainian snickers and Ukraine's white gold.

However, their biggest gripe and country shock—one that I always enjoy hearing about—is the state of Slavic public toilets everywhere, including at their educational institutions. Nothing in their American handbooks prepared them adequately for the reality of dank, urine-saturated squat toilets or regular American-style toilets without seats and toilet paper.

One young American woman told me that when she returns to the U.S. she'll never again look at a toilet seat the same way again, and will never take for granted American public restrooms with their omnipresent toilet seats, bountiful toilet paper and locking doors. Listening to her made me homesick.

Slavic Public Toilets

> *"The unavailability and state of our public toilets reflects official disrespect for our citizens."*
> -view of a Russian babushka

At the outset let me make one thing clear. I do not make it a habit to survey public toilets in Russia and Ukraine (or the U.S.). However, given that I've abandoned my American-car culture and am on foot a good part of the day in Moscow and Kyiv and have been over the past 20 years, I've made quite a few nature calls. Often the need quickly recedes as soon as I've entered one of these facilities. To call them public "restrooms" would be criminal.

Slavic public toilets are not free and most are very old, smelly and in a disgusting state. The elderly female attendant who takes your money also guards and grudgingly doles out a few coarse brown (clearly not baby soft) sheets of toilet paper, and only if asked. Two thoughts come to mind. Who do you need to sleep with to get more than a few squares of sandpaper-quality toilet paper in Slavic public toilets? And thank God I have advanced Boy

Scout training in how to use a square of toilet paper.

Conditions in these public toilets typically are unsanitary, even though you will often see an elderly woman mop the floor around your feet as you use a urinal. Learning that Slavic public toilets are strictly squat toilets is a very rude awakening, especially for weak-kneed Americans.

The stalls generally do not lock, are full of excrement, and flood on to the floor a step below. Moreover, the attendant could make a small fortune if she gave customers clothespins for their noses and galoshes for their feet. Broken faucet taps are common and as for hot water, well "Don't make the chickens laugh," as Slavs like to say.

I'll never forget one of the first and most shocking squat toilets I ever saw. It was in St. Petersburg's main train station in the early 1990s. I arrived early in the morning on a very bumpy overnight train from Moscow and wanted to freshen up in the station's men's room. Rather than have closed squat stalls, it had a handful of waist-high squat stalls with no doors. The men's room was very crowded and all of the stalls were in use, with two or three men waiting in front of each stall for their turn—much less privacy than in American prisons. This was my rude awakening to Slavic squat stalls. Not surprisingly, my urgent need to use one of those stalls quickly vanished.

The toilet paper in public facilities remarkably is the same coarse brown paper used in Soviet times. However, you're lucky if you can find any in academic institutions. During the late 1990s, I spent a great deal of time in Moscow consulting with scholars at a research institute attached to the Russian Academy of Sciences. I remember vividly the thoughtfulness of a mysterious staff member there. In one of the stalls in the institute's men's room (it had a door), a kind soul placed small square sheets from his draft working paper in a wall receptacle, intended for toilet paper, to share with colleagues. No doubt, an unkind Russian staff member might comment that this is all that scholar's work is worth, but I found it to be a thoughtful act.

However, the prize for the most unsanitary and disgusting public toilet goes hands down to Kyiv's national zoo for its state in October 2009, 18 years after Ukraine declared independence from the Soviet Union. Certainly, I've seen worse public toilets in Russia and Ukraine previously but never nearly two decades after the collapse of the U.S.S.R. What was especially disturbing was the fact that the Kyiv zoo had become a beautiful garden-like facility by 2009, unlike its impoverished state in 2003 when I first visited it. In October 2009, it featured a very attractive and well-developed reptile house, manicured grounds, and also had a large board with more than a dozen pictures of leading Ukrainian politicians who contributed to the zoo's upkeep. However, by 2011 dozens of its very large animals were dead as a result of the willful neglect of the zoo's administrators.

After I toured the zoo in 2009 for a few hours and stopped at its café, I made the mistake of using its solitary men's toilet before departing for the metro. What I found almost knocked me over. It's handful of urinals were all caked with a dark orange slime and one of the urinals even had maggots on it.

To add insult to injury, the single sink in this totally neglected facility did not even have running water. I was tempted to complain to a zoo administrator but then I remembered I was in Ukraine. The only explanation for the horrible state of this men's room is the zoo's total disrespect for its citizens and the small children, notably, who visit the zoo. The zoo's staff, no doubt, had its own clean comfort station. Sadly, I found that the state of the men's room at the zoo had not improved at all when I returned in October 2011.

The situation I've found in Ukrainian hospitals for pensioners and the general public, 20 years after the collapse of the Soviet Union, is not as extreme as the zoo's but unpardonable for a medical facility. For example, Kyiv's Pimonenko clinic, a four-story hospital-size facility, has a single basement toilet for visitors' use. It's a tiny dark, dank cave which is not very sanitary and, no doubt, never used by any hospital staff. Moreover, it's is a telling reflection of the hospital's disrespect for its clients and its conspicuous us-versus-them mentality. Interestingly, the same clinic offers staff an elite dining room, café, and massage facilities.

As bad as public toilets generally are in Russia and Ukraine, more troubling still is their scarce availability. The elderly constantly complain about this, but to no avail. During May 2011, for example, outraged citizens in Zhytomyr, a city in northwestern Ukraine, protested publicly for days but with no positive response from their mayor. Significantly, the idea of providing more than a few token public toilets, which serve the needs of disabled persons, is light years away.

The general situation with public toilets is even worse in Ukraine's capital, Kyiv, than in Moscow. In Ukraine, amazingly, public buildings such as national museums, art galleries and local libraries, generally, have no toilet facilities available for visitors. Visitors are shocked to learn this. I recall standing outside of Kyiv's Russian Art Museum in 2009 when a college-age Ukrainian woman darted out and asked me if there was a toilet nearby. I should stress that this is a question that Slavic women never ask a strange man. Obviously she was desperate. Fortunately, I was able to direct her to the toilet in the park just across from the museum. I didn't bother to tell her that this facility was on my "Use only if you're really desperate list" because she obviously was.

When I return to the U.S. after living in Russia and Ukraine for extended periods, I always approach the average American public restroom (yes, the term restroom is appropriate here) with a sense of profound respect and deep longing. I want to fall to my knees and kiss the ground (figuratively speaking, of course) thankful that I'm home.

In addition to finding toilet seats in America's public restrooms, versus knee-shattering Slavic squat toilets, I also find toilet rolls without a Slavic granny tugging at the other end. In fact, a decade ago U.S. government buildings and public libraries, notably, introduced Mega toilet rolls in their restrooms: colossal rolls that are a foot in diameter and theft proof, provided there are no Slavs visiting.

I've learned that anyone who can start such a toilet roll deserves a civic achievement award. Sadly, this is followed by the realization that only an ultra-thin square or two can be torn successfully from this overgrown toilet roll. What sadistic American bureaucrat on the verge of retirement came up with this idea, and what Einstein of a supervisor approved it? No doubt, both received superior performance ratings that year as a result, and both probably carry pocket-size Kleenex packets for personal use when nature calls.

Good news for Russia, however! The 21st century rang in a bright new era in public toilets there. I remember vividly this glorious moment in Russia's post-Soviet history. I had just come off an escalator at Moscow's Frunzenskaya metro station and was about to walk to my apartment just across the Moscow river from

Gorky Park when I spotted a glorious sight just outside the metro entrance. I froze in my tracks and my eyes began to tear. It was a work of beauty and fine American engineering: A plastic John-Boy portable toilet and, yes, it was guarded by a serious looking Russian babushka.

It was heaven-sent and I couldn't resist the urge to use it. The babushka who took my coin insisted on giving me instructions on how to use this advanced technology. I politely listened but really wanted to proudly tell her that I was a veteran user of this American marvel.

Other John-Boys soon graced Russia's landscape, and the exteriors of central Moscow metro stations, in particular. I found several just outside the very busy Lenin Library metro station in the heart of Moscow and other stations. For me this historic breakthrough meant no more descending into the dank, smelly bowels of Soviet-era public toilets, and was no less important than the collapse of the Soviet Union.

But there is even better news and every Russian and Ukrainian, young and old, is keenly aware of it. McDonald's for most Slavs is not primarily the home of the Big Mac or the McFlurry but, first and foremost, it is the home of free, clean, non-squat toilets! Slavic women, in particular, are eternally grateful.

The Sweaty American

> *"Don't sweat the petty things and don't pet the sweaty things."*
>
> -George Carlin

Most of my time in Russia and Ukraine has included very muggy summers with a month typically spent in Moscow and Kyiv as well. However, this changed shortly after Ukraine's democratic Orange Revolution of 2004 when I found Ukraine and its visa regime, in particular, much friendlier to foreigners than Putin's Russia. I don't miss summers in Moscow, especially given its deathly pollution.

Kyiv is no picnic in summers either. It also has very high levels of pollution and is located just 60 miles south of Chornobyl, the 1986 scene of the world's worst civilian nuclear disaster. On the plus side, however, Kyiv has many beautiful parks and countless chestnut trees and even Muscovites refer to it as the Green City and former Miami of the Soviet Union.

During my time in Russia and Ukraine I've always abandoned

American creature comforts and gone native. I find it more challenging and endlessly fascinating. I've never seen an ice cube here in 20 years and would be afraid to have one in a drink even if I could, knowing the horrible state of tap water in these countries.

A few words about my physical build are in order. In my adult history, on average I've been about 15 lbs. overweight, according to international standards, for my almost 6-foot build. By current American standards, this is un-American and I qualify to be called slim.

I know I must have sweated many times during my adult life in America and Washington, D.C. summers, in particular. The string of menial jobs I held from high school up until my first professional job were generally back-breaking and I vividly recall sweating bullets working summers in a propane factory while in college and in a bakery during high school years.

Mid-life memories of sweating don't spring to mind. Oh yes, I can recall breaking into a lather not long ago in the U.S. when I bent over for about five minutes and tried to get a tough knot out of one of my shoes. I became dizzy and nearly lost my balance. However, there's no comparison to my experience on baking days in Russia and Ukraine. The transition from America's car culture to that of a Slavic pack mule weighed down daily with liters of clean drinking water and other articles is not an easy one.

But this is the life I've chosen while living in Russia and Ukraine. To say goodbye to my beloved American—actually Japanese—car that would routinely carry me two blocks to my local convenience store for a 60 ounce, or more, mostly ice drink and often accompanied by a chili-cheese dog. And to say goodbye to the air-conditioned world that most Americans inhabit when temperatures become even slightly uncomfortable for us. Yes, this is my choice: to live on a shoestring in Russia and Ukraine, rather than lie on some tropical beach.

My most vivid early memories of summers in Moscow and Kyiv are of baking sun and stifling heat aggravated by clouds of fumes from countless vehicles without catalytic converters, and from legions of smokers. On foot or in crowded public transport, the picture of a middle-aged American burdened with heavy bags is not a pretty one. On central city streets hordes of unsmiling Slavs would approach me as though I were magnet and violate any sliver of personal space I might guard. As my plastic bags with groceries would grow heavier and drag my arms ever closer to the pavement, I would often find a car slowly sneaking up behind me on the city sidewalk—a common occurrence in both Moscow and Kyiv.

As tiny streams of sweat would flow down my back and temples, I would notice that the army of Slavs around me didn't have a bead of sweat between them. Occasionally I would notice a young Slavic male pass me wearing a black leather jacket in 90-plus degree heat and sucking on a cigarette. This would trigger the release of reserve streams of sweat down my chest and make me feel dizzy.

I would repeat this experience of sweating like ice cream melting in the hot mid-day sun over and over again during the typically 90-plus degree, scorching summer days. But I would dream of a day when I would be able to wear a leather jacket and pants in such temperatures and remain cool and crisp. Typically, I would awake from such a dream in a sweat.

Places where I've set records sweating include the Moscow metro during rush hour and its very long airless, connecting tunnels between stations—and no it's not just like NYC! The cars are so crowded that you often don't need to grab a support if you are standing because you are wedged in on all sides by foreign bodies.

This reminds me of a Russian anecdote: An attractive, young Russian woman standing on a crowded Moscow metro is wedged in on all sides. She turns to one man pressing against her and says angrily, "Sir, back off!" She then turns to an attractive man pressing her similarly and says, "You're OK."

I've been in Moscow metro cars where the temperatures have been reported over 100 degrees and I sweat like a prostitute in church. I hate to admit it but I've often found the heat and crushing bodies so unbearable that I've been tempted to get off at a station before my stop just to get a breath of air. However, I've always resisted, keenly aware that I would have to push my way out of the car only to eventually push my way into another very crowded one.

I can recall often wearing just a dark t-shirt in the scorching summer heat on Kyiv streets and after many hours discovering heavy salt stains on it at home after the sweaty shirt dried in the scorching sun. I never knew my body could release so much salt.

Frankly, I was very impressed.

Many of Kyiv's very narrow underground shopping malls are another sauna during summers and a real fire hazard. They extend for several city blocks and can contain a hundred or more tiny stalls filled beyond capacity with clothing, leather accessories, and home furnishings. Given the serious lack of ventilation in these Slavic catacombs, I often wish I had an oxygen tank with me. However, these narrow underground malls are useful areas to walk through in winter and bad weather, in general.

Minibuses are a major means of post-Soviet public transportation and are usually standing room only. In summer months windows typically remain closed because of the national fear of drafts (a draft is a current of air in any enclosed space). I can recall many summers in Russia when I would have to endure a very long and steamy, standing-room-only bus ride home after riding an airless metro to the end of a line from the center of Moscow.

A few tips to help weak Americans living in Russia and Ukraine cope with miserable summer heat in the asphalt jungle. When you live without a car in the big city and are constantly on the move, you eventually learn to walk long distances on the shady side of the street and ideally plan your activities during the cooler parts of the day. Whenever possible you schedule your morning and afternoon appointments so that you can avoid rush-hour traffic on public transit and city sidewalks. You do most of your serious grocery shopping and carrying on early weekend mornings when there are fewer shoppers and less traffic, including pedestrians, in cities like Moscow and Kyiv; Slavs are often still nursing hangovers.

You also eventually learn to dress sensibly, and in a very un-American manner, for the heat. You no longer wear ties to formal meetings. You follow native common-sense dress tips for the summer, including a pair of those men's thatched, light-weight shoes with holes in them that used to make you laugh. You buy light clothing that doesn't retain sweat. You learn to buy and drink bottled water on the go so that you have less cargo to carry home, and you learn to use the first few metro cars in a train because they are usually less crowded.

When I complain to Slavic friends about the extreme summer heat and lack of ventilation in public transit and most shops, they always say, "With time, you too will get used to it." Twenty years have passed and I'm still not used to it. How long does it take? I'm running out of life!

The sad fact is I will never get used to it. We Americans spend most of our lives, if at all possible, living in an A/C bubble. By middle age, and usually much earlier, we lack the immune system of Slavs and other cultures when it comes to enduring heat. We are bubble people. When temperatures become uncomfortable, we enter the A/C bubble at home, in cars, offices, malls, cinemas, fitness centers, and supermarkets. Interestingly, most Slavs, young and old, that I've met fiercely maintain that air-conditioning is bad for you.

And so we routinely drive rather than walk two or three blocks. We carry groceries with great difficulty no further than the distance from our car to our home. In short, we are very fortunate as long as we do not leave our home, America with all of its underappreciated creature comforts, and live among the natives in a third world country like Russia or Ukraine.

But the summer of 2010 demonstrated unmistakably that Slavs could sweat. Moscow experienced an unprecedented heat wave for several weeks with temperatures reaching 104 degrees. Moscow was blanketed with thick, toxic smoke forcing many citizens who did go out to wear masks or cover themselves with scarves. The heavy smoke even found its way into buildings and the Moscow metro.

Nonetheless, many hardcore Russian smokers continued their habit. Some even joked that doing so was a prophylactic act, with their own clouds of cigarette smoke attacking the thick, omnipresent toxic smoke. Russian authorities claimed that this was the greatest heat wave to hit Russia in 1,000 years.

Regrettably, I missed the sweltering heat wave that blanketed Russia and Ukraine during 2010. I spent the entire summer in the Washington, DC area. It was a sad pleasure, indeed, to watch Slavs melt on TV while sitting in my Lazy-Boy chair, in air-conditioned comfort with an iced tea, in my A/C bubble.

Mayo Heaven

A minute on your lips, a lifetime on your hips.
                                               -a sad fact

American men who are interested in Slavic women from afar typically share a common image. With the aid of numerous Russian and Ukrainian dating and marriage websites, they grow convinced that Slavic women are generally gorgeous and have slim but very shapely bikini bodies. Expats living in Moscow and Kyiv, when they find time to tear away from expat cafes and full-strip bars, often confirm this image in their boastful blogs.

Indeed, many Slavic women fit this stereotype but a great many more do not. In fact, by the time they reach 30 their dimensions often are "meter-meter-meter," as one Russian woman frankly admitted to me.

What explains this dramatic metamorphosis from a tall and thin Slavic vixen into a meaty mama in a culture with no longstanding tradition of pizza, chips, hamburger, and French-fry consumption? In my considered opinion, Slavic women's unabashed addiction to mayonnaise is a key factor.

In Ukraine and Russia, a house is not a home without an uninterrupted supply of fresh, dairy-case mayo. In my American life, as far back as I can remember, mayonnaise has always been a large jar that inhabited the recesses of our refrigerator. It saw the light of day rarely and associated little with its neighbors. Its only real friend was tuna fish. I'm fairly certain that my two grown sons never tried mayo before the age of 18, and I have a sneaking suspicion one in his early 20s has yet to try it.

Here in Ukraine, where I live, mayo has rock-star status and is an acquired taste: It's acquired by the time a child becomes a toddler. In my Kyiv Mega-Supermarket mayonnaise fills a very large dairy case and comes in several dozen types. It typically comes in hand-size plastic pouches and is very fresh, rich and velvety smooth. And it bears little resemblance to the few American brands that have a long shelf life, come in jars, and can be found in store aisles.

Not long ago I found more telling evidence in my supermarket that Slavic women take their mayo very seriously. In a regular aisle I came across green gallon-size tubs of mayo produced by Hellmann's. I was surprised but not shocked. I could easily picture the hefty women who use it generously.

Fat-free or light mayo in Ukraine? "Don't make the chickens laugh," as Slavs like to say. Mention fat-free mayo and you'll likely have a fist fight on your hands. Real mayo is an essential ingredient of Slavic life and not just a cream that lubricates exotic salads and vegetable and meat slices. It's the emergency fix and balm for aching souls that holds families together and keeps women from going over the edge and biting the men in their lives. It's a major national anti-depressant and there is much to be depressed about in Ukraine and Russia. Frankly, I'm surprised it's not available in Slavic drugstores and billed as mayo therapy.

I was saddened to read recently on the Internet that a condition called mayophobia exists. There are no recorded Slavic cases but many Americans apparently suffer from an extreme fear of mayonnaise, "the unspoken white stuff," and even worry about it. One American woman writes: "I literally live my life around my fear. I will not eat at a restaurant if there is a possibility that mayo may be put on my food."

This comment reminds me of my first serious encounter with

mayonnaise in Russia more than a decade ago. It was a very casual get together around a kitchen table and the hostess was making bite-size appetizers in front of me: mouth-size wedges of black bread with thin slices of sausage, onion, tomato, and a shockingly big dab of mayo. My heart raced as she smilingly offered me one. Not to accept would be to insult the hostess. I took a deep breath and then filled my mouth.

These appetizers are made typically to accompany shots of vodka. Before an hour was up, I devoured three more of these appetizers. Today, I am a convert and make them for Slavic friends who never refuse them. I can only imagine the reaction of American mayophobics to these treats.

Many Americans living in Russia and Ukraine admit not liking this white, greasy substance before moving abroad. A few rugged Slavic months later and life without it becomes unthinkable for many of them. Some even joke about how Slavic women seem to use a liter a day.

Mayonnaise is the magic that holds together the many simple but exotic salads that Slavs make typically from whatever ingredients are readily available: diced potatoes, eggs, cheese, onions, pickles, corn, peas, beets, shrimp, herring, meats; lettuce is conspicuously absent from these salads. "Everything tastes better with mayo and things taste best with lots of mayo," Slavic mothers, in particular, are fond of saying.

Interestingly, Slavic salads have very little resemblance to the salads Americans are generally served in restaurants. A middle-aged Russian woman flying back to Moscow after her first visit to the U.S. shared the following story during a long flight. American friends invited her to lunch at a Chili's chain restaurant. She wanted a light lunch and simply ordered a salad. She was shocked by what she received: a huge bowl filled largely with lettuce. Her reaction: "This is enough to feed a small village in my country." Not surprisingly, when the waitress asked what kind of dressing she would like, she said "Mayo." The waitress smiled and said they didn't have mayo as an offering. The Russian woman was shocked and probably even called home that night with the sad news.

The fact is a salad in an America restaurant is typically a huge bowl of foliage and an excuse for the coveted main ingredient, a cupful of blue cheese or other rich and very fattening dressing. If we could have our way in America, we would probably skip the foliage and just have a heaping cup of blue cheese dressing and take little gulps.

I have a warning for Americans fortunate enough to be invited to an average Slav's tiny, modest apartment for dinner. Ketchup isn't considered just a condiment here. I remember the first time I had spaghetti over a Russian friend's apartment in the late 1990s. His wife prepared a spaghetti and chicken cutlet dinner and we sat comfortably around the tiny kitchen table. What I remember most vividly was the sauce that accompanied my spaghetti. Before I could say a word the hostess gave my spaghetti a huge squirt of ketchup from a plastic pouch and then smilingly asked if I would like more. Still trying to recover from the shock, I politely declined. She generously treated me to more, nonetheless.

With time I would learn that American-style ketchup is a delicacy and coveted sauce in Slavic homes, and is considered second only to mayo as an all-purpose Slavic lubricant. Interestingly, ketchup was unknown in Ukraine and Russia until the mid-1990s. It was brought to Ukraine by two young Swedes, Johan Boden and Carl Sturen, who later expanded their business into mayonnaise; in 2010 they had a combined wealth of $26 million. Given Slavs' love affair with ketchup I'm tempted to share the secret of Hobo tomato soup with them: a couple of ketchup packets—the kind normally available free from fast food vendors in the U.S.—boiling hot water, stir and presto!

Objectively speaking, there are two additional reasons why Slavic women often "throw in the towel" after 30 and become meter-meter-meter: very fatty sausages and sweets. The many circles of fat present in virtually all Slavic sausages need to be seen to be believed.

Russian and Ukrainian women do have a very strong cultural love of sweets. This and their slower metabolism after age 30 help explain where the "meters" come from. One Russian woman confessed to me that the favorite exercise and sport of many of these meter gals is "running around the kitchen." In their defense it should be noted that their sweet-tooth addiction is encouraged daily and very easily filled. Slavic cities are littered with convenient kiosks and portable tables near metros that sell inexpensive fresh Slavic pastries, cookies and other sweets. It's very difficult not to indulge.

And who can blame Slavic women for occasionally giving into the temptation of a classic Kyiv tort: three layers of meringue with hazelnuts and a buttercream-like filling. This cake is one of the symbols of this ancient city and was first made in 1950 at Kyiv's Karl Marx Confectionary Factory. I think Marx would turn over in his grave if he knew that a cake factory bears his name and that the owner is one of Ukraine's richest billionaires.

Indeed, obesity is not uncommon among older Slavic women but there is a fundamental difference in their appearance compared to their obese American sisters. Russia's beloved humorist, Mikhail Zadornov, in commenting on obese American women, made the unkind remark that they look like they're wearing Pampers; or, stated differently, like jello shaking on your mother's kitchen table. Obese Slavic women, on the other hand, generally have more of a "built like a brick outhouse" look, more of a meat and potato swimming in mayo obesity. It's the result of not having a tradition of consuming chips, pizza, hamburgers and fries, and especially the need to do a lot of unavoidable walking in a still largely non-car culture.

I thought I had seen everything in the Slavic world of mayo until one day in late 2010 when I was standing in a Kyiv supermarket checkout aisle behind two middle-aged Ukrainian women. The only items they placed on the conveyor belt immediately caught my eye: two liter-size plastic bags of heavy cream and eight pouches of fresh mayonnaise! I couldn't believe my eyes. I was very tempted to ask them if they were going to make something tasty. However, it's rude here for a stranger to ask locals even innocent personal questions.

After some thoughtful reflection, I could only conclude one thing: They were going to have a Slavic "girls gone wild" mayo orgy night. And the only thing that could make the evening more enjoyable would be to have balloons, and invite a male-midget stripper.

If you love mayo, you'll love Russia and Ukraine. You'll be in mayo heaven.

My Khrushchovka

"Life in Russia is repugnant but never boring."
-view of a Russian returning home after a US visit

I'll never forget the first apartment I lived in on the outskirts of Moscow 20 years ago. It was located in what is called a "sleep district"—blocks of grey, identical 20-story buildings—the kind that would easily confuse a man coming home after a night of serious drinking. It was my baptism by fire. My two months there prepared me for the Soviet-style living conditions I would experience over the next two decades in a dozen or more similarly depressing one-room apartments in Moscow and Kyiv.

This one room apartment, about 30 square meters (the size of an average American living room), was located on the 16th floor of a 20-floor high rise. The contents were very Spartan: a tiny bed, writing table, lamp, and chair. The few appliances and wall paper were vintage Soviet.

With hardly a crumb of food in the apartment, it was a mystery how the army of roaches survived. I quickly learned that I wasn't the only one taking a morning shower in my tub. As soon as I would turn on the shower, scores of roaches would run out from behind broken bath tiles and scatter. I eventually learned to run the shower for a minute before entering.

How did I find this treasure of an apartment and many similar ones later? The same way most Russians do. They ask a friend who then also asks friends if anyone would like to move out of their apartment for a month or two and make several hundred dollars. Most Slavs, especially the elderly, jump at this golden opportunity to make quick, easy money just for retreating to their *dacha* (a tiny, often dilapidated, summer cottage) or by moving in with relatives. Unfortunately, my early trips to Russia and Ukraine for up to two months typically meant that I had to rent apartments sight unseen and rely entirely on friends to find decent housing.

From my 16th floor apartment I had a perfect view of at least a dozen other identical, grey concrete block buildings, and to keep me company on most nights a constant whistling, cold wind. The view on the ground outside my building wasn't much better: a grassless, generously-littered lot with a handful of mostly rusty, late-model Russian cars; a lone decaying picnic table with three or four unemployed, middle-aged Russian men, veteran bottle-drainers at work or brainstorming where the next vodka bottle would come from; more of the same picnic tables and occupants in the distance; and a handful of young children playing on the dangerous remnants of an old Soviet-built playground.

I'll never forget the horrible daily commute I had from this impoverished district to the city's center, where I conducted research at several institutes. On a good day I would first spend 20 minutes walking to a bus line where I would have a short wait before boarding a standing-room-only, airless bus for a 30-minute ride to the end of a metro line. There I would ride a crowded airless train, get off after 20 minutes and change to a different line after walking more than 15 minutes in crowded, airless tunnels for a total subway commute of more than 60 minutes. Finally, I would walk more than 20 minutes from the subway station to a research institute.

I still can't believe I made this daily commute for nearly two months and that a Russian friend found this apartment for me; I would hate to think of the kind of apartment an enemy could've found for me. On days when Russian acquaintances would invite me for a few drinks after work in downtown Moscow, the commute home would be unbearable and heroic.

On a bad day, notably, one of the many with torrential rain, I would sit, depressed, in the mornings by my apartment window often for an hour waiting until the rain would let up just enough to allow me to hang on to an umbrella. With all of the high-rise buildings in my neighborhood, it was typically like a wind tunnel on the ground and a nightmare on days with driving rain.

Often I would drag my tired body back to this apartment only to find that seemingly endless *remont* was still underway after 9 P.M. Remont, or remodeling, is a word dreaded by all and it goes on in old and new apartment buildings typically from early morning to late evening including weekends and holidays; it comes in two basic forms, cosmetic and major-capital renovation. Anyone who has lived among the natives is intimately familiar with the vibrating apartment walls that accompany drilling in apartments being remodeled even two or more floors above one's apartment.

After listening to a month of remont noise, I began to think that some of my neighbors were simply running drills and hammering boards with no nails just to torment their neighbors. Leaving this apartment and "sleep district" was one of the happiest days of my life, on a par with the birth of my two sons.

A year later I was back in Moscow living again among poverty-stricken natives for two months. My second Russian apartment was on the first floor of an old 5-story building with only a 30-minute walk to the end of the nearest subway line. The total commute downtown to a research institute was just under two hours and a considerable improvement over my first Russian apartment. I recall much of this two-month stay as a period when I was trying to dry my shoes from the seemingly endless rain.

Upon arriving I learned that this tiny, dilapidated apartment belonged to a doctor and alleged sex therapist, the father of a Russian acquaintance. Barely more than 40 square meters in size, it consisted of a bedroom large enough for the mattress on the floor, and a very small, narrow back room which the doctor equipped for his so-called sex-therapy practice. This area consisted of four tiny partitioned, but not fully enclosed, areas barely large enough to fit a small table with a VCR and chair. I've seen phone booths with more space and privacy than these stalls. This tiny backroom also had a few Emanuella soft-porn tapes (Russian-language edition only) and an ample supply of condoms.

I was devastated when I saw this dilapidated apartment with its mattress on the floor instead of a bed and angry at the person who found it for me. I didn't even want to think about the stories that mattress could tell. I wanted to leave immediately but I had no option but to take the apartment. I had nowhere else to go.

During my stay there I had considerable time to reflect on this so-called sex therapy clinic. I'm not Sherlock Holmes but I concluded from the evidence available (videos, VCRs, condoms) that it was a very dubious sex-clinic which probably provided the kind of "therapy" that many men can do at home—and, in fact, do on their own without anyone's assistance.

Something was not kosher with this alleged sex-therapy clinic. Clearly this "doctor" and sex therapist guru could not have been doing a bustling business if he was willing to rent his private clinic and living quarters to me. The five empty Seagram's whiskey bottles under the kitchen sink suggested the good doctor may also have been involved in another personal therapy.

The doctor was a shifty character, indeed. A day after I moved in he had the phone service to the apartment stopped and tried unsuccessfully to extort additional money for the phone even though it was included as part of the rental agreement. The apartment in general was in a terrible state. Lights would glow bright and dim, the tap water was yellowish, and there was no regular hot water. The toilet did not flush nor did the doctor seem to care. I had to fill the strategically placed bucket with water and empty it into the toilet bowl each time I needed to create a flush. Needless to say, I wasn't very sad when I ended my stay at this sex-therapy clinic and had to say goodbye to the good doctor and Emanuella.

My third Russian apartment seemed promising. A Russian friend said he found a one-room, short-term flat not far from the end of a metro line, near a park and a river. I was excited.

When I arrived I did find a stretch of green across from my building, a tiny river and a park in the distance. The apartment was on the second floor in a building with only seven floors, a good sign. It was owned by a couple in their 70s and looked like it had been neglected for more than 70 years: Soviet-era wall paper peeling everywhere, a wooden floor cracked and raised in many spots due to apparent apartment flooding, and ceilings with signs of extensive water damage. *Welcome to Russia!*

However, the apartment did come equipped with two old refrigerators. One was completely full of over-the-counter and prescription drugs, most of which had expired before the collapse of the Soviet Union (you never know when they might come in handy again). The toilet operated on the same bucket-flush system I learned to operate proficiently at the sex-clinic flat, apparently a time-tested Slavic tradition. Why bother calling a plumber when a bucket is so handy?

This apartment also had a feature lacking in my first two Moscow apartments: very thin walls separating me from very loud neighbors. These were the kind of drunken Russian neighbors who scream while beating and stabbing each other. No joke, and the following sobering fact is worth keeping in mind when thinking about approaching bothersome Russian neighbors: More than half of all murders committed in Russia are alcohol-related and carried out with knives or axes. What loud Russian neighbors? I didn't hear anything.

My excitement with this apartment was very short-lived, indeed. A day after arriving, I went for a morning stroll in the unkempt dog park beyond the nearby river and stepped in a foot-long hole covered with grass. I injured my left ankle terribly and in a day's time it doubled in size. I decided not to turn to the Russian medical system for assistance because my Russian friends had shared many nightmarish stories about it.

Meanwhile, I discovered that my apartment had bedbugs, in addition to hungry mosquitoes from the nearby river and, of course, roaches. Unable to sleep on my mattress and limping with a swollen leg, I went to several drugstores before I found one with a powder to kill bedbugs.

I look back on this apartment and my stay in Moscow as a period when I was eaten alive by mosquitoes and bedbugs (who apparently never tasted an American before), tormented by roaches, and spent much of my stay limping to the metro, grocery stores and work. Interestingly, when I complained to a Russian friend about my living conditions, he looked at me soulfully and said: "You must never forget you are in Russia. Most Russians can only dream about living alone in a one-room apartment like yours."

Many years and many more apartments have passed since these early years of mine in Moscow. Since 2007 I have been living in Kyiv about six months of the year in a Khrushchovka: a five-story brick building with three entrances, each leading to twenty tiny one-room or slightly larger flats, four on each level. Countless Khrushchovkas were built during the 1960s throughout the former Soviet Union and named in honor of the Soviet leader of that period, Nikita Khrushchev.

Each Khrushchovka contains many tiny rotting balconies that hang precariously off the walls and are decorated in eclectic styles—a real eyesore. The combination-lock to the entrance door of my building has been broken for more than three years and the entry, consequently, is urine fragrant; a dank, sour smell that increasingly permeates the stairwell with the passage of time. In addition, the building has stairwell landings with broken windows, trash-littered hallways with crumbling walls and old mail boxes that do not lock. This is typical of most Soviet-era buildings in Ukraine and Russia.

Apartment buildings in Russia and Ukraine, with few exceptions, are managed by a *ZHEK*. He and his several loyal assistants are responsible for building upkeep and managing utilities in a given neighborhood. In fact, the only services a typical ZHEK provides are a daily courtyard sweeper and emergency service if a building's electricity, gas or water shuts down completely. Everyone in Russia and Ukraine, without exception, hates their ZHEK.

Why do I live in this Khrushchovka? It's located in the very center of Kyiv, a beautiful city with more than 1,500 years of history. It's only minutes away from the metro, my toilet flushes and I have no bedbugs. Everything is relative, as they say. On my darkest day in my Khrushchovka I need only to think back to my baptism by fire in Moscow, and any dark mood I may have is gently lifted.

Howling Stray Dogs

> *"Let sleeping dogs lie."*
> -Charles Dickens

Life is challenging enough in Moscow and Kyiv without constantly looking out for dangerous stray dogs. There are sinking sidewalks, missing manhole covers, motorists determined to prevent pedestrians from crossing safely at crosswalks, and massive icicles falling from city rooftops in winter. Add to this picture packs of hungry, diseased and often violent dogs.

During the day these stray dogs are virtually never alone and generally avoid contact with humans. Many of them lie soundly asleep, seemingly dead outside busy metro entrances, in city underpasses and in parks. Typically they appear oblivious to the heavy pedestrian traffic that must maneuver around them, and are often curled up and sleeping with their nose tucked under a hind leg. However, they are very adept at anticipating a kick from a city employee.

Living in Russia and Ukraine, one quickly learns that these stray dogs own the night and are bolder on weekends when car and pedestrian traffic is minimal. During late evening and early morning hours they roam the streets—often in packs of a dozen or more—chase cars, attack dogs that don't belong to their pack, and howl at stumbling drunks. Many Slavic women are afraid to go shopping in the evening because these dogs often follow and even attack them when they spot a grocery bag. It's not even safe for vegetarians to venture out in the evening.

In Kyiv, I'm awakened like clockwork between 2 and 4 A.M. by the packs of angry, howling dogs that frequent my neighborhood. Their anger is palpable, bottled up all day and, no doubt, hunger-driven. On hot summer nights it's impossible to sleep with a window open.

Growing up and living in America does not prepare you adequately to deal with these stray dogs. For one thing, they have no knowledge of English. When they do attack, it's wise to know a few curse words in Russian (Ukrainians also speak Russian). Otherwise you may shout something in English which may sound like the Russian equivalent of, "I have sausage in my pocket." Secondly, keep moving when they do attack. Typically they will lunge at you, pause, and then do the same a few more times rather than immediately back off—even if you swing something at them.

How do I know these things? Experience is the best teacher. I've been a magnet for stray dogs on more than one occasion in the past. And I've learned that when a pack of four or more stray dogs appears to be sleeping soundly during the day, one of them is always on guard and is the designated attack dog; generally, only his slightly-opened eyes give him away.

I learned this one lovely, golden autumn day in the heart of Kyiv when I observed a handful of stray dogs asleep on a big nest of leaves. I took a photo—not realizing that stray dogs, like criminals, do not like to be photographed—and walked past them at a distance of about ten feet to get a closer look. A big mistake! I apparently violated their comfort zone because one of the dogs snuck up behind me when I was about thirty feet away, greatly startled me, and started barking viciously. He looked like a miniature version of the demonic Hound of the Baskervilles.

Fortunately, in keeping with sacred Slavic tradition, I never leave home without a large sturdy plastic bag. On this occasion it contained a couple of hefty books. I instinctively swung it at the dog but was careful not to hit him, remembering he had backup and I didn't. He backed off briefly but continued barking angrily, then lunged again, not caring that other pedestrians were approaching him. Frankly, I was hoping he would shift his attention and go after one of them, but no such luck. He soon stopped and smugly swaggered back to his pack. I think his excessive display of force was intended primarily to earn points with his canine clan.

Kyiv and Moscow both have a growing canine problem. Kyiv, for example, had an estimated 30,000 stray dogs in 2009, up from 6,000 two years earlier. Ukrainian animal rights activists estimate the number could grow to 80,000 in a few years. During the first quarter of 2009 alone, Kyiv registered 747 dog bites, a record number. Packs of stray dogs even roamed Kyiv's beaches during summer 2010 and attacked natives with food.

It should be stressed that these stray dogs lead a very tragic life. In Ukraine and Russia they are treated no better than in barbaric medieval times. In 1996 a German filmmaker made a documentary showing a slaughterhouse in Kyiv where stray dogs were routinely clubbed and beaten to death. Authorities closed the slaughterhouse due to international criticism and the facility was taken over by a private group. They turned it into an SOS shelter and veterinary clinic for stray animals funded by European donations.

Foreign funding for the shelter dried up in 2008 and the Ukrainian government remains callously indifferent to the problem of stray dogs. The shelter has received no state funding for its sterilization and vaccination program in 12 years; its annual budget for 2009 was a paltry $63,000.

The shelter is in a dire state. Its dedicated staff of 10 employees works a 24/7 schedule in inhumane conditions. During 2010 the shelter reportedly operated with little heat and electricity, no running water and without even a toilet in their facility. Ukraine's parliament of 450 members, incidentally, has more than 300 millionaires and a handful of billionaires.

Ukraine's stray-dog population, in particular, will likely face increasingly cruel treatment as officials frantically prepare Kyiv and other Ukrainian cities for the Eurocup 2012 games. Rather than sterilize dogs on the street and eliminate the problem in a few years, brutal methods are being used to deal with the situation. In just one month during 2010, 85 dogs were poisoned in the

Ukrainian city of Vinnitsia. The government's priorities are clear. During 2010 it even found millions of dollars to launch an early effort to hold the 2020 Winter Olympics in Ukraine.

Other animals also suffer in Ukraine because of callous and incompetent government leaders. Kyiv's national, state-operated zoo is recognized as one of the world's worst, according to Ukrainian animal activists. The death toll for 2010 included eight large animals: an elephant, giraffe, camel, zebra, tiger, bear, bison and an armadillo. Animal activists cited poor living conditions, malnutrition, and mismanagement as the reasons for the tragic deaths.

On a much lighter life-goes-on note, I recall the following 2008 scene near my apartment in downtown Kyiv during the morning rush hour. I was walking on the sidewalk and noticed two stray dogs just ahead, one with a crushed hind leg; many of these dogs are maimed because they fail to safely cross multi-lane city streets full of reckless, speeding drivers. The dogs were fornicating, with the disabled dog at the controls, in full view of bumper-to-bumper morning rush-hour traffic. Not wanting to interrupt the love-making on the narrow sidewalk, I stopped in my tracks hoping the union would be quickly consummated.

Like a terrible car wreck, it was a difficult to turn away from the action. Other pedestrians respectfully stopped, a few politely sidestepped the action. I must say from where I was standing the dog's disability and undernourished appearance did not seem to hold him back in the slightest from pursing his mission. In my opinion, he functioned on a par equal to any four-legged canine. Life has its moments, even for God's poor creatures.

My Weak American Cat

> *"The unexamined life is not worth living."*
> -Socrates

Once again I hear the whining sound of two very scrawny young cats outside of my Moscow apartment building this autumn morning. It's not mating season that's driving them but a daily ritual where they beg for food. Eventually a poor babushka from my building makes her way to a bench in our unkempt, beer-bottle-strewn, tiny courtyard. The whining subsides and the cats follow her frantically.

From my third floor window I see a familiar sight. The babushka takes a slab of heavily buttered white bread from a plastic bag, meticulously breaks off bite-size morsels and lovingly feeds the cats by hand. The cats gratefully gobble up the bits. Their lives differ dramatically from those of pampered American cats.

Five thousand miles across the Atlantic in a suburb of Washington, D.C. our family's two cats routinely turn their noses up at non-albacore tuna, and find the sight of a sardine repulsive. My wife is a real cat person. I'm not and for good reasons. The biggest reason is her large ginger cat, Tigger. He's a real outdoor cat who comes indoors to use the litter, eat, and hide, no doubt from his many enemies.

Tigger constantly sits on the roof of my car and is probably doing it this very minute as I sit here in Moscow. I think he does this deliberately to annoy me and provide himself with a defensive position against his many enemies. He's a regular fixture there, especially just after I've finished washing the car. And after I drive home on cold days, he often jumps on the hood of my car to gather warmth from the recently running engine, but only as soon as I'm out of sight. He's a very shifty character, indeed.

In getting to the roof of my car Tigger always makes sure to leave plenty of cat prints on my front window and curiously always on the driver's side. Where did he learn this vile practice and why doesn't he ever climb to the roof of the car using the back window? Why is it that no other cats in our neighborhood sit on the roofs of cars? I suppose I'm lucky that he doesn't invite other cats to join him, but then again he doesn't seem to have any friends.

I think the reason for this behavior of Tigger's is rather obvious: to torment me constantly. I privately look forward to being a pallbearer at his funeral. The only problem is that he will probably set a record and outlive me. I can just picture him atop my casket and funeral car, with cat prints on the driver's side window. If he tried any of his car buffing antics in Moscow, I'm sure he would be found floating in the Moscow River the very next day.

I should note that Tigger is a rather unfriendly cat with poor interpersonal skills. Oh, he feigns friendliness with some of the neighbors. He apparently knows better than to put all of his eggs in one basket. And I'm sure he leads a secret life and has a second home. However, I've never seen him atop any other cars in the neighborhood.

My wife constantly defends Tigger stressing that he was a semi-feral rescue cat when we acquired him. I often reply that I can understand perfectly why someone would've abandoned him. During his private moments at home, he often enjoys biting holes in metal window blinds and bending them to gaze furtively outdoors.

Tigger keeps to a very rigid schedule. He sleeps indoors all day often with one eye open, and lurks around the neighborhood stealthily all night long. Then at 6 A.M. like clockwork he's outside the driveway door whining to come in. Of course, if I'm the only one who hears him; I let him sing for at least another half hour.

Tigger and I have a long history of clashes of which my wife is only vaguely aware. Typically these occur when she is away from the house and Tigger is sleeping in secret quarters such as the bathtub behind a shower curtain or in the large bathroom hamper on a pile of fresh towels. Unaware of his presence, I will innocently approach the bathtub or bathroom hamper only to be startled and almost go into cardiac arrest by his disgusting hiss that sounds worse than that of a cobra snake, and is accompanied by a facial expression that begs for the services of an exorcist. Of course, I immediately back off since I'm not wearing garlic or a cross around my neck.

However, I do believe in paybacks. Often when my wife isn't home and I'm in the kitchen and hear Tigger gently ascending toward my area from the basement unaware of my presence, I surprise him with a cobra-like hiss and a demonic facial expression. His startled expression is priceless. No doubt, my paybacks reinforce the long-simmering cold war between us and help explain his sleeping with one eye open. However, I feel my actions are fully justified and lose no sleep over them.

For some reason when I see my wife's two cats and Tigger in particular, I always think of the classic expression; "The unexamined life is not worth living." Of course, it's silly to expect Tigger to thoughtfully ponder his life of leisure and dirty habits. However, if I had my way the best payback for Tigger would be to parachute him at night into one of the very poor Russian neighborhoods I've lived in. There he could experience the life of a Slavic cat firsthand and queue mornings for a crust of buttered bread, should he even be so lucky. He could also try to survive with Russians driving on sidewalks and with loose and missing manhole covers. I'm certain that Tigger would soon be very aware of his dramatically new surroundings and would be examining closely his new Slavic life.

Yes, Tigger your days of wine and roses would be over. Just try sitting on the warm engine hood of a Russian's car or playing king of the hill on his car's roof. You'll be seeing stars. Yes, no more surreptitious sleeping in the bathtub and cozy bathroom hamper, and forget about using an indoor cat litter. You'll only be able to dream about having a sardine or some non-albacore tuna.

And Tigger don't forget about the language barrier—how's your Russian? Oh, and did I mention the army of stray, howling, homeless dogs who own the night, your favorite playtime? Welcome to Russia Tigger! A trash cat you once were and would be again if you lived in Russia.

Meet My Slavic Neighbors

> *"How do you make a Russian happy?*
> *Burn down his neighbor's house."*
> — a Russian anecdote

Growing up in America, my immigrant parents taught me to practice good neighborliness: to be polite and respectful to neighbors in the apartment buildings we lived in, and later in our detached-home neighborhood. Occasionally the neighbors next door seemed undeserving of our respect, but we always practiced civility and avoided any petty squabbles. With time this family practice became an ingrained habit of mine.

Neither this culture of civility nor time spent living with ten wild, physical education-recreation majors (jocks for short) in a small three-bedroom Cape Cod style house in a college town in upstate New York adequately prepared me for my Russian and Ukrainian neighbors.

Since 2007 I've spent about six months of the year living in Kyiv in a crumbling five-story Khrushchovka, one of countless identical brick buildings constructed during the 1960s throughout the former Soviet Union. The neighbors in my building and its living conditions are typical of those I've experienced in well over a dozen Soviet-built apartments I've lived in Russia and Ukraine during the past 20 years.

Meet My Current Neighbors:

The chronic urinator. Tolya is a perpetually jobless young man in his late 20s who lives with his retired mother in an apartment two doors down from me on the third floor of our Khrushchovka. He has the dubious reputation of being an unabashed, chronic urinator who leaves nocturnal puddles on the tiny stairwell landing between our floor and the one beneath. No, he does not have a tragic medical condition.

How do I know Tolya is the guilty party? One day an elderly neighbor, Tamara, who lives on the fifth floor, ranted endlessly about the horrors of the communal areas of our building as she inched along the steps in front of me. She said the chronic urinator's identity is well known to most residents in our building and that he stubbornly refuses to cease his flagrant, nightly desecration of our hallway.

Tamara said Tolya drinks and smokes with two or three male friends every evening by the window on the landing between the second and third floors. She speculated that Tolya and friends urinate in the hallway out of respect for his mother: he does not want to enter their tiny one-room flat and wake up his mother because she provides him with beer and cigarette money. His selfless and very tolerant mother works very hard as a cleaning lady to supplement her meager monthly pension of less than $100.

Two floors down from my apartment we have the *chronic apartment-door slammer.* Between 6 and 7 P.M. Konstantin, a short, thin man in his 50s who lives alone (not surprisingly!) begins his daily ritual of slamming his apartment door a half-dozen times at intervals of about 15–20 seconds for about 10 minutes. He then takes a short break, apparently to refresh himself, only to resume the same banging procedure two or three more times. Konstantin is very conscientious and rarely misses a day of door slamming. When he does miss a day, I pray that he may have passed on to the pearly gates. I can only imagine that his annoying behavior is a cosmic payback for one of his hated neighbors.

Surprisingly, I have never seen a single neighbor, even those with small school-age children, come out of any of the other 18 apartments in our section of this Khrushchovka and complain about this door slamming or Tolya's loud nightly ritual of stairwell drinking with friends. Apparently they are keenly aware that nothing good results from such interventions and usually some sort of retaliation can be expected.

Call the police? Locals know better. The police are more of a problem than any hooligans. They typically take hours to arrive and when they do appear any noise and partying typically has stopped. They then accuse the caller of having fabricated the story and give him a hard time and even a fine.

I've asked Ukrainian friends about this "My house is at the end of the village, I know nothing" mentality of Ukrainians and Russians. They say that neighbors in apartment buildings typically are reserved, mind their own business and their close family's welfare. They try to "fly below the radar" of the tax police and other authorities. Their principal interests are family, close friends, good food, and alcohol.

My next door neighbors: In 2009 an attractive couple in their mid-20s moved into the one room flat next door to me. As is customary, there were no pleasant introductions and no delivery of cookies. Instead neighbors typically meet when there is an emergency involving mutual apartments, most frequently a bathroom flooding a neighbor below.

And so it was with my new neighbors. For weeks I listened to constant drilling and hammering accompanying the major remodeling of their newly-purchased flat. With my patience tested to the limit daily by this and the unnerving activity of other neighbors, I noticed a cloud of drywall powder coming steadily through the small electrical-fuse box located in a common wall separating our two apartments and located near my entrance.

I listened to the continuing drilling in the area of my electrical box and watched the drywall powder pour out. Finally my nerves gave out and I rang the neighbor's door. A young woman answered and behind her was a workman holding a power tool. I told her they were drilling into my wall and electrical box and that they would soon be through the wall. The woman responded with an expression that reminded me of a deer caught in one's headlights. I returned to my flat and found that the drilling stopped.

Less than an hour later the young woman's husband, dressed in a suit, rang my doorbell. He introduced himself and said he heard I had a problem with their effort to improve their flat's electricity. I bit my tongue and explained diplomatically that their workman was apparently attempting to join their electric service to my upgraded electrical box. He said that they too wanted such service. I told him fine but not on my dime, and warned him that if my electrical service was interrupted he would have to pay for a licensed electrician to repair any damage.

He left very annoyed but their effort to join my electrical box stopped. Needless to say, I won't be getting an invitation for dinner and drinks from these neighbors any time soon, nor will I be asking them to keep an eye on my flat when I am out of the country. However, I do intend to open my electrical box periodically to ensure I don't have a clear view of them in their apartment.

Vika and Kolya, my trusted neighbors: After living in my Khrushchovka for about six months I developed a courteous relationship with Vika, her unemployed husband Kolya and their two barely school-age daughters; they live on the fifth floor of our building. Vika is our apartment building's courtyard sweeper and works for our local ZHEK, the building and utilities manager.

On major holidays I would give the family a box of chocolates, cookies and some fruits. With time I thought I could trust them, especially since Vika had worked for the apartment manager for 10 years.

I was leaving Ukraine for three months and, rather than not pay the monthly bills for my communal apartment and telephone services, I contacted Vika and Kolya. I gave them enough money to cover the fees and a generous tip for their help. While in the U.S. for three months I had peace of mind knowing that Vika would tend to my apartment-related bills and empty the junk mail quickly accumulating in my tiny, broken mail box.

Upon returning to Ukraine, I prepared an envelope with a thank you card, additional money for services rendered and a box of chocolates for Vika's family. When I tried to call her on my apartment phone, a recorded message informed me that my phone service had been stopped due to non-payment. A few days later I found a bill in my mail box indicating that Vika and Kolya also had not paid my apartment's communal services for the last three months as agreed. Apparently, they spent the money I gave them on personal expenses and alcohol, no doubt. So much for my trusted neighbors.

Finally, there are the *"working girls" and their sisters the pole-dancers* who live in my Khrushchovka. They are there, no doubt, because it's convenient. The building is in the very heart of Kyiv, a playground for many foreign male visitors and rich locals as well. According to Tamara, the building gossip, four working girls, or elite prostitutes as she calls them, live just above her in a small one room apartment on the fifth floor with noisy nocturnal visitors dropping by all the time. Tamara believes they get referrals from so-called escort agencies at all hours of the night and this explains why they are always zooming off in waiting cabs.

Their presence in our building is quite conspicuous. They're all tall and thin, in their early to mid 20s, with dyed blonde or red hair, skin-tight clothing, and mandatory stilettos—real role models for the young school girls in my building.

My only interaction with them is in our building's stairwell. Many evenings upon entering our building I see them descending the stairs in their clickety-clak stilettos like firemen answering an emergency call. When I hear them coming I react as I do for all emergency vehicles. I pull over and wait until they pass. After that I pinch myself to see if I'm invisible to them. I never see them return to our building because this is way past my bedtime.

When I leave my apartment in the morning I routinely find the working girls' Slim-cigarette butts on my doormat, used Q tips and fast food wrappers in the stairwell. They must constantly curse the fact that they live on the fifth floor and that Khrushchovkas were constructed without elevators.

The two pole-dancers in our building live on Tamara's fourth floor. They are both attractive blondes and look very supple and springy, no doubt an essential requirement for their job. Unlike our working girls' porno-glamour style, they are often dressed in fashionable fitness outfits.

Pole-dancing is not easy work. It is fraught with serious orthopedic consequences, the competition is fierce and the turnover in

Kyiv is very high; club managers and their loyal customers like to see fresh talent. Nevertheless, ambitious young beauties from all over Russia and Ukraine flock to Moscow and Kyiv, respectively, hoping to have a chance at the pole.

Tamara is certain that the girls on her floor are pole-dancers because she has seen them enter the Penthouse Gentlemen's Club on many occasions. It's just a block away from our building—a short commute for the girls—and is fittingly located in the basement of a seven-story residential building.

Believe it or not, the Penthouse full-strip bar is located next to Ukraine's Constitutional Court, and joined to it by a common courtyard. Ukraine's highest court is composed mostly of old men and has earned the reputation of being a corrupt, politically-manipulated institution. Rumor has it that there is an underground passage that conveniently connects the Constitutional Court building to the Penthouse Club, which coincidentally happens to be located underground.

Interestingly, the Penthouse full-strip bar also offers a buffet business lunch! What kind of man comes to a full-strip bar to eat during daylight hours? Hmm, I wonder where Ukraine's arthritic, male chief justices go to break bread at lunchtime. I'll have to investigate this matter further.

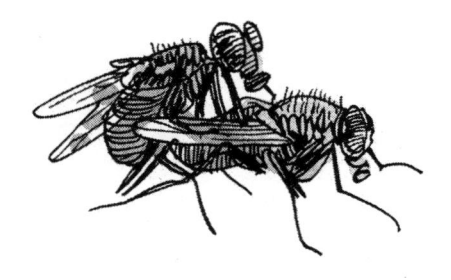

Fornicating Flies

> "*If you keep your mouth shut, the flies won't get in.*"
> -a Spanish proverb

In America, I've always found indoor flies to be a nuisance. I can't ever recall being happy to see one. However, my encounters were never noteworthy. Regrettably, I can't say the same about my experience in Kyiv during August 2002.

At the time I was renting a tiny one-room, seventh floor apartment in a sturdy Stalin-era building in the heart of the city. The apartment had unusually high ceilings and southern exposure which made for very hot August days. Like most apartments in Kyiv, it lacked air-conditioning or even a fan. Evenings I would leave all of the windows open to fight the high humidity and heat.

There came a day, however, when I was no longer able to do this. Late one afternoon I returned to my apartment to find more than a dozen flies mysteriously on my walls and zooming about wildly. I had just spent two weeks in this flat and had rented it several summers previously without any fly problems. In addition to being very annoyed I was perplexed by the source of these invaders. With no fly swatter available, I grabbed a dishtowel and tried to direct them out of one of the several windows. However, these were not the typical American flies that I was used to. These were hungry Ukrainian flies and several were soon nipping at me.

I should note that a dishtowel is a poor substitute for a flyswatter, especially for a novice. It catches a lot of air when in motion and this slows it down greatly. After about 30 minutes I observed that the number of flies had increased noticeably to several dozen. At that point I directed my attention to the windows and saw several more enter.

My anxiety was growing by the minute. It was another very hot day and this activity was not agreeing with me. After an afternoon of running around the city, I wanted to sit down and relax with a cold drink. Instead, I was standing with a very puzzled expression and waving a dish towel with little success.

Where were these flies coming from and why were they coming into my apartment? I quickly surveyed my one room and tiny kitchen. No trash. I emptied what little I had that morning. No food left out and at this point I was getting quite hungry. I had entertained the idea of having a sandwich when I got home but now this was hardly an option. What were my options I wondered?

It became increasingly apparent that one option I did not have was to leave my screenless windows open. More flies were entering and I did not see any exodus. The only option I could think of was to close all of the windows and begin eliminating these Ukrainian invaders. However, this was easier said than done.

My apartment had 11-foot ceilings which I was initially glad to see, a 7-foot high wardrobe closet, and an even taller china cabinet and enclosed book case. Ukrainian flies, I quickly learned, are not stupid. After I waved a dish towel at them for half an hour with few casualties, they quickly got the message. They scattered and went to higher ground. Some attached themselves to a high chandelier in the center of the room, others parked atop the very high cabinets, and the bold ones just continued buzzing around me.

At this point I was very hot and thirsty. I seriously considered leaving my apartment but was not ready to accept defeat. Instead, I opened the door to the tiny semi-enclosed balcony hoping to get a breath of air without letting more flies in through a window. I sat at the small table on the balcony wondering why the gods had forsaken me. Before long a handful of flies were nibbling at me.

I quickly retreated back into my apartment. As I surveyed my

30 square meter apartment (the size of an average American living room) I saw something quite surprising. Several of the flies were resting on the ceiling, a surface out of my reach. I had never observed this kind of fly capability before. Of course, I never really cared. Was this something all flies could do or only Ukrainian ones? I decided to probe this question on the Internet at a later date.

Over the next few hours I devoted considerable effort to attack the problem at hand. My results were rather meager but I was developing a decent backhand swing with the dishtowel. I was also learning to anticipate the movements of the flies and occasionally strike them not directly, but a few inches in the direction I anticipated they would fly; at first this was fun.

Unfortunately, southern exposure was turning my apartment with closed windows into a steamy sauna. I gasped for air. Desperate, I finally opened a window. Within seconds more flies entered. Where could they be coming from I wondered? My apartment building's large trash receptacles were located a good distance across our courtyard and my flat was far above the ground floor. I continued to attack my fly population intermittently but with very modest results.

Eventually it was bedtime and I hoped that we would all turn in and get some much-needed rest once the lights were out. However, I quickly learned more about fly behavior. Apparently, these Ukrainian flies were well rested and liked to party at night. Although I covered my head with a sheet the flies continued buzzing around my head and landing on me. Moreover, the evening heat and closed windows made sleep virtually impossible and left me in a sweaty, agitated state.

To add insult to injury, the next morning I awoke to find more than a few flies fornicating on the walls in my tiny kitchen, and they were out of reach. It was a painful X-rated scene to watch. *Welcome to Ukraine!* Could things possibly get any worse and would I ever be able to look at two flies again without imagining them having sex?

The good news was that I had to leave my flat that day to attend a local conference. The bad news was that I was an exhausted wreck and could barely stand up. Still, I was happy to evacuate my apartment and leave my new neighbors behind.

When I returned late that afternoon I noticed that there were even more flies—baby flies! Over the next few days, I diligently continued to attack my fly population hoping that they would eventually die a natural death.

Just prior to the arrival of my fly problem, I invited a Ukrainian acquaintance, Oleksandr, a retired Soviet army colonel, to stop by my apartment over the weekend for drinks and a bite to eat. I had two days left before his scheduled visit to try to eliminate my flies. I was making progress with the windows closed and also losing some weight in my sauna environment.

I decided not to cancel my meeting with Oleksandr and instead to retreat with him to my tiny balcony with its table and chairs. I also decided not to mention my fly problem. When Oleksandr arrived I immediately escorted him to the balcony and gave him a cold drink while I prepared some food. As I was doing this I noticed he was periodically slapping his arms. I must admit I enjoyed seeing someone else suffer. I joined Oleksandr on the balcony and before long he remarked that I had some very hungry flies. I said that I too noticed that and was puzzled by it.

Oleksandr then advanced several theories based on his lifetime in Ukraine and Russia. The first one shocked me. He said there could be a dead granny in the flat beneath me. The second one was less worrisome. He suggested that a neighbor in a flat below may have acted in a customary Ukrainian manner reserved for village life and inappropriate for the big city. He may have gone fishing and returned with a large batch of small river fish which he then hung on a balcony close line to dry out in the hot sun before leaving to spend a week at his dacha.

Ukrainian and Russian men like to nibble on salty, dry fish called *taranka* with their beer and vodka. Lastly, he offered a very alarming theory. He said a neighbor may have hung fish out to dry on a line and then may have died. I was keeping my fingers crossed for theory number two.

In any event, a few days after my meeting with Oleksandr the fly problem ended. It was only many months later, when this wound finally began to heal, that I started to research flies out of curiosity. What did I discover?

Strictly speaking, there are two basic types of flies: house and garbage (as far as I'm concerned they're both garbage). Based upon Oleksandr's theory about decaying fish and the fact that my flies did not sleep on vertical surfaces, I eliminated house flies as a possibility.

I learned that garbage flies like to lay their eggs in decaying meats and fish and then garbage-fly larvae leave their developmental site to seek out drier and more protected areas for pupation—a sweet sounding term. And lucky me, I should be honored that they chose my apartment over many others in the building.

This information didn't lessen the pain inflicted upon me by these invading Slavs. Perhaps, one day I'll be able to make peace with flies. Until then I never go overseas without a sturdy American flyswatter handy, and I still shudder every time I recall flies fornicating in my Kyiv apartment.

Slavic Attack Pigeons

> *"Kill no more pigeons than you can eat."*
> -Benjamin Franklin

The opinionated French call pigeons "rats with wings"—how gracious of them. Many people call the French frogs—touché. Those same people often say, "Nice country, too bad about the French." But the topic here is not the French but rather Slavic pigeons.

I must admit I've never been a big fan of these stout-bodied birds. Like most people I've tolerated their presence and gotten terribly offended when they've left an unsolicited deposit on me. They say it's good luck when a pigeon leaves droppings on you, but the "they" is usually the person with you who is chuckling heartily at your expense.

My father loved pigeons. He grew up in a tiny Ukrainian village, far from any big city, and never had the opportunity to get much schooling. He was displaced during WWII and along with my mother became a refugee in Germany. In America, he kept and even bred pigeons in our family garage in upstate New York for most of his adult life. He was especially fond of turtle-neck doves and would even expertly imitate their distinct cooing.

I never shared my father's fascination with pigeons, nor gave it much thought while I was growing up. To me it seemed an odd preoccupation at the time. But after many years in Russia and Ukraine, including many trips to simple villages, I now know that many Slavic men find raising pigeons an enjoyable, traditional hobby.

My mother, on the other had, was not enamored with the pigeons often running loose in the rafters of our garage. I can still see her angry as a wet hen and scolding my father after his birds repeatedly desecrated the family car beneath them. My father would only smile in response. He never dared say that it was good luck.

Fast forward several decades and my life in Moscow would inevitably bring me in frequent contact with hordes of pigeons. Moscow can be a very cold, bleak and depressing city. Moreover, without the many creature comforts which Americans take for granted—heat, hot water, uncontaminated tap water, a car, friendly customer service—the days can be harsh and unbearably long. Add to this picture hordes of pigeons often flying directly at you, close enough to part your hair or take an eye out, as you drag your tired body around the city.

After more than a few of these encounters, and Moscow's guaranteed "no-customer service" environment, I really began to dislike these pigeons. I even started thinking of them as anti-American Russian pigeons. This only increased my hatred of them.

Whenever I passed through a city park or square with scores of low-flying pigeons coming right at me, I learned to quickly raise both arms as though directing a plane on a runway. This would always surprise them and they would immediately part like the Red Sea and increase their altitude. This made me feel that I had the upper hand with these anti-American dive bombers.

However, these Russian pigeons were very crafty. One day while I was on full alert for flocks of pigeons to attack me head on, a lone pigeon caught me totally off guard and attacked from nine o'clock. It came so close that I could identify its sex (female). After that incident I was on heightened full alert, and periodically would even check behind me for Russian attack pigeons.

It was only after more than a decade in Russia and Ukraine that my attitude toward Slavic pigeons began to dramatically change. I was more adjusted to the country and culture shock that foreigners inevitably encounter when they live and work among average Slavs, and this improved my general mood. But one day, in particular, I had a real "aha moment." In the course of a single day, I spotted two pigeons that had been squashed like pancakes on Kyiv's downtown streets by speeding cars. I started to connect these fatalities and the almost weekly reports of pedestrians killed at crosswalks throughout Ukraine and Russia by reckless drivers.

Soon I came to the realization that these Slavic pigeons and I had a much in common: we were on the same side of the barricade, team members here in the East. Theirs was not an easy life with tragedy literally at every corner, flattened friends and family taken from them forever. We were both struggling to survive in an often unfriendly and hazardous environment, and battling many of the same elements: reckless, speeding drivers maiming and killing our brethren, the rude behavior of many Slavic pedestrians (many try to kick pigeons and also routinely violate my personal space), toxic exhaust emitted by cars flooding city streets, and a sea of smokers on city sidewalks.

The conclusion was inescapable. More than empathy and understanding was needed for these once stout-bodied birds. I had to act immediately, talk is cheap.

Any school kid (most are overweight in America) knows that you should stay away from white flour as much as possible, and I do. However, in Ukraine and Russia there is a tasty loaf of white bread with a crispy crust called a baton—3x12 inches, that's available fresh daily and costs about 40 cents in Ukraine. I love the golden, crisp crust but don't care at all for the white doughy center.

With my Slavic pigeons in mind, these days I slice the very bottom of a fresh crisp baton, open it carefully and remove in one large piece the huge, often still warm center. I buy this loaf no more than three times a week (I don't want to give Slavs more ammunition for their stereotype that all Americans are fat), visit the pigeons in a park every few days, and scatter half of a baton's finely shredded center.

Whole wheat bread naturally would be much more nutritious

but I'm not running a Club Med for pigeons, nor am I a Rockefeller. I think I've found a win-win solution here for both sides, versus the zero-sum mentality of the Cold War, as we fight the elements. The pigeons are able to build fat to take them through darker days ahead, and I receive surprising satisfaction each time I see them gobble up the bread I bring; we both enjoy this baton and it's very inexpensive. Moreover, I know I am making a small but important difference in their difficult lives and it never fails to lift my spirits.

With time I began to study carefully the behavior of Slavic pigeons and to understand the attraction these birds held for my father. I observed an amazing variety of color and pattern that I previously had ignored: the blue-bars, silver-backed, blue-headed birds that resemble wild rock doves; pieds, birds with big white splotches; checkers, dark birds with checkered backs; spreads, all-dark birds; reds; whites; and red-bars, reddish birds with a pattern similar to the blue-bar.

I also found their behavior fascinating. For example, I found that even after observing a flock for a few minutes, members were starting to get frisky (an American word) with one another (Slavs just call it copulation). Typically the male bird would clap his wings together in a kind of advertising flight with wings held in a V formation and tails spread. But that's all I'm going to describe for an American audience.

I'm not sure if American pigeons are as sexually active as Slavic ones. This will have to remain an open research question. I do know that Slavs, in general, are not at all prudish like Americans. Nude public beaches exist today and did even in Soviet times. Moreover, a Slavic male isn't allowed on a regular beach unless he's wearing a speedo; bad news for American men visiting beaches!

Currently, I'm on very good terms with Slavic pigeons. However, ours is a fragile peace that could easily be shattered by significant bird emissions. I'm sure I could forgive an accidental bird dropping or two on me by excited pigeons. But any more than that and we could be back to our Cold War days.

Dr. Kovalenko, Master of Sports Medicine

> "A waist is a terrible thing to mind."
> -Tom Wilson

Shortly after arriving in Moscow one August during the late 1990s, I had the misfortune to greatly aggravate a previous knee injury. One morning I went for a stroll in an overgrown park on the outskirts of the city where I was staying and stepped into a foot-long hole apparently dug by an animal. I injured my ankle and in a few days my right knee doubled in size.

Fortunately, a Russian friend quickly arranged an appointment for me with an acquaintance of his, Dr. Nikolai Vladimirovich Kovalenko. He told me that Dr. Kovalenko was a famous doctor of sports medicine and that I would be in good hands. My friend also told me I could pay for the doctor's services by making a modest contribution in an envelope, as locals do customarily.

I arrived early for my appointment the next morning at the Sports Medicine Clinic. A young nurse met me and said the doctor had stepped out briefly for a meeting. A short while later a tall, heavy-set man in his 60s with a Chekhovian beard and stern expression charged into the office holding a pack of cigarettes and a disposable lighter. After record-brief introductions, we entered a room where he examined my knee but ordered no X-rays. He then drained a considerable amount of fluid from it and injected it with cortisone. He asked if I knew what this treatment would do. I answered, "No." He replied, "Very little."

He then offered me a simple prescription. He said I must lose 20 lbs. within a month to reduce the strain on my knees. At almost 6-feet tall and 185 lbs., I understood that the doctor had a good point. I told him I would do my best to reach that goal. He replied, "Do it, or don't bother coming back to me." Needless to say, we didn't hug as we parted.

A month passed since I had arrived in Moscow and it was time to return to Dr. Kovalenko. I remember that morning vividly. I was in very good spirits. I had lost 15 lbs. and was sure the doctor would be pleased. At the clinic Dr. Kovalenko looked at me severely and said, "Let's see what we have here." He pulled out a thin sheet of old, yellow loose-leaf paper from a file which contained notes about our first meeting. Without asking me a word about how I felt he said, "Let's weigh you."

Still feeling upbeat, I stepped on the ancient scale and was happy to see that I, indeed, had lost just over 15 lbs. I expected his sour expression to be replaced by at least a half smile but I was very mistaken. He blurted out, "15 lbs. in one month? A wealthy American from superpower America could not lose 20 lbs. as prescribed in one month? You are a weak American! During the next month I want you to lose another 15 lbs. or do not come back to see me."

He then examined my knee very carefully, commenting that he noticed no swelling and that even a loss of 15 lbs. was already having a positive impact. He handed me two 15 lb. weights and said, "See how much less your poor knees will not have to carry once you lose the additional weight?" I nodded obediently. Before leaving, he demonstrated and had me perform some knee-strengthening exercises.

I left his office very depressed. I did not mention that my right knee was bothering me daily after just 30–45 minutes of walking. Moreover, I didn't think I could possibly lose another 15 lbs. I was now at 170, light-headed much of the time and depressed with life, in general, after a grueling month in Moscow, lugging liters of drinkable water daily, riding crowded airless public transport, shopping misery, washing clothes in a tub, and life without a car.

I didn't see how I could possibly lose another 15 lbs. I was hungry all the time and thought I would probably put on weight. But in the back of my mind I could hear Dr. Kovalenko's words echoing: "Do not come back to see me if you do not lose the weight." And his crushing words, "You are a weak American. Superpower? Ha!"

I was determined not to give up and to make this Russian eat his words about America and me. The next month was tortuous. Autumn had just arrived and it was very windy, unusually cold and raining most of the time. The fresh vegetables and fruits available on street stands throughout Moscow during the summer had disappeared. Muscovites had collectively changed their attire overnight into dark, warm, dirt-concealing clothing. The steady, heavy rain made daily travel, chores and exercise much more difficult and requiring more fuel. Instead, I was expected to diet.

The natural urge for any true American, under these trying circumstances, would be to get a deep-dish family size pizza with extra cheese and a medley of other toppings and wash it down with at least a liter of soda or beer. A true Russian, on the other hand, would probably fry some onions and potatoes, get a jar of salty pickles, some herring and wash it down with vodka and beer. But this also was not to be. For the next month I lived on watery soup, Slavic carrot and cabbage salads, a few eggs, endless cups of tea, oatmeal, apples, and some dried fruits and nuts.

A week before my scheduled return to the sports clinic I still had 6 lbs. to lose. Depressed but not defeated, I eliminated eggs and nuts from my diet. With two days to go, I had 2 more pounds to lose, felt very weak and could only think of food: big portions, greasy cheeseburgers, Mexican food, and huge cups of coffee with frothy heavy cream—all of the things that sustain a superpower.

The month ended and I prepared to return to Dr. Kovalenko. I had lost 15 more pounds but felt terrible. No longer did my right knee seem to bother me. I now had new ailments. I constantly felt weak and light-headed and occasionally dizzy. My sleep was interrupted nightly by agonizing food cravings. One night I even dreamt of being at a party with buffet tables collapsing from every imaginable kind of delicacy. I didn't even know if I could gather the energy to make my way back to the sports clinic.

I mustered what little strength I had left and put on an American happy face. I greeted Dr. Kovalenko and said I thought he would be pleased with my progress. He responded gruffly, "We'll see." His next words stunned me. He said, "You look horrible, very pale and haggard. What have you been doing?" I said, "It's not what I've been doing, it's what I haven't been doing, eating! I've been following your orders."

He then reviewed his handwritten notes from our previous meetings, weighed me and noted my additional 15 lb. weight loss. His only reaction was to raise a single eyebrow. I wanted to ask, "Weak American?" But I didn't want to provoke him. He was a heavy set man with a big beer-barrel stomach that looked like it was no stranger to sizzling sausages and frothy beer. In fact, his fingers reminded me of little pork-link sausages but I may have been hallucinating at that point.

Next he asked me to lift two 15 lb. weights off of the floor to illustrate how much weight my knees no longer had to carry. I leaned over, almost lost my balance, grabbed the weights but had difficulty lifting them. As I did I looked over to Dr. Kovalenko who had a scowl on his face, I'm certain I heard him whisper, "Weak American." We ended our meeting with my doing a few more knee-strengthening exercises and his words, "You know where to find me, if you need me."

To celebrate I stopped at Patio Pizza, an elite restaurant located near Pushkin Museum and the fabulously restored Christ the Savior Cathedral, and always loaded with filthy rich Russians and their bratty kids. Needless to say, I didn't invite Dr. Kovalenko.

Given my weak malnourished condition, I asked the waiter for a table as close to the buffet table as possible. I then ordered a large Greek pizza with two types of olives, peppers and feta cheese, and a frosty pint of unfiltered Russian beer. Before eating, I first toasted Dr. Nikolai Vladimirovich Kovalenko, Master of Sports Medicine.

Fortified by the pizza, I then made several trips to their famous salad bar which is unlike anything we have in the States. In addition to a wide assortment of rich Slavic salads with various choice meats, it also offered a medley of exotic fish dishes. I had generous portions of most of the delicacies which I washed down slowly with a second and third pint of Russian beer.

I left Patio Pizza with a party going on in my stomach and certain that I had gained 5 lbs. I was on the road to recovery!—weight recovery. That night I slept like a baby.

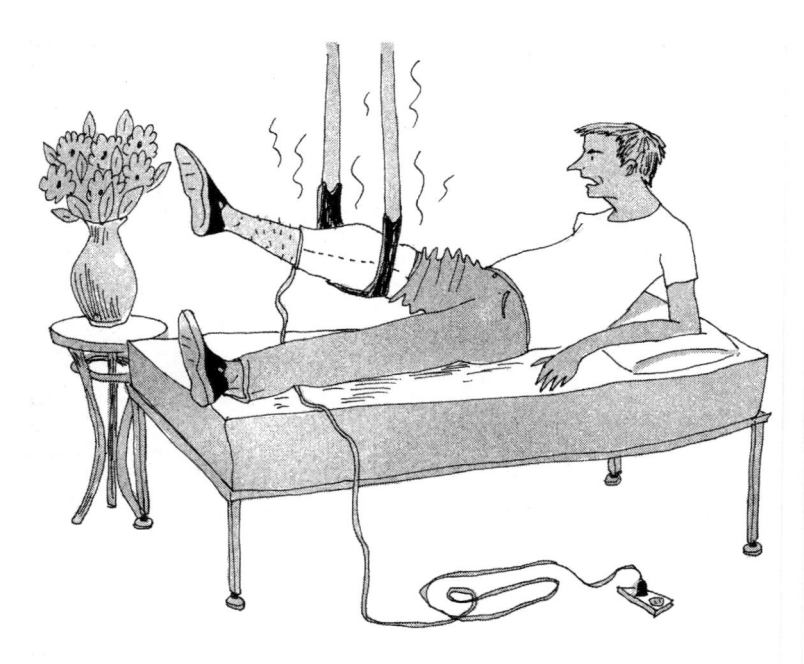

Inside Ukraine's Collapsing Medical System

> *A man wakes up in a Ukrainian ambulance and asks the doctor, "Where are we going?" He replies, "To the morgue." "But I'm not dead yet!" the man protests. The doctor replies, "But we're not there yet."*
>
>   -a Ukrainian anecdote

As luck would have it, I was destined to experience Ukraine's collapsing medical system during 2004. I developed an urgent need for medical attention shortly after arriving in Ukraine for a 9-month stay. An injury I received a few years earlier was greatly aggravated by weeks of climbing the steep streets of Kyiv and the endless steps leading to street underpasses and metro areas. As a result, my right knee had swollen to twice its original size and I had sharp shooting pain in it. Hoping against hope, I rested the knee for almost a week saying a silent prayer for the swelling to go down. But my prayer went unanswered.

I had used the American Medical Center in Kyiv earlier but it was very costly and it relied for the most part on the same Ukrainian doctors and facilities available to natives. I decided to try to cut out the middle man. In Ukraine and Russia it's who you know that counts. Good connections are most important to survive and prosper, and payment of cash on top of meager salaries is a fact of life that makes the Slavic world go 'round.

The Soviet free medical system had been collapsing steadily in Russia and Ukraine for a dozen years when I turned to it in Kyiv in 2004. Doctors were drawing meager salaries of about $100 per month and required cash contributions in envelopes from patients in order to survive. Impoverished, elderly patients, meanwhile, typically waited hours in the dark, dingy corridors of hospitals and outpatient clinics to see a doctor. Once hospitalized, they were required to provide their own medications, food, linen, and contributions for staff as well as doctors.

Over my many years in Ukraine, I was fortunate to develop several close friends who would always offer unconditional support in my darkest hour of need. One of these friends was Valya, a dentist, who worked at a large, hospital-size outpatient clinic that served pensioners and Ukrainian residents living in its district. I failed to meet these requirements, so Valya's assistance was crucial. She told me not to worry and promised to take me to meet a surgeon who worked at her clinic.

It was February and the streets were snow-covered and icy. Getting to the clinic with my bad knee, even with the assistance of a cab, was very difficult. The only entrance to the clinic had very steep, crumbling stairs coated with ice, and its poorly lit interior had not been upgraded since Soviet times. I arrived at the clinic shortly before noon and just before the start of Valya's shift at the dental dispensary. Although the hall was crammed with patients waiting to see her, she quickly changed into her doctor's frock and immediately escorted me to the surgeon's office, a floor below, and cut ahead of a large group of elderly, grumbling natives waiting outside that office without blinking an eye.

In keeping with Slavic tradition, I had a large box of chocolates for Valya and an envelope with $50 (more than traditional). She instructed me to give the chocolates to the doctor who would treat me. She repeatedly refused the money in keeping with Slavic tradition, but finally accepted it saying that she would share it with the other doctor and her assistant.

Valya introduced me to the surgeon, Natasha, who was sitting at an old wooden desk with her female assistant at her side. Valya quickly explained my predicament and lack of authorization to use the clinic. The doctor instructed her assistant to immediately prepare a small treatment booklet which would allow me to receive care at their facility. I then gave the large box of chocolates to the doctor who in turn gave it to her nurses.

At that point in the small office, Natasha told me to drop my pants for a look at my knee. For a shy American, this scene with three Slavic women in attendance was a bit embarassing. Slavic men, however, are accustomed to this. They grow up receiving treatment from a medical community consisting mostly of female doctors, dentists, and other medical staff.

Without so much as an X-ray, Natasha immediately told me I had deformed knees and suggested a 10-day therapy regime to include 10 sessions of electro-therapy, a total of 30 injections in my right knee and vitamins. Happy to receive quick attention, I readily agreed. Natasha then began to write feverishly for five minutes filling three medium-size notebook pages. I thanked her and went with Valya to the clinic's drugstore where I was able to purchase enough medicines and hypodermic needles for a few days of treatment at the cost of about two dollars.

Valya next escorted me further down the same corridor to the electro-therapy room. There a grandmotherly-type doctor in her seventies recorded my name, age and place of employment. She then asked me to sit on a bed in a curtained corner of the room while she prepared my knee for electro-therapy. After about 20 minutes of treatment, the therapist told me to come back the next day about the same time.

I then went to the office where nurses give various types of injections. Once again I gave my name and age, presented the hypodermic needles and medicine to the two young nurses working there. One then told me to go into their treatment room. After asking me where the pain was, she gave me three injections in my right knee. At that point I thought the injections for the day were finished. However, the nurse then instructed me to lower my shorts and brace myself for an injection in my bottom. To my further surprise, I received a second injection in my other cheek, and a third one. These last two injections were the vitamins the surgeon had mentioned earlier and which I naively thought were to be taken orally. I took a deep breath when she finished and thought: Only nine more days of treatment!

Things were going smoothly until I went to a local drugstore as directed to purchase drugs and needles for my next injections at the clinic. Neither of the two attendants on duty could decipher the doctor's illegible handwriting. Finally, to try to solve the riddle, I called Valya, the dentist, who knew the name of the injection, plazmol. I returned to the same drugstore but learned it was temporarily out of stock.

Barely able to walk, I went to the opposite end of the same very icy avenue in search of another drugstore. Luckily the next drugstore had plazmol and I purchased 27 vials, enough for the remainder of my therapy. I then made my way back to the clinic for my second day of treatment.

I thought my second electro-therapy treatment went smoothly until the elderly doctor returned and removed the pad from my knee to find that it had been burned. She seemed really upset and asked why I didn't turn down the knob on the wall. I told her I thought I was supposed to feel a burning sensation. Instead of remaining in the treatment room, she left for the full 20 minutes of my therapy session and now was worried that I would complain to a clinic administrator and that she might lose her job. I assured her I wouldn't make a fuss. As a reminder of that day, I still have a small scar on my right knee.

I continued receiving electro-therapy and three injections into my knee and bottom for the full 10-day therapy, for a total of 60 injections—more injections than I've probably received during my entire life in America. The swelling in my knee did eventually begin to go down but I still had a sharp, shooting pain in my knee. After a week I decided to go back to the clinic and again see Natasha, the surgeon.

However, when I reached the clinic I found that another elderly surgeon, Volodymyr Volodymyrovich Kononenko, was on duty. I explained the course of therapy Natasha had prescribed for me and my continuing pain to the grey-haired, good-humored doctor. Volodymyrovich carefully examined my injured knee, bending it in various directions. He then asked me pointedly, "Do you know what this 10-day therapy has done for you?" I said no. He replied, "Nothing!" He dismissed my earlier prescribed therapy as useless and said the only thing the electro-therapy did for me was to burn my knee in several places. He also similarly dismissed the anti-inflammatory plazmol injections into my knee and the B vitamin injections.

Instead, he wrote a prescription for a single injection of cortisone which I purchased at the clinic's drugstore. When I returned with it, he first drained my knee, then gave me a very deep injection and suggested a return visit in three days.

Did the shooting pain in my knee stop after I finished visiting this clinic? Not at all. However, I did learn to manage the pain by circumventing Kyiv's many steep hills and limiting my use of steps whenever possible.

Did I feel better after I stopped visiting the clinic? I was very grateful that I no longer had to search Kyiv's drugstores for medical supplies, make my way through ice, snow and slush, and climb the steep, crumbling steps to the clinic. And this made me feel better.

Navigating Slavic Minefields

> *"Step on a crack, break your mother's back."*
> -an American proverb

In large American cities it is increasingly common to see Americans walking to the metro or elsewhere and multi-tasking, for example, reading a newspaper, texting, checking e-mail. If you do this in Moscow or Kyiv you will quickly get a rude introduction to a collapsing and corrupt medical system.

Slavs do chat on cell phones as they walk the streets of these cities but they do this with eyes wide open. They never take their eyes off of the sidewalk, the road and, in winter, the icy roofs of tall buildings. This behavior is learned and ingrained in early childhood and often reinforced by personal accidents and news reports of pedestrian fatalities.

The city is a minefield. The sidewalks of Moscow and Kyiv are pock-marked with cracked and sinking pavement, loose and missing manhole covers. Each year falling icicles and sliding sheets of ice from tall city buildings kill innocent pedestrians, and aggressive, reckless motorists taunt citizens daily at crosswalks and even on sidewalks. During December 2010, for example, a mother and her 3-year-old child were run down at a Kyiv crosswalk by a speeding driver in an Audi. Overgrown city parks and greens also include danger zones for inattentive strollers.

These dangers are aggravated by official indifference to these accidents waiting to happen. In Kyiv I've monitored how long dangerous pavement, even in the city's very center, goes unaddressed. Daily for a month and a half in 2008 I sidestepped a hole, a foot-wide and nearly as deep, at the bottom of a set of steps leading to the perpetually busy Tolstoho metro station. Thousands of commuters passed this danger zone daily. After a few weeks it did receive some attention. It became a convenient trash receptacle for cigarette butts, empty drink containers, and candy and food wrappers.

During 2009 there was a foot-long stretch of sunken sidewalk near a large trash bin in front of my Kyiv apartment that received no attention for many months. Each day I had to remind myself of this danger. One day I saw a homeless person wrench her ankle there as she approached to search our trash bin.

Americans visiting Moscow and Kyiv need to be very alert when entering metro stations. The Soviet-era swinging glass doors are called "widow-makers" by the locals, because they are extremely heavy and swing quickly with knock-out force. More than 20 years after the collapse of the Soviet Union, these same doors continue to be added to new metro stations, making access for disabled persons and the very elderly virtually impossible.

Moscow and Kyiv's parks and overgrown city greens can also be a danger zone. I learned my lesson during the summer of 1996 while I was staying in a rundown apartment on the outskirts of Moscow. Before undertaking the long daily commute to the city's center, I often went for an early morning walk in the large wooded park across the road from my apartment. The park had tall, grass trails, instead of sidewalks, and was very unkempt. Many locals unleashed their dogs there daily.

To avoid oncoming, unfriendly-looking dogs, I would often go off the beaten path and cut across the overgrown green. One day I did just that, but soon found my right leg knee-deep in a hole covered with grass. It seems that some dogs like to dig and not just walk in this park. Rather than experience the greater pain of entering Russia's crumbling and corrupt medical system, a Slavic circle of hell, I chose to limp for a few weeks and let nature take its course.

Interestingly, you will virtually never see a Russian or Ukrainian step on any of the countless manhole covers on city sidewalks and streets. They know better. Too often they are loose and they are often stolen during the night. I remember being in Moscow in the late 1990s and standing near a street corner in the heart of the city. A Russian woman who worked at a research institute I had visited many times before walked by, noticed me and shrieked, "What are you doing?" Perplexed, I asked for an explanation. She said, "You're standing on a manhole cover. You don't have enough problems?" With time I realized the practical wisdom in her statement.

In 2006 I was reminded of this manhole incident when I heard a very tragic, heart-wrenching news report on Ukrainian radio. A mother in a remote Ukrainian village rode home on a bus with her 4-year-old daughter one very dark evening after work. The driver pulled up to a bus stop shelter and the two stepped off the bus. The child immediately fell through an open manhole. Authorities searched for five hours before they found the little girl who had been carried 180 meters and was dead.

Since 2006 I have heard many more horror stories where missing or stolen manhole covers have created life-threatening situations in Russia and Ukraine. Kyiv is a city with more than 1,000 manholes and nine scrap metal points; several of them admittedly pay $10 for an intact manhole cover. City officials refuse to seriously address this problem and protect their citizens and visitors. During 2010, for example, an elderly woman who was walking her dog along a Kyiv street suddenly slipped down an uncovered manhole. She received third-degree burns from the hot water flowing below and her dog was boiled alive.

Ukraine's pedestrian minefield became even more dangerous during the winter of 2009–2010. A record snowfall covered the country and even paralyzed its capital Kyiv. To add insult to injury, the usual pedestrian mines, including icy and sunken sidewalks and loose manhole covers, were all dangerously concealed with ice and a layer of snow. Not surprisingly, city officials reported a record number of pedestrian accidents and hospitals were flooded with patients that winter.

Living the life of a pedestrian in Moscow and Kyiv, I feel like I take my life into my hands every morning I step out of my apartment. It's a strange feeling of uncertainty. I often wonder whether I'll hit one of these many mines on the way to work or whether a speeding motorist will hit me at a crosswalk or even on a sidewalk. The option of driving is even less appealing. It means joining a sea of reckless, speeding Slavic drivers and frequently being forced to pay a bribe to the corrupt traffic police.

Instead, I follow the example of the AAA (American Automobile Association). Before leaving my Kyiv apartment mornings I take a few minutes to prepare a mental "Trip Tik" which takes into consideration potential mines along my trip path, including ever-present construction which makes sidewalks inaccessible, areas with dangerous icicles, rotting apartment building balconies and packs of starving, stray dogs.

I've also learned never to leave my apartment in Kyiv or Moscow without some form of personal identification and at least the local equivalent of five dollars, an acceptable bribe for any annoying police officer who may stop me for no good reason. The ID is not just for police, it's also a courtesy just in case I hit a serious, unexpected minefield: It will be easier for authorities to identify my body.

Slavic Bat Radar

> *"Stay in your own lane."*
> -an American saying

Americans are great believers in the concept of "stay in your own lane" and its sister concept "good fences make good neighbors." Our average homes, by international standards, are enormous in size and have been growing steadily over the past few decades. Some are so large (the so-called "McMansions") that people can avoid their own family should they choose to do so. In short, we are great believers in private space and this includes keeping a good distance when speaking even to close friends. Other cultures feel comfortable with close talkers.

In addition to American history and geography, this culturally-ingrained and shared American norm is reinforced by our car culture and resistance to mass public transit. Only in an absolute emergency would most Americans, given a choice, even consider public transport. Even the idea of car-pooling to work is generally considered offensive and out of the question unless it buys us access to an express lane. Driving to work alone gives American white-collar workers, for example, the option to sneak out early—with a persuasive excuse of course—rather than wait daily for three additional riders to appear at a prescribed hour.

Russians and Ukrainians generally have some very un-American concepts of private space, public transport and socially acceptable public behavior. One needs to grasp that most Slavs have lived as huddled masses throughout the Soviet era and now two decades after the collapse. This means that three generations typically live in a two-room—not to be confused with a two-bedroom—apartment—and often four members of a single family live in a one-room apartment measuring 30 square meters (about the size of an average American living room). Given such typically tight quarters, it is not surprising that Russians and Ukrainians inhabit parks as often as possible and go for daily strolls to "air out," as they like to say.

It's important to comprehend that the Soviet Union was a non-car culture. Only in recent years has the idea of affording a car in one's lifetime become a reality for many Russians and Ukrainians. However, the international economic crisis of 2008–2009 dashed this dream for many. The vast majority of these Slavs still rely daily on public transport (a mix of metro, bus and minibus) which is a national contact sport. I've seen canned sardines that have more wiggle room than Slavs in the sea of post-Soviet minibuses flooding Russia and Ukraine today.

Despite spending a good bit of the last two decades living and working in Moscow and Kyiv, and having lived in bustling cities such as New York and London, I still find it difficult at times to get used to typical Slavic behavior on the metro, city streets, sidewalks and supermarkets in Moscow and Kyiv. It differs dramatically from what you encounter, for example, in New York and London.

An American walking the crowded, central sidewalks of Moscow or Kyiv quickly realizes that the average native has no concept whatsoever of "right of way" or walking in a straight path. It seems genetically absent. Their movements more often resemble those of a raging bull expecting everyone to jump out of their path. You need to experience it to believe it, and daily there are endless opportunities. After a while you begin to think you are invisible. A few examples will illustrate this behavior.

Example one: Imagine you are walking down a crowded central sidewalk in Kyiv or Moscow in a straight path on the far right hand side of a sidewalk easily large enough for four persons to walk abreast. In the space of a city block a dozen or more natives walking toward you from different lanes will instinctively "lock into" your path from a good distance and leave you with the uncomfortable feeling that they will collide into you if you don't move.

Example two: It's morning rush hour and you and a few natives are walking two city blocks to reach the metro. You are walking toward a wall of pedestrians apparently just off the metro and taking up the entire very wide sidewalk. You walk in a single, straight lane to the far right with a few others but none of the oncoming natives yields even an inch. Consequently, you are forced to push through the crowd. The same scene recurs at the underpass leading to the metro and before you can even reach the metro doors, and this is a daily occurrence.

Example three: Kyiv and Moscow have the deepest metro escalators in the world. Virtually all of the stations have escalators. After getting off a train there is always, to put it mildly, a mad stampede to the escalator. And there's always a mob of people pressing and pushing against one another until finally the mob splits into two rows at the foot of the escalator.

Just like New York City you say? Not quite. The body contact you feel in these scenes in Moscow and Kyiv would definitely result in a few stabbings or fist fights, at a minimum, in New York. At first I was very offended by this pushing but with time you realize that this behavior is ingrained from childhood; it is generally not intended to be offensive, although objectively speaking it is.

Example four: Observe Moscow and Kyiv drivers even for a day and you will realize that they have no concept of or respect for lanes. Most also consider pedestrian crosswalks a terrible nuisance and a waste of their precious time, and attempt to shoot around people already in the green-light, zebra crosswalk. Moreover, these Slavic motorists routinely drive and park on sidewalks, and commonly drive in reverse on busy sidewalks.

Example five: Slavic shoppers armed with shopping carts in enormous 12-aisle, or more, supermarkets conspicuously lack any concept of right-of-way or stay-in-your-own-lane behavior, which is equally evident on their sidewalks, streets and metro areas.

With time I've learned to cope with the above rude, culturally ingrained behavior. A few tips for any Americans planning to live and work among the natives in Russia and Ukraine.

Tip one: What to do when oncoming natives "lock into" your straight path from different lanes expecting you to jump out of their way? After a while you will spot these types a mile away. Avoid direct eye contact with them. Turn your eyes slightly away from them but always keep them in your peripheral vision. You'll see them change course at the last second and slide off of you as though they have bat radar. I've run this experiment countless times and each time there is a Slavic teflon, non-stick reaction. Once in a great while a thug will purposely run into you.

Tip two: In large supermarkets with Slavic shoppers stay very alert, learn to jump out of the way of staff obliviously operating heavy equipment, and wear padded clothing.

And finally *tip three:* To increase your chances of making it alive across pedestrian crosswalks, zebra and those with green lights, avoid being the first to cross and try to have a buffer of several pedestrians on the side of oncoming traffic. Ideal buffers include mothers with baby carriages or small children, and hefty babushkas.

Slavic Formula-1 Drivers

> "They say Mother Teresa loved mankind, but that's probably because she never had to drive in Moscow during rush hour."
>
> -Slavic humor

For most people, Formula-1 racing is a special event that occurs once a year with great fanfare. However, in Moscow and Kyiv Formula-1 type drivers can be found wherever there is any virtually clear city block. In this short space many reach speeds of 70 mph and greater. Watching them is breathtaking. I often expect many to pop parachutes in order to stop at a red light. Instead, many of them sail right through. The more courteous ones kindly blast their car horns to alert oncoming cars as they run red lights.

At times I get the impression that the roads are flooded exclusively with inexperienced 16-year-old boys who've just received their driver's license and are racing their dad's luxury SUV. With all of the emergency, high-speed braking that's done to avoid crashes, you might think that brake work is offered free in Russia and Ukraine.

I remember the first time I witnessed this Slavic style of driving. It reminded me of my joy-riding days with rental cars. As a young thrill-seeking man I would occasionally take them through extremely grueling road tests and then return them with a sheepish, guilty expression. Lesson of the day: Don't ever buy a used American rental car.

This obvious Slavic disrespect for one's own vehicle, not to mention other motorists and pedestrians, is very curious. In Soviet times it was a dream come true for an average citizen to ever obtain a car. The last 20 years have witnessed a sea of vehicles added to Russian and Ukrainian roads. Except for the countless, filthy "newly rich," buying even a modest car is still a very special acquisition for average Slavs.

How can we better understand this pervasive, very dangerous Formula-1 style of driving in heavily populated Slavic cities? A Ukrainian friend and cab driver in Kyiv for over 20 years shared his insights with me. He said that most drivers in Ukraine and Russia have limited and poor training, and fairly limited experience on the road. It's not uncommon for them to bribe inspectors in order to pass driving tests, or even buy their driving licenses. Moreover, traffic fines are light and bribing the poorly paid police is a norm. None of this is surprising given that total corruption is endemic in both of these countries.

My friend added that these new drivers then "learn to drive" in this dangerous soup by copying the habits of older drivers whose skills are actually modeled after watching real Formula-1 drivers in action. However, unlike real Frormula-1 drivers, most Slavs aren't professional drivers and they don't even wear seatbelts.

Each time I use a seat belt, Slavic cab drivers smile and, without exception, tell me, "It's not necessary here." By using a seatbelt here, you insult the driver. Interestingly, most Slavic drivers do keep a tiny religious icon on their dashboard—probably a good idea.

The results of this driving culture are often very tragic. Compared to Germans who are known to drive at high speeds, Ukrainians had nine times the number of accidents in 2008, and four times more than the French. According to a 2009 World Bank report, alcohol, smoking, and traffic accidents account for 94 percent of Ukraine's mortality. The situation in Russia, with its greater incidence of alcoholism than Ukraine, is no better.

Pedestrians are truly an endangered species in Russia and Ukraine. Here you take your life in your hands every time you step out of your apartment, walk city sidewalks with moving cars, and attempt to navigate crosswalks with or without stop lights.

A walk light for pedestrians does not mean walk. It means count how many cars with blacked-out windows will shoot through your right of way and narrowly miss hitting you. Drivers also routinely ignore and force others to ignore the ubiquitous zebra–pedestrian crossings.

And you don't even need to step off the curb to suffer. For example, during October 2010 in the eastern Ukrainian city of Dnipropetrovsk, a speeding motorist in a huge Toyota Landcruiser Prado SUV jumped a curb and killed three pedestrians waiting at a corner to cross. After many years in Russia and Ukraine, I can no longer approach an American crosswalk in the same casual way I once could.

The situation on public sidewalks in Moscow and Kyiv reminds me of the Wild, Wild West. I learned this firsthand more than a dozen years ago on a sidewalk in busy downtown Moscow. I was walking and, as usual, looking out for sinking sidewalks, craters and missing manhole covers when a quiet-running car nudged me from behind. I couldn't believe it. Before I could even express my anger, the driver angrily motioned for me to get out of his way.

It's clearly not enough to navigate the minefield ahead of you on Slavic sidewalks and street crossings. You also need to watch your back. In the picturesque heart of Kyiv there is a kilometer-long street with very wide, cobblestone sidewalks called Khreshchatik. Once a care-free area to stroll any day of the week, today it is the scene of parked and often speeding cars.

The sad fact is that Slavic motorists typically view pedestrians to be a nuisance, much like potholes but bumpier. They tolerate them only because hitting one would create an annoying dent in the car and require much paper work, loss of valuable time and, no doubt, a sizeable bribe for the police. Pedestrians on sidewalks especially irritate the drivers of black luxury SUVs with blacked-out windows because they take up precious parking and driving space. Speedbumps on Slavic sidewalks could save lives.

The luxury-car decadence of Ukraine and Russia's political elite is disgustingly conspicuous outside of parliament and government offices, in general. They are some of the most egregious violators of the rights of pedestrians. Their SUV weapons of choice are: Toyota Landcruiser Prado, Range Rover, Lexus, BMW, Mercedes, Audi, Porsche and Cadillac. Blacked-out windows seem to be standard on virtually all cars driven in Russia and Ukraine. This encourages rude and dangerous driving practices and denies a pedestrian the right to see and identify who is threatening his life daily.

What about rootin-tootin Putin? Is Russia's little macho man taming his country's crazy drivers? Au contraire! Believe it or not, real Formula-1 drivers raced around the Kremlin during July 2010. Russian fans had a chance to see Russia's first Formula-1 driver, Vitaly Petrov, speed around the Kremlin—yes, including around Lenin's tomb! Thank God he's not alive to see this, it would kill him.

Unfortunately, there is no reason to think that Slavic driving practices and sidewalk safety will improve in the near future as more cars are steadily added to roadways. Frankly, I would not be surprised if I saw two Slavs on a street corner, waiting for a green walk light, make the sign of the cross and then turn to each other and say, "Good luck. I hope you make it to the other side."

Nor would I be terribly surprised if Toyota and Range Rover soon come out with even bigger and better special-edition SUVs for Russia and Ukraine's newly rich called Toyota Sidewalk Cruiser and Sidewalk Rover, respectively. I think the not-too-swift, filthy rich, so-called VIP of these countries would quickly snap them up.

Finally, I would not be surprised if more and more Slavic mothers soon began to admonish their young school children, while dressing for school, the way many American mothers often do: "Put on clean underwear! You never know when you might get into an accident."

My Slavic Mega-Market

> *"Have a nice day."*
> -American politeness

Major changes in grocery shopping have taken place in the 20 years since I first started living and working in Russia and Ukraine. The small, single-room grocery stores characteristic of the Soviet era, and still active a decade after the collapse of the U.S.S.R., are thankfully gone. Thinking about them still makes me shudder.

By the year 2000, modern American-style supermarkets finally began to spring up. Most were fancy and too expensive for average natives to frequent. However, after 2005 enormous discount supermarkets, many on the outskirts of Moscow and Kyiv, were affordable for average workers and even retired persons on meager pensions. In Moscow, Auchan, a French mega-market chain, opened its doors in 2002 and Ashan in Kyiv a few years later.

In Kyiv I frequent my nearby Mega-Market, part of a chain of stores much larger than the average American supermarket. Although it's located in the center of Kyiv just two city blocks from my apartment, I always have to plan my purchases carefully and calculate the weight and bulk of the items I plan to purchase. This is because I intentionally don't use a car in Kyiv or Moscow for the simple reason that most Slavs drive as though they're NASCAR or Formula-1 drivers.

The first impression of any American entering my Mega-Market, no doubt, would be that it's a high-security liquor market and this is understandable. For starters, there's serious face control at the entrance. Just beyond the entry there are half a dozen heavy-set, alert men in black suits standing almost equidistant behind thirty young, female cashiers. Most of their time is spent keeping an eye on the cashiers and shoppers in the long aisles directly in front of them. At the other end of the store there are another half-dozen similar men also watching shoppers in their respective aisles.

Just beyond the stores turnstile entrance there are four very long aisles of alcohol with countless brands of vodka, beer and wine. *Welcome to Ukraine!* If this wasn't enough, there's a very large room full of exclusive wines and spirits with two security guards just behind these aisles of alcohol. By now you should have guessed that there is a Slavic national tradition of stealing with very deep Soviet roots, and management likes to show customers conspicuous physical security in addition to the video surveillance visible throughout the store.

Beyond this abundance of alcohol (great product placement by the way), presuming you even need to go any further, there are two aisles of real food, canned and boxed. Then more Slavic essentials: nearly two aisles of very fancy chocolates followed by two aisles of cakes, pastries and cookies. In fairness I should note that this supermarket also has a modest fruit and vegetable section, a large deli with dozens of the world's most fatty sausages and a large dairy case. Moreover, all of this supermarket's aisles are constantly being restocked by an army of meagerly paid mostly college-age workers, who don't go to college and typically work 12-hour shifts.

Significantly, this Mega-Market, with more than 50 percent of its stock devoted to alcohol and sweets, is typical of most Slavic supermarkets. Add heavy smoking to the diet of Slavs and it is not surprising that the average male life expectancy in 2012 was 59 for Russians and 62 for Ukrainians, compared to 76 for German men.

A few words are in order about Slavic shoppers' etiquette in large supermarkets. It's a sight to behold and can best be described in two words: bulldozer and roadblock. I often get the sensation that I must be invisible when I shop in my Mega-Market and that I have some magnetic power that draws Slavs and their carts into me. I deliberately never use a shopping cart despite the store's wide aisles. I find that using a shopping basket allows me to maneuver more quickly and leave the store with fewer bruises.

Slavs typically drive shopping carts as though they were bulldozers and instruments to clear the path in front of them. It's important to understand that supermarkets and shopping carts are essentially alien, post-Soviet concepts for Slavs. Most are very inexperienced at operating a shopping cart and drive them recklessly, never yielding the right of way, just as they do with their cars on the road.

Operating a shopping cart is obviously not rocket science but I've noticed that many natives pull rather than push their carts, and often do so from either side. For a long time I thought this was ridiculous but I eventually found the logic in this social norm. Apparently, it's easier to get through the many road blocks created by Slavic shoppers in the aisles if you are pulling your cart and pushing others out of the way with your free hand.

I often find it impossible to get through aisles even with just a shopping basket. Shoppers routinely position their carts horizontally in the aisles and take their sweet time to study products on shelves and shake the contents of canned and bottled products, even when they see you coming. You can wait forever and they won't move their carts.

But the real fun is in the deli line. Shoppers line up alongside the deli case. Slavic queue jumpers typically wedge between shoppers lined up next to the deli case and strain their eyes for minutes to look at the various meats. They do this several times with different people in the line and eventually find a victim and nestle in, usually toward the front of the line. Most people can easily spot these veterans but generally avoid making a scene because they know these queue jumpers love confrontation and always have the last word.

The largely female staff of these modern Slavic supermarkets is another joy to behold. They're not much of an improvement over the surly, snarling sales people who ran small Soviet grocery stores. They clearly lack a "service gene" and never heard of "the customer is always right" business philosophy. Their Soviet-style mentality is best reflected in the words, "Why do we need to be nice to the customers, we have all of the goods?" Stated differently, it's an "I'm not getting paid to be nice to customers" attitude. Not surprisingly, it's virtually impossible to get a response from these cashiers when you greet them. I often feel as though I need to snap my fingers several times to bring them out of a trance.

But these are all mini gripes. Slavic modern supermarkets are paradise compared to the Soviet-style *kassa* system in the small grocery stores which I endured in most districts of Moscow and Kyiv until about 2005. Kassa literally means cash register and refers to the Soviet system of having one or more tiny cash register booths in a food store.

Just imagine the following shopping experience on a very humid summer day in an airless tiny store. To get meat or cheese you need to stand in one line, let's call it section one, with lots of women (Slavic men conveniently leave food shopping in their traditional gender role's culture to their wives or mothers) pushing into you and complaining until it's their turn and a store clerk weighs their meat or cheese and tells them the cost. They then go to the line at the meat and cheese cash-register booth (kassa), one of several, pay and get a receipt to bring back to section one's store clerk, but only after waiting for her to finish with a customer. To get bread and baked goods you enter a queue for a different section and go through exactly the same procedure. For dairy and fish you would have to join two additional queues and repeat the process.

Often shoppers, including myself, would muddle the figures one needed to remember while going from one section of the store to a line at the proper kassa, and this would give overweight salesladies a chance to express rage and impatience and publicly belittle a customer. I recall how I would often have to build up my courage to go into my local kassa-system grocery and join the multiple queues. I hate to admit it but there were days when I was under the weather and would drop out of a store queue after a long wait without buying what I needed.

Hower, the kassa system did have a Soviet logic. It kept food behind counters and away from shoppers' sticky fingers. Moreover, the cashier booth theoretically made theft by staff more difficult. In fact, in Soviet times there was a great deal of theft of store goods by store staff. The kassa system, to put it mildly, was a Slavic circle of hell you wouldn't wish on your worst enemy. By entering it you were guaranteed to be pushed, humiliated and ridiculed with every visit.

Several years ago I had an opportunity to conduct a supermarket experiment on a Russian friend, Oleg, who was attending a conference in Washington and visiting the US for the first time. Oleg stayed at my home during the conference and when it was over I gave him a tour of Washington sites. As a sign of appreciation, Oleg asked that I take him to an American supermarket so that he could make some purchases and help prepare a family dinner.

I drove out of my way and took Oleg to a state-of-the-art American supermarket, an enormous Wegman's, a recent winner of the Dale Carnegie award for leadership and innovation in the field. At Wegman's I decided I would let Oleg do all the shopping and simply observe and answer any questions he might have. Oleg, not surprisingly, behaved just as he would have in a large Moscow supermarket. He grabbed a large cart and, thankfully, did not pull it through the store. However, his driving ability left much to be desired. He quickly ran into the carts of several women moving slowing in a single lane, when they failed to get out of his way; their angry eyes expressed their emotions. Of course, there was no reaction or apology from Oleg, who simply continued to plow forward.

Things got more interesting quickly. Oleg went to the deli section of the store, refused to take a number and tried unsuccessfully to jump the queue; I think he was offended when he was denied this Slavic right. When his turn finally came, he picked out several cuts of meat and some cold cuts and indicated the desired amount in grams. This created an interesting, lengthy exchange which made me wish I hadn't set Oleg up for all of this.

Oleg continued to get things on his shopping list. Without a single "Excuse me," he reached in front of several shoppers looking at items on shelves, each time receiving very unfriendly stares. At this point, I was thankful we were not in a supermarket in a rough part of New York City.

One more item and our shopping would be complete. Oleg went up to a store clerk in the beer section and asked him where the vodka was. The clerk looked at Oleg with a huge smile and started to laugh. Oleg grew impatient and asked again. The clerk explained that American supermarkets don't carry vodka. Oleg was in a state of profound disbelief and told the clerk he thought it was shameful for supermarkets not to carry vodka.

To interrupt their conversation, I told Oleg we really needed to get back home. I followed a visibly disappointed Oleg to the checkout line. The female cashier at the busy checkout greeted Oleg with eye contact and the standard, "Hi, how are you?" Oleg responded with a sour expression and a squint. And then the roof almost caved in. The cashier glibly and politely asked Oleg, "Did you find everything OK?" Before Oleg could set off any fireworks regarding the store's inexcusable lack of vodka I grabbed his arm and in Russian quietly said, "ne nada" meaning you "don't need" to respond.

Before the cashier even started to ring up our groceries, Oleg asked to buy two large plastic bags (you buy them in Russia and Ukraine) and was told they were free. He immediately took the bagging responsibility over from the cashier as you're required to do back home. Finally, when the transaction was over the cashier thanked Oleg and said, "Have a nice day!" Oleg responded, "Yes, I will," and we exited.

Feeling a bit guilty, I stopped at a Virginia ABC Liquor store on the way home and picked up a very big bottle of vodka while Oleg smoked nervously outside. I think it's fair to say that Oleg experienced some mild country and culture shock that day, and may even have felt a bit like a fish out of water in an American supermarket. However, no lasting damage was done and certainly none that vodka couldn't quickly repair.

For me visiting a large American supermarket after living and shopping in Ukrainian and Russian supermarkets is like dying and going to heaven. However, everything is relative as they say. And I'm not sure Oleg, and other Russians, would agree with me.

School of Defensive Walking

> "Rudeness is a weak man's imitation of strength."
> -Eric Hoffer

How can one best deal with Slavic Bat Radar and all of the other egregious Slavic violations of personal space that drive a civilized person in Russia or Ukraine mad daily, or worse yet to Slavic-style drinking? How can I save foreigners planning to live and work there the aggravation that I've suffered daily over many years? I finally broke the code and developed a coping system after years of being plowed down by unleashed herds of Slavs, unwilling to yield even a sliver of a lane for anyone advancing in their direction.

These questions haunted me for years. Eventually, I decided to channel my anger, and at times rage, into a positive, almost scientific method to defend against dreaded Slavic Bat Radar and worse.

The answer is my School of Defensive Walking, knowledge and training which I am willing to impart to interested individuals, groups, and governments for a reasonable fee, of course. My system begins with an important acknowledgement and obvious fact: average Americans are not equipped with the bat radar capability and Teflon quality of most Slavs. Consequently, they cannot easily slide off of aggressive, oncoming locals who often monopolize sidewalks and brazenly violate a foreign visitor's personal space on streets and in stores, change lanes recklessly and routinely cause near-collisions.

Americans generally tend to view this behavior as very rude, rather than simply as culturally-conditioned behavior, and understandably continue to be angered by it with each daily encounter. They typically try to avoid as much as possible situations where this kind of offensive behavior occurs. However, this is a very unsatisfying, defeatist response.

In fact, Slavic Bat Radar and the rude public behavior of locals figure prominently among the reasons why American Embassy staff, their families, and foreign contractors are eager to leave after their tour of duty is over. This and the fact that staples of American life, notably, Doritos, Cheetos and Pop Tarts must be flown in regularly from America.

My target audience includes new U.S. Embassy staff, their families, the countless U.S. State Department contractors in Russia and Ukraine, American scholars and students participating in academic exchange programs, and the expat community, in general.

It is a pernicious myth to think that there is nothing foreigners can do to help themselves take control and cope better with this very common and annoying, Slavic public behavior. Make no mistake, there is no simple solution. Concerned with the physical security of my fellow countrymen in Russia, Ukraine and beyond, many sleepless nights have led me to develop the concept and practice of defensive walking.

My School of Defensive Walking begins with a seminar on defensive walking principles, an off-the-street training program with real Slavs who employ reckless and rude walking techniques, and one-on-one sessions on Slavic streets which will allow my trainers to evaluate your walking skills and coach you to change any weak habits. I also recommend periodic evaluations.

My Training Program

Students trained in my program internalize five fundamental elements of defensive walking: think and look ahead, identify hazards, keep your options open, manage the risk, and control with finesse. To avoid collisions and to provide "space for cushion-walking," they are drilled to get the big picture, keep their eyes moving, leave themselves an out, and make sure Slavs see them.

I don't want to give away all of the secrets of my defensive walking system, but I will provide a few concrete examples of what students will learn in my program. To break through the reckless herds of Slavic workers and students exiting metro stations and taking up entire city sidewalks during peak morning and evening hours you will use the "blocker system." Thinking and looking ahead, you will pause for a few seconds, identify two or more sturdy male Slavs advancing against the herd in your desired direction (a single burly babushka also will do), and follow closely behind, imitating the same blocking system used in American football. You'll be surprised how effective this can be; this tip alone is worth the price of my course. Ideally, you will try to avoid travel during pedestrian rush-hour traffic but you will no longer fear it.

During non-peak pedestrian hours, you will learn to actively use your peripheral vision to be on the lookout for Slavs who try to overtake you on city sidewalks only to cut sharply in front of you and make a sharp right-hand turn, which in any civilized country could, and should, have been made easily behind you. Keenly aware of their presence and style, here you have the option to slow down or even come to an abrupt unexpected stop to avoid playing their game. In other words, students will learn to use their eyes effectively to identify activity on sidewalks and underpasses ahead, on either side and to the rear, and to get the big picture so that they're not forced to make snap decisions. Maintaining a "cushion of safety" will become second nature.

Students will also be drilled to become attentive to the ever present uneven and dangerous sidewalk surfaces, motorists driving on sidewalks, stray dogs (often in packs), and falling icicles and sheets of ice from apartment and city buildings in winter. All of my students, incidentally, must undergo a thorough eye examination as part of the application process.

As a bonus my students will also be taught defensive walking and shopping tips in huge Slavic supermarkets. It's not enough to avoid peak shopping hours there. My students will receive a guided tour of a very large Slavic supermarket during peak hours with one of my experienced trainers, who will shield them with his body from attacking natives if necessary. *Tips for my students include the following:* Make an initial visit to the supermarket simply to learn the layout of products, observe native shoppers' reckless habits and, at first, purchase no more than a few articles using only a hand basket.

In general, never use a shopping cart. This, of course, means more trips to the supermarket but this will provide you with more practice as well. You'll thank me for using a shopping basket when you see how locals block even wide aisles with their carts and bodies, and how cashiers provide customers with no time at all to bag their groceries before taking the next customer.

Electing to use a shopping cart opens you up to numerous collisions and guaranteed frustration. Believe it or not, I witnessed the following scene in my Mega-Market in Kyiv. A 20-year-old Ukrainian female, a model wannabe in stiletto heels, rammed her supermarket cart into two carts that entirely blocked a dairy aisle. She did so without hesitating and with no show of emotion, as if it was routine for her.

My advice to students: If you witness such a ramming incident by a native—and they are not at all uncommon—retreat! There is no disgrace in this tactic. With shopping basket in hand, turn around and go through another aisle but watch carefully to ensure that the narcissistic rammer has not turned into your new aisle.

I also suggest you bring your own sturdy, reusable shopping bag as this will buy precious seconds to bag your items and help save what little is left of the environment, especially in Moscow. And remember, if you always expect native shoppers to run into you with their carts and look at you angrily, you'll never be surprised and eventually even learn to slide off of them in bat-radar fashion.

Additional supermarket tips: Place any bottles (your vodka) or boxes you purchase flat on the checkout conveyor belt or expect a stern scolding from the cashier. And expect cashiers even in the largest supermarkets to ask you for correct change for your purchase and to give you a sour expression if you fail to do so; scolding customers and sour expressions are the few perks that make up for their meager wage.

If you bring a cart full of food to the checkout, be aware that you will have no time to bag your groceries and will have to place them back in your shopping cart to bag elsewhere. Most importantly, under no circumstance say, "Have a nice day!" to the cashier after you have completed your transaction. If you do so, they will look at you as though you've spit in their borscht or escaped from an insane asylum.

Once you've graduated and accumulated several weeks of on-the-ground experience successfully, I want you to have some well-deserved fun. On a day when you are feeling particularly robust and confident, I want you to do some role playing. Pretend you are a Slav in the big city with typical non-civilized walking habits but also equipped with Slavic Bat Radar. Arbitrarily violate the personal space and right of way of men, women and children (but not stray dogs) in your path. Overtake them from behind only to cut their path off and make a sharp turn directly in front of them, or stop abruptly for no good reason in front of someone following closely behind (don't worry they'll slide off of you, they're equipped with bat radar). And most importantly, do not—repeat, do not—say "Excuse me" or "I'm sorry" to anyone for your behavior; this will immediately identify you as a foreigner. Enjoy being a Slav with bat radar but only for a day, and then retreat back to our defensive walking techniques.

I'm not expecting a Nobel Prize for my pioneering work in Defensive Walking, although I would not turn one down. A plaque in my honor prominently displayed in the Hall of Honor of the U.S. State Department building in Washington will suffice. I do hope, however, that one day soon the U.S. State Department will honor my School of Defensive Walking Program with a prominent place alongside the important, traditional coping mechanisms it steadfastly supports for Embassy staff and their families in countries such as Russia and Ukraine, namely, timely shipments of Doritos, Cheetos, diet soft drinks and, of course, Pop Tarts.

Sexpats on the Post-Soviet Playground

> "Middle age is when your age starts to show around your middle."
>
> -Bob Hope

The collapse of the Soviet Union in 1991 left a massive post-Soviet playground for foreign men, a thriving destination for sex tourists or "sexpats," as they are frequently called. Nowhere is it more active and visited in the former Soviet Union than in Ukraine, where a 90-day–visa-free regime for citizens of the EU, America and Canada has been in effect since 2005. Russia, which also has a booming sex industry, does not offer sexpats a visa-free regime and requires AIDS-test results for foreigners wishing to remain longer than 30 days.

Ukraine still lags far behind Thailand as a favorite destination for sex tourists but it's catching up quickly thanks to the Internet. There one can find contact information for thousands of young and not-so-young Slavic women and international sex forums with candid information about prostitution in the former Soviet

Union and elsewhere.

What exactly attracts sexpats to this post-Soviet playground? Could it be the soulful eyes and high cheekbones of Slavic women? It could be, but there are greater attractions for average sexpats. Foreign men, many of them middle-aged, generally stress the enormous volume of beautiful and easily available young women who dress very revealingly. The list of attractions includes long-legged blondes in skin-tight jeans and even tighter stretch pants, waist-length, breast-hugging, black-leather jackets and knee-length high-heel leather boots; whips and chains are all that's missing from this picture and they can easily be arranged. And in the summer, there's lots of flesh on display: micro-mini skirts, hot pants, see-through blouses and pants and, of course, stiletto heels.

Twenty years after independence, Ukraine remains an impoverished but highly educated country where the average monthly wage in 2012 was only about $250 and where prostitution is commonplace. Given this harsh reality, it's easy for many sexpats to meet beautiful young women and prostitutes almost anywhere, especially in expat bars and clubs where they tend to congregate nightly. In short, it's the lure of the young berry that draws many middle-aged sexpats here.

What kind of sexpats visit Ukraine and Russia? In my experience there are two basic types: pro-sexpats and first-timers. The goal for each is the same but their approach and results differ dramatically. Turks are a prime example of pro-sexpats. I've met many Turkish men in Kyiv and their message about Ukrainian women is always the same. They find them very beautiful, available and inexpensive, and not at all like their very conservative and unapproachable Turkish women. Thus, it's no surprise that Turkish men, usually in groups, repeatedly spend their summer vacations in nearby Ukraine.

Unlike many American and British novice sexpats, Turkish, Italian and Spanish sexpats typically don't waste their time and money wining and dining young Slavic women and taking them on shopping sprees, nor are they easily scammed by them. You won't find Turks wasting their time on Internet correspondence with young Slavic women, nor walking hand-in-hand with them in downtown Kyiv. Their interaction is straightforward and generally takes place behind closed doors.

In the resort city of Odessa, for example, there are hotels where tour groups of Turkish men stay for a weekend for the sole purpose of having sex with a busload of poor, young Ukrainian girls from provincial areas. And during warm summer days, Turks, Italians and Spaniards typically stroll along the central streets of Kyiv and Odessa and simply enjoy the eye candy on display.

American and British novice sexpats, on the other hand, can be easily spotted downtown in Kyiv and Moscow. They often walk hand-in-hand with a Slavic girl half their age or younger who is dressed in porno-glamour style with heavy make-up, speaks very broken English and is oblivious to the angry stares of passing locals. Novice sexpats easily find these women on enticing dating websites and fly East generally at great personal expense. Upon arriving, these hot young women greet them affectionately and offer them a personal tour of their city.

The tour will include essential activities: wining and dining her, shopping at malls for lingerie (which she promises to model for him), perfume, cosmetics, skin-tight jeans and, of course, Italian stiletto heels—all for his pleasure, she repeatedly tells him. By the end of the day, his credit card is almost maxed out and, unaccustomed to walking many miles daily like average Slavs, this middle-aged American or Brit will gladly accept her suggestion that they meet early the next day. A stiff drink and a hot bath may seem like heaven to him at this point.

Often this will be the first and last time the novice sexpat sees this predatory young woman. American and British first-time sexpats are easy prey. Many of these very young women are pro-daters who string along three or four foreign men at a time on the Internet, hoping one or two will make the trip to their country. They're also known as pro-shoppers for obvious reasons. After they've fleeced one victim, they retreat momentarily and then move on to the next. Most are content never to leave their country unless one of their foreign victims offers them an exotic vacation. As a rule, they deliver as little sex as possible in return for their loot. Turks, Italians and Spaniards are too savvy to waste their time on these scammers.

Virtually everyone in the U.S. associates the words "girls gone wild" with the spring-break antics of wild, intoxicated American college girls in sunny Mexico (caught on video to the chagrin of their parents). Kyiv and Moscow also have their moments. Once darkness descends upon these cities, sexpats—many in their 40s, 50s and 60s—fill their favorite bars, clubs and hotels and with the aid of alcohol and plenty of young Slavic women become "old men gone wild" who "let their genie out of the bottle."

During my many years in Ukraine and Russia I've seen many strange couples walking hand-in-hand downtown in daylight, especially sexpats and young Slavic women. Two examples in particular spring to mind, both in Kyiv in recent years. One day in the upscale, downtown shopping district of Kyiv, I spotted a very tall, frail-looking man, at least 75 years old and resembling Father Time, with a very attractive, average height 20ish blonde hanging on to his arm. Naturally, I froze in my tracks in a state of disbelief.

At first I thought the young woman might be taking her elderly grandfather for a walk or to a nearby health clinic. I approached the two gingerly to gather more information and walked slowly behind them. His American English, her very limited, painful English and their turn into a posh boutique made clear to me that something non-kosher was going on here.

Still I can't be too hard on this old timer. I guess I need to give some credit to a 75-year-old man who not only can put his pants on by himself when he wakes up (I hope) but also can fly across the Atlantic and beyond and keep pace with a 20-year-old pro-shopper. Certainly he's not naïve. He simply wants the company and attention of a young, attractive woman. As one sympathetic Ukrainian friend put it, "He just wants a little bit of heaven before he gets to heaven."

But my favorite strange couple consisted of a striking blonde in her mid 20s, at least 6' 6" with lots of curves, dressed like a porno-pop star in skin-tight black-leather pants, leather vest, spike heels and wearing heavy make-up. Her hand-holding companion was a pudgy little man barely 5' tall, about 40 years old, wearing glasses and resembling a NASA engineer.

It was mid-day in downtown Kyiv when I first spotted them and my first reaction was that there must be a circus in town. My second reaction was *Welcome to Ukraine!* Not surprisingly, I noticed many locals staring at this strolling couple, as though a meteor was dropping from the sky.

I was dying to confirm that the little man was an American and the woman a Slav. I followed them for a short distance as they unabashedly strolled along the city center. Eventually I approached closer and overtook them as they were speaking. Indeed, he was an American judging by his English accent, she a Russian-speaking Ukrainian, and not surprisingly she was taking him to the nearby shopping mall.

I have to give the little guy credit. My typically male reaction to this couple was, "Go for it little man!" Make your colleagues at NASA envious. Birthday wishes can come true!

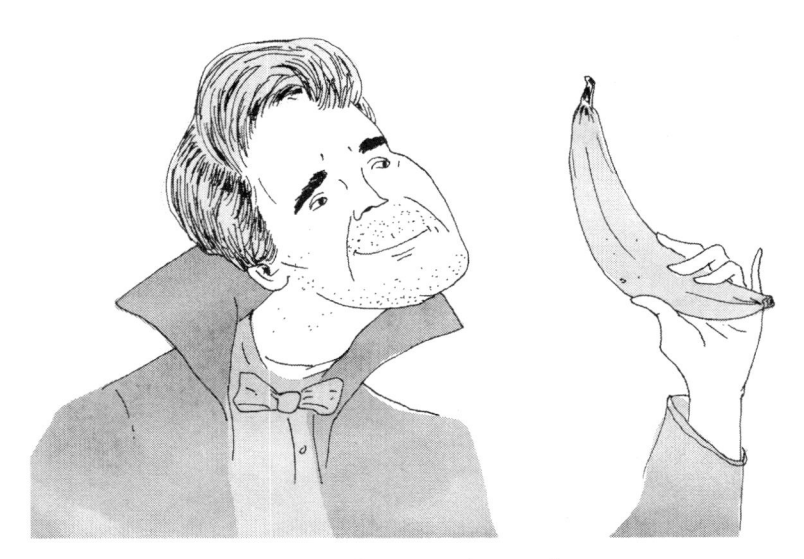

Khytrist, a Key to Understanding Slavic Women

"If you're going to steal, steal a million; if you're going to sleep with someone, sleep with a king."
-Slavic pro-daters' code of conduct

History has been unkind to Slavic women. During the 20th century, notably, it has stolen millions of their men in wars, famines, Stalinist purges, and to widespread alcoholism. Ukrainian women in particular continue to be hard hit in the 21st century by economics. Several million of their best men have been forced to live illegally in Europe and perform hard labor in order to send money home to their impoverished families; nearly 300,000 Ukrainians work in Russia, most legally, for the same reason. Consequently, Slavic women often have the lion's share of family responsibilities placed on their shoulders, in addition to full-time jobs.

Genetics, however, have smiled upon Slavic women. The ancient history of their lands, with protracted Viking and Mongol Tartar presence, clearly shows in the genes of apple-cheeked village girls and their big-city sisters. It is not by accident, as locals like to say, that Ukraine has become the foreign "bridebasket" of Europe and a major destination for sex tourism. The beauty of Ukrainian and Russian women is no international secret.

Almost with their first steps, Slavic girls learn from their mothers and grandmothers how to be *khytri* in the presence of males. *Khytrist* is defined as slyness, cunning, craftiness, and the ability to outfox. It is, unarguably, a strong traditional characteristic of Slavic women, especially in their relations with men, passed down and refined through the ages. Slavic men clearly lack this quality and are easily disarmed by their women. Interestingly, many Slavic women will smile, rather than get offended, if caught being crafty toward a man by another woman.

Slavic women are forced to be more cunning and competitive than Western women because decent, marriage-minded men are a very scarce resource in Russia and Ukraine, and gender inequality and sexism prevail in the workplace. These harsh realities, along with very poor economies, force Slavic women to be strong and compete fiercely for men, especially those on a higher social and economic level.

In Soviet times this meant that grandmothers would ensure that little girls were dressed nicely, often like little princesses, before they went out in public. Beauty and charm were the goals then. Several years ago Marina, a Moscow university professor in her mid-40s, provided me with an additional insight. Despite growing up poor in St. Petersburg, she said her grandmother never allowed her to leave their apartment, even as a young adult, unless her hair, make-up, clothes, and stockings were perfect. And she stressed that this was a very common practice among her peers.

With the collapse of Communism and the introduction of wild capitalism and wild foreign men, many young and not-so-young Slavic women strive to be even more khytri than their mothers and grandmothers in Soviet times. An army of young women in tight, revealing garb can easily be found patrolling the streets of Moscow and Kyiv daily and frequenting expat bars and clubs in the evenings. Men with deep pockets, fat wallets and foreign passports are always a welcome sight. For desperate Slavic women the stakes are very high, indeed, and include a possible ticket out of their *durdom* (insane asylum), as many call it, to a life of financial security and comfort.

Toward this goal there are several new post-Soviet resources to help Slavic women reach this goal. One is *sterva.org*, an amusing and sexy Russian-language Internet informational site which instructs Slavic women how to bring men to their knees in a relationship. The word *sterva* traditionally described a wretched witch or bitch, but in modern usage refers simply to a woman skillful in the art of manipulating men; in other words, a khytra woman with advanced training.

S*terva.org* contains interesting and informative Russian-language articles such as, "How I Became a Sterva" and "How to Become a Sterva" and a forum for stervas. It also features the latest styles in astronomically high heels and other essential dress for stervas. The site's motto is, "Want to be a sterva? Then be one! Stervas of the world, unite!!!"

But my favorite resource for the new post-Soviet times is a course with the pretentious, scientific-sounding name Stervologia taught by Vladimir Rakovsky. He's a 45-year-old randy Russian and a former worker with Russia's Emergencies Ministry who is now relieving Russian and Ukrainian women of $300 for a 2-day session on how to manipulate and exploit men (the average monthly income for an honest worker in Ukraine is just over $200). Touting his master's degree in psychology from Moscow State University, he presents himself to women with money and ambition as a guru in the art of male seduction.

Dressed in slimming, black clothes and with bushy, black eyebrows, Rakovsky resembles Count Dracula more than he does any Don Juan. Yet women seem to flock to his classes which he has been holding regularly in Ukraine since 2005 and Russia since 1997. At his side is his 25-year-old saucy wife Yevgenia who is a teacher in his School of Seduction class and proficient in pole dancing and striptease. Together they unravel the mystery of how to bring men to their knees by acting like little girls (the Lolita class includes women 18–56!), how to sit and walk seductively, how to dress seductively, and how to disarm and manipulate men with feminine charm.

The curriculum presents some challenges and has its moments. In addition to pole dancing and striptease lessons (with students 18–56!), Rakovsky also teaches woman how to perform oral sex on bananas. I've seen actual photos of smiling women in his classes pleasuring bananas. It's unclear whether Rakovsky developed his banana-pleasuring skills during his time with Russia's Emergencies Ministry or Moscow State University. Interestingly, he stresses that his classes offer information and skills that a mother should pass on to a daughter. Hopefully, such skills do not include a mother-daughter banana session.

On a more serious note, khytri Slavic women even with sterva training can and often are outfoxed. A typical case in point is Oksana, an attractive and highly educated researcher with the Academy of Sciences in Ukraine. At the age of 25 she became involved with much older, influential foreign men while pursuing advanced degrees in Warsaw and Paris. In the best tradition of a *khytra zhinka*, a cunning woman, she chose further education as a vehicle to repeatedly but unsuccessfully evacuate her home country.

At first she attracted and brought a Polish Colonel, twice her age, to his knees while simultaneously earning an advanced degree in Polish. This relationship went back and forth and lasted several years. Fluent in French, in addition to Russian and Ukrainian, she then ensnared a French general more than twice her age while getting a degree at the Sorbonne. With his considerable influence, she then spent a half-dozen years going back and forth from Ukraine to France for alleged academic programs.

The married French general was always generous. In return for her charms and special favors, he typically sent her home with an exploding suitcase of gifts but no golden ring and no ticket off the sinking ship called Ukraine.

But the years roll by quickly. Today at 36 Oksana still works as a Ukrainian researcher and aggressively seeks foreign travel. Still desperate to evacuate Ukraine, she continues to post her profile on dating and marriage websites, looking for men twice her age from North America, Australia and Western Europe.

Slavic co-eds refer unkindly to Oksana types as retreads: sly women who manage to ensnare foreign men with their charm and intelligence, win several foreign trips but ultimately fail to receive a marriage proposal, and have no realistic prospect of ever having a child or a family of their own.

Good news, however. Not to worry! If all else fails, Professor Rakovsky has an additional weapon in his Stervologia bag of tricks. His wife Yevgenia also teaches a class on lap dancing (with students 18–56!) that's guaranteed to win the heart of any man, especially those with deep pockets, fat wallets and foreign passports.

Looking for Love in all the Wrong Places

> *"You have to pay to play."*
> -street wisdom

Six A.M. at my 24-hour Kyiv Internet café is a time when the city still sleeps and I always find the Internet easily available. One early morning during September 2009 as I sat at a computer in a virtually empty Internet café, I overheard a loud American in his mid-40s, with Molson (beer) muscles that showed years of dedicated effort, babbling non-stop to the young English-speaking Ukrainian college student on duty. When I finished using the Internet, I couldn't resist the urge to ask the American where he was from.

He responded joyfully like someone who had just won the lottery, "Oh, you speak English, you're an American?" I assured him I was. He told me his name was Bill and that he lived in North Carolina. He had just returned from the resort city of Odessa where he went to meet a young Ukrainian woman with whom he had been corresponding on the Internet for several months. He then asked if I'd go for a coffee with him.

I agreed reluctantly. Over the years I've grown very weary of typical expats in Moscow and Kyiv and their well-known bar and club hangouts. But Bill was visiting for a short while and seemed desperate to speak to an American.

Over a cup of coffee I learned that Bill was very disappointed and angry about his recent trip to Odessa. Irina, the woman waiting for him there, bore little resemblance to the beautiful young woman he corresponded with online and, over the course of a few days, took Bill for quite a lot of money: shopping for clothes, perfume, cosmetics; wining and dining; and the cost of having a translator present, who also ate at Bill's expense, and a car and driver. After a few days of this routine, Bill realized that Irina was a pro-dater who was scamming him, together with her translator and driver friends. He was especially angry because he "didn't even get lucky" with Irina, as he put it. I listened attentively.

Bill was so angry that he planned to blow the lid off of these female scammers with the aid of the Internet when he returned home. I broke the news to him gently. I told him it had already been done by countless foreign men, many of whom are now die-hard women haters.

I asked Bill if he knew that Ukraine is the AIDS capital of Europe and was not surprised to learn that he didn't know. I often ask foreign men seeking Ukrainian or Russian women if they are aware of the dangers out there, and they are typically only vaguely aware and seemingly indifferent. I took advantage of the opportunity to share some harsh realities with Bill about the post-Soviet playground he had entered.

Ukraine is facing a growing AIDS epidemic. In 2009 the World Health Organization estimated that 1.6 percent of Ukraine's less than 46 million population is infected with HIV/AIDS compared to 0.1 percent of Germany's population. Odessa, a popular resort destination, is estimated to have about 150,000 infected people. It should be stressed that these are conservative estimates because Ukrainians generally refuse to be tested.

Russia closely trails Ukraine. It had an estimated one million HIV cases in 2010 with new cases growing at an annual rate of 8 percent. More than 40 percent of new HIV cases there are among women of childbearing age.

Ukraine also faces a general epidemic of STDs. The busy circle road around Kyiv and Moscow where non-elite prostitutes flock, many very young and from the impoverished provinces of distant cities and the train stations that homeless prostitutes inhabit, are a hothouse for the spread of STDs. Ukrainian health authorities estimate 1 out of 3 of these women are infected with syphilis. Moscow's more active circle road makes Kyiv's look provincial.

By comparison, an estimated 70 million Americans have STDs, nearly one quarter of the population. No reliable statistics are available for STDs among Ukraine's general population. However, given Ukraine's solid reputation as a sex tourism haven and the "bridebasket" of Europe, and with the highest rate of HIV/AIDS in Europe, there is little doubt that the country's STD epidemic will also continue to grow.

Ukraine and Russia also face a long-running epidemic of tuberculosis (TB) affecting the general population, and prison, drug-addicted, and sex-industry populations, in particular. Many HIV-infected prostitutes have TB, including the drug-resistant strain, which can be transmitted sexually.

Several factors contribute to these growing epidemics. Many Ukrainians still refuse to use condoms, believing that using a condom is a sign that you don't trust your partner. During 2010 the Ukrainian Ministry of Health reported that nearly half of Ukrainians aged 25–49, who had more than one sexual partner in a year, did not use condoms.

Add to this disturbing picture the combination of sex and alcohol. Here it is important to note that in addition to high adult alcoholism, Ukraine has the highest rate of teenage alcoholism in the whole of Europe. Moreover, any man can tell you that heavy alcohol consumption coupled with sex can lead to impaired judgment and unsafe sex practices. Recall the old Russian joke: "What is non-traditional Russian sex? Sex without vodka." It's not just a joke, it's the truth.

Finally, the Ukrainian government has shown a callous indifference to their AIDS epidemic. They have gladly accepted international support but have refused to budget adequately for the prevention and treatment of HIV/AIDS. Instead, they have made major funding for Ukraine's multi-city preparations for the 2012 Eurocup finals a top priority. In October 2010 they went a step further and made the incredible announcement that they planned to budget more than $60 million in an effort to win a bid for the

2020 Winter Olympics.

To add insult to injury, Ukraine's new president sanctioned the closure of Kyiv's premier HIV/AIDS treatment facility during July 2010 to make room for a new VIP hotel. The clinic treated one thousand of Kyiv's HIV patients on an out-patient basis and was a center for the advanced training of infectious disease doctors in Ukraine.

Can men like Bill from North Carolina grow tired of looking at the army of young women on the streets of Kyiv, Odessa or Moscow, clad in skin-tight jeans, even tighter stretch pants, and in micro-miniskirts, and offering generous displays of cleavage and bare midriffs in the summer heat? I've been told by Slavic men that you can get more than tired: You can even get an eye infection by staring too long at these women. They say it's like looking directly at the sun. However, there are much greater dangers than this to be found everywhere on the post-Soviet playground. Knowing the alarming facts about this playground should be enough to help men break the Siren-like spell this army of young, parading women casts upon them.

Unfortunately, I don't think my message about Ukraine's sexually transmitted epidemics hit home with Bill. Before parting, he told me he was meeting several new expat buddies that evening at O'Briens' Pub, a well known expat hangout in downtown Kyiv. Bill assured me there would be a lot of young *devushki* (Russian for girls) there. I politely declined, wished him the best and reminded him he had my phone number should he need to call. I also reminded him that he was lucky he "did not get lucky" in Odessa. But life goes on and old habits die hard.

My Lovely Russian Rose

> *"Not everything that smells like church incense is holy."*
> -a Slavic saying

By age 50, and often much earlier, men experience a mid-life crisis. That's when a man starts facing his mortality and tries to regain his youth by robbing the cradle or buying a little red sports car.

Sultry images of young Slavic women are all over the Internet these days and many middle-aged foreign men, especially those in the grips of a mid-life crisis, are thanking their lucky stars. In visiting Slavic dating and bride sites, lo and behold, they discover an entire culture of young women, mostly 18-25, purportedly searching for father figures up to the ripe old age of 60 to caress their firm young bodies.

Could this really be true? Hardly. These very young, mostly spoiled, big city girls (very different from the masses who live in towns and villages) are typically looking for a ticket off of the sinking ships of Ukraine or Russia, or a least a domestic–sugar daddy.

Enticed by Internet photos and blinded by loving emails from perfect strangers, arthritic men (many armed with Viagara and Rogaine) make the arduous journey across the Atlantic and beyond to finally meet their lovely Russian or Ukrainian rose. What they see, as one young woman candidly admitted, is what we want them to see, no more, no less.

Their Internet profiles read the same. They all seem to love kittens, knitting, walking on beaches and seek a loving and kind man to cuddle in the evenings. They fail to mention that they like to drink and smoke on social occasions, meaning when they meet their friends daily. The sad fact is that a whole generation of huntresses exists, notably in Moscow and Kyiv, 20 years after the collapse of the U.S.S.R. and the introduction of wild capitalism. Today there's an enormous fresh crop of 18–20 year olds. Many are poor but dressed in porno-glamour fashion. They have a false sense of entitlement when it comes to the good life, and a fierce determination to get it at any cost.

Intoxicated and drawn by the nectar of the young Slavic berry, middle-aged foreign men quickly fall under their spell. For many it's the first time their fat wallets open wide. And these young, big city pro-daters are experts at draining fat wallets in record time. *Step 1*, they identify a fat wallet. *Step 2*, they try to drain it in record time. *Step 3*, they move on to the next fat wallet. *Step 4*, they admire their loot. At the top of their wish list are jewelry, furs, high-end perfume and cosmetics, as well as designer handbags, and clothes: jeans, leather jackets, pants, boots, and, of course, Italian high heels.

In return, they'll convince the fatherly foreigner that they love him like no other man they've ever known, and they'll provide him with some casual sex but only shortly before he leaves the country. Then they'll send him a month or more of passionate, sexy emails begging him (and the other two or three other middle-aged foreign men they regularly correspond with) to return as soon as possible.

And then tragedy will strike. Dear family members, mothers, grandmothers, aunts or uncles, will become deathly ill and need costly hospitalization and medicines. A close relative will inevitably die as a result of the reported illness and no money for burial costs will be available. When *Make a Wish Foundation* refuses to answer her plea, she will turn to you as a last resort in her hour of need. How can you possibly turn her down? Of course, she will not tell you that operations and hospitalization, even under their crumbling and very corrupt medical system, still cost only a few hundred dollars and simple burials a few hundred more. Instead, she'll ask for thousands. These women, after all, see foreign men as a potential ATM machine.

But worse things can happen to love-struck foreign men. There can be an even darker side to the lovely Russian or Ukrainian rose who manages to become a foreign bride. Despite even careful scrutiny, these men often bring back to the U.S. or UK a Slavic bride who turns out to be their worst nightmare: a woman who quickly makes it clear that she is not the traditional, feminine model he dreamed about and she pretended to be, but rather someone who'll be a cold companion until the blessed day when her green card arrives. Then she'll shuttle back and forth between the U.S. and her Slavic homeland; she'll have her cake and eat it too. Meanwhile, she will be spending lots of quality time with Slavic women (and young Slavic men), in her American city who already have their green cards. Together they'll party Slavic-style just as they did in Moscow or Kyiv.

And if her American husband tries to disrupt her master plan and makes unwanted sexual advances—and there will be many— she will do what many Slavic women, new American brides, have been doing for years: she'll repeatedly file false domestic battery charges against him, obtain a restraining order and gain possession of their home. Typically, she'll become pregnant or already have a baby before she takes this course of action to ensure that she is on track for a green card, and to make her false domestic battery charges more compelling.

For the new husband this will be an endless living nightmare: jail time, loss of a home, enormous legal fees, and child support. He'll likely bear the psychological scars for life. Can't happen? Just read the countless similar horror stories documented online by American and foreign men, in general.

Foreign men seeking to resolve a midlife crisis in Russia or Ukraine, or simply sample the nectar of a young Slavic berry, should heed the words of a Ukrainian mother to her adult son, echoed in a recent novel by Iren Rozdobudko, one of Ukraine's most popular contemporary novelists: *You must understand son, the times have changed. Today there are no good girls. Each one is either a drug addict, a prostitute or a huntress at someone's expense. We simply want to protect you. We don't want you to suffer should you marry suddenly.*

Elderly Slavic women often offer middle-aged foreign men seeking young Slavic women the following sound advice: "Just look closely in a mirror five minutes and you'll understand everything. You are not a match."

So much for trying to resolve a midlife crisis by dragging arthritic bones across the Atlantic and marrying a much younger Slavic woman from a big city. What other options are available? Experts suggest the following: take a daily vitamin, eat well, get enough rest, share your feelings, keep fit, and get aerobic exercise. *Thank you, experts!* However, my preferred option for dealing with a mid-life crisis is to buy a little red sports car, for reasons I'll explain in the next chapter.

In Defense of Little Red Sports Cars

"Middle-age is the awkward period when Father Time catches up with Mother Nature."
-Harold Coffin

Given a choice between a young Slavic bride (i.e. this applies only to the two-faced young ones from hell and not all Slavic women) and a little reds sports car to manage a mid-life crisis, why would I unhesitatingly choose the latter? Let me count the reasons:

A little red sports car:

Won't ever deny you entrance into its plush, soft, cavernous interior unlike...

Won't continually ask you to buy it designer clothes and expensive jewelry.

Won't force you to come along on weekly shop-till-you-drop sprees that deplete you of what little cartilage remains in your osteo-arthritic knees.

Won't ever ask you to buy it a huge, gas-guzzling black prestige SUV with black-tinted windows, the kind "newly rich" Russians and Ukrainians each have two or three of.

Won't rant for hours about how Americans are boring, fat, soulless, don't have any friends and never go anywhere fun.

Won't ever tell you that you dress slovenly like most Americans.

Won't put you into cardiac arrest every time you check your monthly credit card and bank statements.

Won't file false domestic battery charges against you to build a case for a green card.

Won't unfairly get a restraining order against you to prevent you from returning to your own home.

Won't make hundreds of dollars of phone calls monthly to Russia or Ukraine.

Won't abandon you daily to spend evenings and weekends with Slavic-American women who already have their green cards.

Won't empty your joint savings account.

Won't hire a lawyer at your expense to drain you of any remaining wealth.

Won't get you a dirty look from middle-aged women if they see you out with her during daylight.

But a little red sports car:

Will give you the new car smell that drives men crazy.

Will break the boredom of your middle-age life daily by giving you hours of driving pleasure without breaking you at the bank.

Will allow you to pick up attractive women who would like to go for a spin.

Will turn over every time you ask it to on cold mornings, unlike a young Slavic wife.

Will only ask you for periodic oil changes and no expensive accessories.

Will never complain if you look at, approach, or even touch other little sports cars.

Will have a fair resale value if you take care of it, and will allow you to buy a younger, cuter little sports car.

Finally, your little red sports car

Will never give you an STD, unlike a young Slavic wife who likes to party with her Slavic-American girl friends and their young Slavic-American male companions.

In Defense of Slavic Women

> *"American boy, American joy, American boy for always time, American boy I leave with you, Moscow goodbye!"*
>
> -a popular Russian song

There is a common image of foreign men who come to Russia and Ukraine in search of young brides and happiness ("lovepats" as they are called), as losers: middle-aged men who couldn't get the time of day from an attractive American woman. This unflattering stereotype of American and other foreign men, who come in search of a Slavic bride, undoubtedly has some basis in fact. However, the score or more of lovepats I've met in Russia and Ukraine over the past 20 years defy simple classification. They come from varied social, economic, and geographic backgrounds, and vary greatly in appearance.

For example, on a flight from New York City to Kyiv in 1998 I sat next to John, a 40-year-old man from Arkansas. I learned that he was an average, hardworking American, with a modest home, stable income, and a great deal of loneliness in his life. Soft spoken and not unattractive in appearance, he did not at all fit the loser stereotype of lovepats. After a few months of Internet correspondence, a Ukrainian marriage bureau helped him arrange the all-important first meeting in Kyiv.

During our long flight across the Atlantic and beyond, I learned that John was very anxious and had serious doubts about whether he was acting wisely. He was going to a totally foreign country and did not know any Ukrainian or Russian, both essential for basic communication in bilingual, largely non-English speaking Ukraine. Moreover, the airfare, hotel, required translator, marriage bureau fees, and other related expenses placed a significant strain on his modest budget. Learning that I spend a great deal of time in Ukraine and Russia, John had many questions for me about Slavic women and, in particular, whether one could find a sincere one; he had read about the many scams that foreign men can encounter.

I told him Slavic women, like women everywhere, are all different. However, most, especially the older ones, are united by their traditional Slavic culture with its many unique and honorable traditions. I assured him that there were many sincere, kind and very attractive women to be found in Ukraine. I also told him his decision to come to Ukraine was a bold and courageous one, and that only about one out of every 10 lovepats ever goes from home computer dating-matchmaking to visit Russia or Ukraine, according to dating websites. Before we parted we exchanged contact information and I sensed John was more at ease.

Over the course of the next decade I had an opportunity to gather many insights from Slavic women of various ages and social backgrounds about why so many of them turn to dating and marriage websites and bureaus, and seriously consider leaving their homeland. The common, rigid stereotype of Slavic women seeking to become American brides as gold-diggers, predatory tramps and sly tarts becomes untenable when exposed to corrective evidence over time.

I should note there was not much gold to dig out of most of the lovepats I met in Russia and Ukraine. Most seemed to max out their credit cards in a flash after they wined and dined one or two Svetlanas and took them on a mandatory shopping spree in the hopes of getting lucky.

Certainly there is no shortage of Slavic female scammers, especially in major Russian and Ukrainian cities where middle-aged foreign men tend to flock: Luhansk in eastern Ukraine is a striking example. Moreover, a casual survey of the Internet yields many horror stories of marriages between foreign men and Slavic women that reinforce this stereotype.

However, most Slavic women who seek foreign husbands and are willing to leave their homeland do not fit this unflattering stereotype. Instead, they face harsh domestic realities that compel them to take this difficult step.

First and foremost, millions of Slavic women face dismal marriage possibilities because of demographic and socio-economic realities, and are desperate to find a decent Slavic husband. Women significantly outnumber men, a post-WWII and post-Soviet phenomenon. Significantly, since the collapse of the U.S.S.R. in 1991, average male life expectancy has declined measurably: 59 years in Russia and 62 in Ukraine in 2012.

The pool of potential Slavic husbands is further reduced by widespread alcoholism and drug use. Slavic men also like to have fun but are allergic to marriage and are prone to domestic violence and multiple affairs when they do settle down with a women. This is reflected in declining marriage rates and increased divorce rates since independence in 1991. Meanwhile, a Slavic wife must work, take care of the children, shop and prepare food, clean the apartment, and wash clothes.

Poverty is also an important factor underlying a Slavic woman's decision to look beyond her borders for a husband. Even doctors, teachers, economists, and accountants typically earn little more than $200 a month in Russia and Ukraine in 2012. In addition to being poorly paid, women rarely have the opportunity to pursue a promising career because they are the victims of discrimination in the workplace and live in a very sexist, male-dominated culture.

The main reason millions of Slavic women seek the foreign option is to create a family: to have a decent, non-violent husband, children, to live in a stable and secure environment and, hopefully, to be treated as an equal partner. These are mostly average women who live outside the huge, glitzy cities of Moscow and Kyiv and dress in a style other than porno-glamour.

As the saying goes, "Moscow is not Russia" and "Kyiv is not

Ukraine." The women you'll typically find in these capital cities are not typical of average Russian and Ukrainian women, respectively, who seek foreign husbands. They're not dying to leave their trendy metropolis to live in suburban Idaho or North Dakota.

The alternative to the foreign option for many is to lead a single, solitary life, the fate of millions of Slavic women. Significantly, unmarried women in Slavic society not only are deprived of a family, they also hold a lower social status than married women.

One should not underestimate the sacrifices a Slavic woman must make in pursuing the foreign option. In making this important decision she must leave behind family and friends and her homeland. She must move to a foreign country where she knows no one besides her husband, where she will not hear her native language, and where she will most likely be largely housebound for her first few months in a remote American-suburban setting. Thus, she may face the very real fear that she may be going from the fry pan into the fire in choosing a foreign husband in a foreign land.

In return for her sacrifices, she hopes her foreign husband will be a decent man and good partner, that he will not drink and womanize like Slavic men, that he will be attentive to her views and needs, will help raise their children, and assist with the household tasks. Lastly, because Slavic women who make such a monumental change are ambitious and typically very well educated, they hope their husband will understand and respect their desire to eventually pursue a career that will allow them to realize themselves and add to the security of the family.

Nearly two years after I met John, I received a letter from Arkansas. By that time I had forgotten about John and our soulful conversation but he had not forgotten about me. There was a lengthy letter and a photo inside the envelope. He thanked me for my thoughtful remarks during our shared flight and said I had given him the added strength he needed to get through his trip. He said that he met the woman he corresponded with, a young Kyiv resident, but there was no chemistry between them.

However, John did not give up his search. The marriage agency he employed introduced him to Irina, a nurse in her early 30s living in the provincial town of Fastiv on the outskirts of Kyiv. She, in turn, introduced John to her caring, extended family. The two of them quickly found a strong connection and, according to John, are happily married. He provided me with a photo of Irina, an attractive woman, preparing dinner in their Arkansas kitchen.

A typical matchmaking story? Hardly. Irina's provincial roots, her age (30 versus 20), and nursing-humanitarian background probably made living in Arkansas more inviting and less of a difficult transition than it might have been for a young woman from a big city.

Not many young Slavs are impressed with life in suburban America. More than one Muscovite after visiting the U.S. has told me that he would hang himself if he had to live in an American suburb for more than two weeks. I've always been too polite to say that most Americans visiting Moscow for the same period probably feel the same way.

> "American boy, American joy, American boy for always time,
> American boy I'll leave with you, goodbye Moscow, hello Arkansas!"

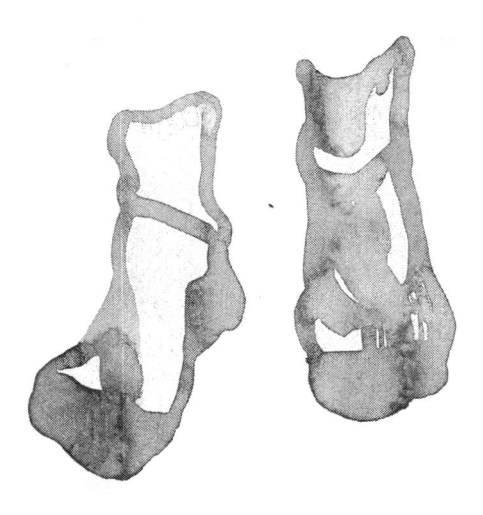

In Defense of Slavic Men

"Life is very hard, but fortunately short."
                                            -a Slavic saying

Slavic men are heavy drinkers and smokers, drug addicts, sexist womanizers, weak, lazy, non-intellectual, ill-mannered, spoiled mamas' boys, unhygienic and, in general, irresponsible. This is a stereotype with which many Slavic women would unhesitatingly agree.

It is no secret that stereotypes, although essentially distorting and misleading, generally contain some element of truth. How can we better understand why many Slavic men reflect the negative qualities in this common stereotype? What are the harsh realities that shape their daily lives?

To begin with, it is impossible for average married Slavic men to earn a wage that allows them to support their family and live with dignity: in 2012 the average monthly wage in Ukraine and Russia was about $250 per month, and the average pension less than $150 per month. Over time these dismal earnings gradually erode the self-esteem of men who are supposed to be breadwinners in this culture of very traditional gender roles.

Add to this picture the extremely difficult living conditions Slavic men must cope with daily. If he is newly married or even middle-aged, he will most likely live in two tiny rooms (30 square meters, the size of an average American living room) with his wife, daughter and mother. Although new, larger apartments are available 20 years after independence for anyone to buy at Western prices, it is impossible for average Slavs to do so given their meager salaries. Thus, the average Slavic male is helpless to change his family's cramped living arrangements.

To live in such cramped, tiny quarters, especially during the long, cold winter months greatly tests the patience and tolerance of all family members, especially the failed breadwinner. And with the constant shortage of money for bare essentials, family arguments are inevitable and frequent.

Viewed in this light, it is not surprising that many Slavic men have low self-esteem after listening to their wives' often non-stop chorus of, "What kind of man are you? You can't provide for your family. I bring home more money than you do." I hear this regularly through my Kyiv apartment's thin walls and even on city streets.

Moreover, to add insult to injury, these Slavic men must cope daily with the conspicuous in-your-face wealth of Russia and Ukraine's so-called elite who brazenly stole their country's prime assets with the collapse of the U.S.S.R., and now flaunt their wealth daily with their prestige SUVs, designer clothes, homes, and exotic vacations. Slavic grannies aptly capture the bitter post-Soviet life of most citizens when they say: "Today everything is available but unaffordable. The country is one big museum, and if you look too long you will cry."

To cope with this poverty-level existence and a future which many view as hopeless, Slavic men typically try to escape it: They turn to the bottle to self-medicate and leave their tiny apartments to drink with close male friends—a deep Slavic tradition—who understand and share their pain; they womanize in the hopes of finding some tenderness; others lose control and turn to domestic violence.

But for everything in life you need to pay, sooner or later. Too often the so-called non-boring life of Slavic men comes to an early end. The hard lifestyle first takes their health and then their lives. Average male life expectancy in Russia and Ukraine in 2012 was

59 and 62 years, respectively. Any American man living among average Russians or Ukrainians for even a few months will quickly understand how easy it is to self-medicate with alcohol here and become an alcoholic.

Is there any defense against the charge that married Slavic men generally are lazy and often shirk household and childcare responsibilities? Apparently not and not surprising given the matriarchal society which exists and arose out of necessity: men dying early in wars and from alcoholism. Slavic mothers are traditionally very authoritarian in their child-rearing practices and are often intrusively involved in the lives of their adult children. They especially like to pamper and overprotect their sons and expect their sons' wives to do the same; the wife, in effect, becomes a second mother. Moreover, they often intrude into their married lives to enforce this practice. In short, Slavic women bear some responsibility for the shirking habits of their men.

Slavic men generally accept this easy, sexist lifestyle which places very heavy burdens on their wives. Slavic wives must have the patience and tolerance of a saint to put up with their husbands' ways. To their credit, they generally do not divorce their husbands. I've often heard middle-aged Slavic women wryly compare their husbands to a suitcase without a handle saying: "It's not at all useful, but it's a shame to throw it out."

Interestingly, Slavic men virtually never divorce their wives unless they have another woman lined up who'll care for them like a second mother, and usually is much younger than their first wife.

Yes, many Slavic men are "nogoodniks" and their culture tolerates such behavior, but we shouldn't paint them all with the same brush. Labeling every Slavic man as weak, non-intellectual, drunk, and sexist is just as unfair as labeling every young Slavic woman a gold-digger.

Millions of Slavic men can also be caring, loving, responsible, model fathers, husbands and citizens. Take, for example, the four million Ukrainians working in Europe, three million of them illegally. The majority are men working selflessly at hard labor to earn a dignified wage in order to provide a better life for families back in Ukraine. To do so they have no choice but to be separated from their children and wives. Similarly, tens of thousands of Ukrainian men work at hard labor in Russia to provide income for their families in Ukraine.

Finally, there is one area where there can be no defense of the habits of many Slavic men, hygiene. Women are quick to point this out with sour expressions. They list as egregious violations the following: men who don't seem to know that their socks can be changed daily—one gets the impression that their socks could walk about independently; men who don't shower—it seems their mothers never showed them how to use water to wash themselves; men for whom deodorant is an alien substance; men who blow the contents of their nose out on public sidewalks and even subway platforms—apparently their mothers never taught them how to use handkerchiefs or Kleenex; men who spit unabashedly on public sidewalks; and, finally, men whose teeth are mustard-colored due to heavy smoking. Personally, I think Ukraine should not be seriously considered for European Union membership until their men agree to use handkerchiefs or Kleenex when in public.

Interestingly, during October 2010 the Ukrainian government announced a campaign to encourage men ages 27–50 to be more active, to exercise regularly and adopt a healthy lifestyle. This was motivated by the low average male life expectancy of 62 years and, no doubt, mostly by recent IMF pressure on the government to increase the pension age for men to 65 in the next few years as a condition for major loans. Inexplicably, the Ukrainian government's campaign does not target men over 50. I asked a close Ukrainian friend in his late 40s for his reaction to this initiative of the newly elected government. He smiled and said, "I'll drink to that."

P.S. FYI, the procedure for Slavic nose blowing on public streets is as follows: press the forefinger of your right hand (thumb may be used if forefinger has been lost in an agricultural or industrial accident) on your right nostril, blow hard out of your left nostril then alternate this procedure placing your left forefinger (again, thumb if necessary) on your left nostril and blow hard. Novices should come to a complete stop when doing this and spring forward ideally almost 90 degrees; experienced nose blowers on public streets can perform this habit while moving at a slow pace. Be sure to take daily wind velocity into consideration.

Po-nashemu—"It's a Slavic Thing, You Wouldn't Understand"

> *"I love you like salo, I love you like beer."*
> -a line from a popular Ukrainian song

In simple terms, culture is how people spend their free time and how they behave towards each other. The longer you live in Russia and Ukraine and interact with the locals, the more you'll realize that Slavs are hard core believers in their culture and traditions. They are also very opinionated and believe their customs and ways of celebrating, in particular, to be better than those in America.

Po-nashemu, or "our way," and conversely *ne po-nashemu*, "not our way," are expressions foreigners will often hear in Ukraine and Russia if they break bread with Slavs. Slavs, for example, drink their vodka straight and in shots. Many women will exhale a blast of air before downing a shot, believing that this allows them to increase their vodka intake. Macho Slavic men will often sniff a piece of black bread or a cucumber slice after a shot instead of taking a bite of an appetizer.

Ukrainian men drink lots of vodka on weekends, while Russian men tend to drink it as though every day was a holiday. Russian women often complain that their men drink vodka as though it were water.

Ukrainians have a very special po-nashemu, our way tradition. For centuries, they have had a love affair with salo and jokingly refer to it as Ukraine's white gold or Snickers. Russians often make fun of Ukrainians and their salo but also love it. Ukrainians who visit America have even been caught trying to sneak personal amounts of salo into the U.S.; occasionally very ripe salo has even turned up in lost suitcases. When asked by customs officials if they have anything valuable to declare, Ukrainians sometimes jokingly respond, "Only salo."

Salo is an acquired taste which typically elicits fear and frowns from foreigners. It's really quite tasty and is generally eaten in very small amounts as an appetizer with vodka by working-class Slavs. The proper method to enjoy salo is to place a very thin slice on a small wedge of black bread, add a sliver of onion or garlic, and a few grains of salt. This is guaranteed to make a Ukrainian's mouth water.

Slavic train travel is another striking example of po-nashemu behavior. Ukraine is a large country the size of Texas, and most trains are composed of sleeper cars. They average about 10 hours to reach their destination and typically depart late afternoon and arrive early the next morning.

Train travel in Russia and Ukraine is always an adventure. I've traveled by train in both countries many times and recall vividly my first po-nashemu adventure. It was on a Kyiv to Moscow overnight train. I had a ticket for a sleep compartment for four, a real luxury compared to the open-sleep carriage for 50 that routinely fills with a 150, not counting the occasional goat or two. To my surprise, the other three travelers in my compartment were women: a 40-year-old engineer returning home to Moscow and two college-age girls on vacation. I was especially happy to see there was no goat in our compartment.

During our trip I was richly exposed to Slavic generosity and their art of conversation. Each of these women came prepared with a bagful of treats to share: sandwiches, fruit, chocolate, and even wine. The women skillfully organized a communal table shortly after we left the station. After brief introductions we had our first toast of the evening, "To our acquaintance!" This was followed by more detailed personal histories and more toasts. I made the third toast, which is always to women, and did so standing as customary. Fascinating conversation flowed non-stop for five hours before anyone even thought of going to sleep.

Shortly before midnight we had a nocturnal visitor. A middle-aged, vodka-soaked Russian dressed only in boxer shorts and a striped Russian navy t-shirt appeared on our threshold. This gruff Don Juan asked if he could help even out the ratio of men to women in our compartment. Our 40-year-old engineer sent him running with just a few choice words. The women laughed uncontrollably after he was gone.

Loud parties with vodka, champagne, lots of food, and singing were still raging after midnight throughout the train. Someone even brought a guitar. The scene was very different from anything I had ever experienced in the U.S. or Western Europe. Slavs were partying, mostly with strangers they had just met, like there was no tomorrow. It was only after many more train trips that I realized this was a typical Slavic scene. Slavs really seem to enjoy and live in the moment. They always seem to be in search of new impressions and memorable events.

In my experience, however, a Slavic birthday party is the best opportunity to witness a real po-nashemu celebration in action. It's an evening-long celebration and a feast, usually with no more than a half-dozen guests in order to ensure an intimate atmosphere: close friends, a co-worker or two, and a visiting foreigner all crowded into a tiny one or two-room apartment. The celebration usually starts early in the evening and does not end before midnight.

I'll never forget the birthday party of my Russian friend Nikolai's wife, Maya, who was in her mid-40s. Like most Slavic women, she spent the entire day preparing a feast for the half-dozen guests. Nikolai added a leaf to the small kitchen table and we moved it into the living room/bedroom. Chairs were scarce and the large sofa provided the needed additional seating.

Maya set the table with her finest embroidered table cloth, dishware and crystal. She prepared a half-dozen tasty, cold dishes, including exotic salads, in addition to the evening's hot main course. The table also had fine wines, champagne and vodka, and a large bowl of fruit.

Music played and we looked at family albums until everyone arrived. Maya received flowers, flowers and more flowers from the guests, chocolates, wine and some more personal gifts. We spent most of the next six hours seated at the table. In keeping with Slavic tradition, each guest made a lengthy toast in honor of Maya, many told anecdotes and shared their recollections of first meeting Maya, working with her in a high school and other memorable moments. Men left the table periodically to smoke in the kitchen and tell some spicier jokes in private.

Interestingly, one of the guests was a Russian-Czech sculptor (Russian father, Czech mother) who shared funny stories illustrating how Czechs do not know how to party like Russians. As the evening progressed there was even dancing, despite the size of the tiny apartment. Sveta, an unmarried high-school teacher and Maya's best friend, singled out the Russian-Czech sculptor for special attention. She dragged him to a tiny corner of the room which she designated as our dance floor and, with a Russian top 40 rock radio station playing, she went to work.

The wine was clearly having an effect upon Sveta and her dancing was a sight to behold. An attractive woman in her late 30s, her movements were uninhibited and marked by a lot of torso and shoulder thrusting and thrashing of arms. Sveta also appeared to be a big fan of River Dance, peppering her dance with their foot movements. Clearly, she had a "let's-have-fun, devil-may-care" attitude. Her sculptor dance partner stood almost motionless apparently mesmerized by Sveta's high-energy, eclectic dance moves.

A short while later Igor, a childhood friend of Valery's, was busy playing a guitar and singing a favorite Russian ballad. The room grew very quiet and the mood was pensive. Before long Maya brought a large, multi-layered Russian tort into the room and also treated guests to tea and cognac. The old table creaked under the weight of all of the food and drink, and reminded me that average Slavs with little money spare no expense to celebrate a special occasion with friends and visitors.

The many eloquent and lengthy toasts honoring Maya and the ritual of telling jokes and recalling shared history, the art of conversation, made clear to me that Slavic birthdays are a very special po-nashemu celebration. The evening was an unusual and very enjoyable blend of sentimental, funny and wild moments, and one of the most memorable parties I've ever attended.

Every culture has its share of po-nashemu, "our way" customs. America is no different. During America's often turbulent 1960s and 70s, for example, African-Americans often wore t-shirts with the bold statement, "It's a Black Thing, You Wouldn't Understand." It was meant to underscore their separate culture, unique traditions and the often harsh world they found themselves in.

Culture, they say, is an entire system of survival and coping skills. Most Russians and Ukrainians still cling to their age-old culture and traditions because they help them cope and survive the typical impoverished existence. Twenty years after the collapse of Communism, Slavs embrace much that is new, while preserving what is time-tested. Without immersion in Slavic life, many of "their ways" will inevitably seem odd and alien to foreign observers.

One of my favorite examples of a po-nashemu Slavic custom is their tradition of sitting quietly at home for less than a minute before departing on a major trip. I was first exposed to it in Moscow about 20 years ago. I was packed and ready to leave my rented Moscow apartment for the airport and waiting for a ride from a Russian friend. He arrived with the landlady and, before we could leave, the two suggested we sit for a moment. We sat quietly with heads bowed for about 30 seconds until they said they were ready to leave.

I left not knowing what had just transpired. Sometime later I learned that sitting quietly before such a departure is an age-old Slavic tradition. It dates back to when simple villagers would sit with family and say a brief prayer followed by *iz Bohom*—go "with God"—before setting off on a long journey. The prayer and reference to God largely disappeared during 70 years of Soviet Communism, but the custom remains ingrained and alive today.

Not long ago I was home in the U.S. waiting for one of my sons to drive me to the airport for a flight to Ukraine. I was packed and ready to go when he arrived. Instead of leaving, I asked him to sit quietly with me for a few seconds. After about 30 seconds, I told my son I was ready to go. He asked me what that was all about. I said, "It's a Slavic thing, you wouldn't understand. I'll explain it to you later."

Slavic Go-Slow Lifestyle

> *"The slower you go, the further you'll get."*
> -age-old Slavic wisdom

There is a popular Slavic myth that Russian and Ukrainian men are very hard working. Clearly many of them can work in incredible spurts as deadlines approach. This is their renowned maximalism. However, they can also do nothing with even greater intensity. This is their exceptional minimalism and it helps fuel widespread alcoholism.

Their go-slow lifestyle and culture has deep Soviet roots and is reinforced by the wild capitalism of the past two decades. The Soviet legacy is essentially a "they pretend to pay us, we pretend to work" ethic. Soviet propaganda enjoyed portraying the masses as selfless, workaholic builders of communism but the reality was often starkly different. Three men on a state farm, for example, could chase a pig all day and still receive their paltry, set monthly wage. Similarly, three women working in a small Russian grocery store, with mostly empty shelves, could stand idle most of the day. Two of them might eventually hold a salami on a cutting board as a third woman cut slices off for a customer. In both cases there was little or no incentive to work harder or even pretend to, given their miserly wages and guaranteed jobs.

Twenty years after the collapse of Soviet Communism, fast forward to the introduction of wild capitalism. Many of the hardest working and poorest Slavs, notably Ukrainians, have left their country since 1991 and are among the 3 million illegal and 1 million legal Ukrainians in Western Europe, and nearly 300,000 legal ones in Russia, working mostly at hard labor to support families back home.

However, the vast majority of Russians and Ukrainians today are hardly workaholics, and for good reasons. "No one gets rich through hard work," as Slavs like to say, and the evidence is indisputable: The average wage in Ukraine in 2012 was about $250 per month and not much higher in Russia. Slavs also are keenly aware that personal connections are more important than skills in landing a good job in their system. Without these connections they tend to seek positions that require minimal effort because most jobs essentially pay the same meager wage.

Nor is it a secret that the newly rich in both Russia and Ukraine became millionaires virtually overnight, and billionaires a few years later, because they were in a position to steal the rich natural resources and property of their respective countries when the U.S.S.R. collapsed. Thus, it's perfectly understandable that average Slavs continue to embrace a "they pretend to pay us, we pretend to work" ethic. This is not America where hard work and discipline can advance the average worker.

Significantly, Slavs follow a "work-to-live" philosophy, one that is very European. They see work as a necessary and unavoidable evil, a place to recharge, chat and drink lots of tea with co-workers, perform as many personal tasks as possible and make a few useful contacts. Slavs seem to instinctively embrace a laid back, "live-for-today" lifestyle that most Americans are programmed not to accept or feel comfortable with. They view the "live-to-work" philosophy of Americans as obsessive, unhealthy and unattractive.

Interestingly, Slavic grandmothers and mothers traditionally teach their young "the slower you go, the further you'll get" in life.

It's a thoughtful, culturally rooted expression that suggests rushing into things won't get individuals far in their system, and that it's more prudent to proceed cautiously and avoid risky behavior.

Viewed in this light, it is not surprising that chronic tardiness, rather than American punctuality, is a characteristic of Slavs. During my many years in Russia and Ukraine, I've experienced "Slavic punctuality" firsthand on many occasions. Nothing you may have experienced growing up and working in America can adequately prepare you for this culture shock. I first experienced it during the 1990s when cell phones were very rare. I like to tell Americans planning to live and work in Ukraine that the difference between Washington and Kyiv time is an additional seven hours, plus two for the chronic tardiness of any Ukrainians or Russians with whom you may have scheduled a casual meeting (that's eight hours, plus two for Moscow).

I can't remember how many times, especially before cell phones were commonplace, I arranged to meet a Slavic friend or acquaintance at a café and they failed to arrive for an hour or more for no good reason, and later indignantly asked why I wasn't there when they did arrive. Eventually, I learned to wait for them outside of cafes and whenever possible to arrange meetings at my apartment in Moscow or Kyiv, but things hardly improved.

On one occasion, not at all atypical, a friend and his visiting cousin agreed to stop by my Moscow apartment around 7 P.M. for an evening of casual conversation and drinks. They eventually arrived around 11 P.M. with 2 liters of beer, a smoked fish, big smiles, and no apology. They said they lost track of time while having a few drinks at a bar and forgot to call on their cell phone.

I now always ask Slavic acquaintances and friends if we're meeting according to Slavic or German time; the latter implies precision and is a phrase recognized by Slavs. All this does, however, is to get an amusing reaction from them. Slavs see Americans as obsessed with time. "Time is money," Americans like to say, but not here.

Slavic chronic tardiness has deep Soviet roots. It was very common in the Soviet workplace and not grounds for disciplinary action. Often it was a way for a worker to protest one's lousy job and contempt for the system. Today's paltry wages keep this practice alive and well. Significantly "Slavic-style punctuality" is offset by their uncommon patience, a quality they inevitably develop in coping with their maddening living conditions and rude, non-service oriented bureaucracy.

But do Slavs really know how to relax? When I heard this topic announced on a Ukrainian radio talk show several years ago, I dropped my spoon in my borsch and nearly fell out of my chair. I had to pinch myself to see if I wasn't dreaming. You see, Slavs are masters of relaxation and have turned its practice into a near science. In fact, I'm convinced Slavs could probably win Olympic gold for relaxing if only there were such an event.

What evidence have I found in Russia and Ukraine to support this claim?

1. First and foremost, there is the go-slow, social-club atmosphere of the workplace for the majority of Slavs, with endless cups of tea and chit-chatting interrupted by the need to take frequent cigarette breaks, talk on cell phones, surf the Internet, play computer games, scan glossy fashion magazines, and take a leisurely lunch break. But don't go home yet. Happy hour often begins before the work day is over with a weekly celebration for various reasons, complete with appetizers and alcohol for mandatory toasts. "We live but once, life is short," they like to say.

2. And what about the endless Slavic holidays and long vacations? What fool said, "Christmas comes but once a year?" Not for Slavs. Religious or not, most celebrate two (Orthodox, old-calendar Christmas is January 7) and two New Years (old-calendar is January 14). And by celebrate I mean you can hear glasses clinking for two weeks straight with work across Russia and Ukraine grinding to a halt—a two-week national drinking binge. Then there are the official May holidays which last an entire week, after which Slavs come back to work and immediately discuss plans for their summer vacations which typically last an entire month.

No money for a summer vacation to escape city life? No problem! Even poor Slavs can stay with extended family in villages with no running water but plenty of fresh air, fruit and vegetables, beautiful countryside, and typically a river in which to bathe and swim. These month-long vacations allow Slavs to rest up and get ready for the next season of endless Slavic holidays.

3. And then there is the ritualistic culture of serious vodka

drinking and smoking. You won't find Slavic men crying in their beer because of poor wages. Friday, in particular, is vodka drinking night, a chance to spend six or seven therapeutic hours in communion with their closest male companions, and a chance to badmouth wives and girlfriends while recalling and exaggerating their womanizing adventures.

 4. A café and park-bench culture, where Slavs regularly sit for hours and practice the fine art of conversation is also always within in easy reach. Slavs love to chat in cafes, at home over endless cups of tea or while strolling in parks. The Slavic art of conversation is well developed because it requires a go-slow culture in contrast to the "got-to-run, time is money" American culture.

 5. Picnics and love of nature in general are traditional Slavic passions. Slavs love to go on picnics almost any time of the year. It's a time to barbecue, drink, bring along a guitar and sing songs with close friends and family.

 6. Strolling daily in parks with close friends is also a favorite Slavic pastime. It allows married women, in particular, an opportunity to "air out," as they call it, and to complain about their lazy, drunken husbands. Russian and Ukrainian cities and towns are designed with plenty of room to stroll.

What do all of these "go-slow" Slavic passions have in common? All of them permit Slavs to get out of their typically postage-stamp-size apartments. Imagine an American male in his 40s living in a one-room apartment about the size of an average American living room (30 square meters) along with his wife, teenage daughter and mother (or mother-in-law), a very common situation. Then add months of severe winter weather and no welcoming malls to retreat to for hours. Getting out of these flats as much as possible allows family members to unwind and "release stress," as they like to say.

Finally, how likely is it that an American "go-fast, live-to-work" culture will take root in Russia and Ukraine in the not too distant future? Many Slavs, after visiting America on temporary work visas for even a few months, complain about the "mad pace of American life" and say they are glad to return home.

Less glad to return home is Gloria Jean's Gourmet Coffee House, a chain with Chicago roots and more than 100 outlets in America alone. Not long ago they closed several stores they had for only a short time in downtown Kyiv. Their experiment in trying to make expensive "coffee-to-go" infectious among Ukrainians was a big flop.

Gloria Jean failed to adequately grasp that most Ukrainians get their coffee-to-go in tiny thimbles from the countless city kiosks near bus and metro stops around town for one-tenth of the cost of a Gloria Jean gourmet coffee. Moreover, when they do go to a coffee house-café setting, it's a special event and they expect to spend a few, unrushed hours relaxing and chatting with friends. Thus, the typical Slavic response to Gloria Jean's "coffee-to-go" campaign was, "Go where? We're not in a hurry, we're not Americans."

Determined not to give up, Gloria Jean even erected a summer patio complete with Burberry-style blankets to allow customers to snuggle on chilly evenings; no doubt Kyiv's many homeless looked at these blankets covetously as they passed by. But even this desperate effort failed. The only thing "to-go" in this coffee-to-go, culturally insensitive experiment was Gloria Jean. And knowing Slavs, as I do, probably a few of those lovely Burberry-style blankets.

Vodka and the Weak American

> *"Goodbye brain, tomorrow we'll meet again."*
> -a popular Slavic toast

I have never been able to stand the taste of straight vodka, but that's never stopped me from drinking it with Slavic friends. Living in America most of my life, my contact with vodka was very limited, always in mixed drinks and typically at small social gatherings. Thus, when I started living and working with Slavs in Russia and Ukraine, I was in for quite a surprise. To even suggest to a Slav that one might drink vodka in a fashion other than straight will receive a look of bewilderment and the comment, "What kind of idiot mixes good vodka with non-alcohol?"

Living and working with locals in Russia and Ukraine over a period of 20 years I've learned a great deal, mostly through trial and error, about their beloved vodka culture. One of the most pernicious myths existing about Russia and Ukraine is that drinking among Slavic men is a time for fun and relaxation.

Nothing could be further from the truth. Drinking vodka is hard, dangerous work and communion with close friends. It's an often dreaded, but essential, experience of Slavic life. Not to accept an invitation to drink with a close friend, even if it hurts your health, is considered a "sin." It's very insulting and rude.

Drinking vodka by the glassful or in shot glasses in the company of Slavic friends is always purposeful, unhurried and accompanied by numerous toasts and hours of soulful conversation and crude laughs. The vodka is always consumed straight, never sipped, and once a bottle is opened it must be finished on the spot. The ironclad rule is that by agreeing to participate you set aside your health until the last drop has been drunk.

After several hours the vodka has taken hold and conversations become more relaxed and candid. Drinking is interrupted with frequent smoking on a tiny balcony; a non-smoker must go as well to provide moral support to smokers and to continue in the conversation. Soon six or seven hours have passed and all the bottles have been drained. One might understandably expect that the drinking is over. Instead there is a brief pause followed by serious discussion of who will go to the nearby 24-hour kiosk for more vodka, beer and cigarettes.

Here there is always a danger that the designated person will not return (becomes a Slavic MIA), finding new drinking buddies along the way. This happens very often. The designated bottle retriever is admonished by all present to hurry back and usually does. With more vodka, beer and cigarettes at hand the marathon typically continues for a few more hours. Then some of the party struggle into a cab for the early morning trip home to face their wives or partners, while others have collapsed and may be asleep on a sofa or with their head on the kitchen table.

Serious hangovers are treated without hesitation the next day with beer or any alcohol readily available. Children are truly a godsend in this situation. Fathers routinely send a teenage child to a corner kiosk to retrieve beer from a sympathetic attendant.

This regaining of consciousness is followed by a routine examination of one's body, first in the mirror, to see if any injuries were incurred. Recollections of the previous night are often hazy due to blackouts, time travel as I call it, and all the drinking buddies eventually regain consciousness and compare notes to see if everyone survived. I advise participating Americans to bring along a camera, as there is often little to remember the next day.

Such serious drinking bouts, Slavs like to note, build strong friendships and over time provide a rich tapestry of near-death experiences and funny stories to recall and toast when they next reunite. Slavs are fond of saying, "Memories are the only paradise no one can cast us out of."

Any American living and working closely with Slavs in Russia and Ukraine is generally delighted and honored if he finally receives an invitation to visit a Slavic acquaintance's very modest one or two-room flat (not to be confused with a two-bedroom flat) and partake in some ritualistic, weekend drinking and non-stop conversation with two or three of his host's Slavic friends. It marks a potential turning point in their relationship, an opportunity for soulful conversation and the potential starting point on the very long road to a true friendship.

Americans who are not veteran-vodka drinkers typically try to impress their Slavic acquaintances with their drinking ability. I know I did my first time. However, I was an amateur, lacking Slavic experience and stamina. In our seven hour marathon-endurance test, I soon fell by the wayside and blacked out for a few hours only to awake several hours later to find my Slavic drinking partners still going strong. At that point they poured me another shot of vodka which I forced down, and regretted shortly thereafter.

For Slavs, drinking vodka with a new acquaintance is all about taking the measure of a man. It's a great equalizer and humanizer, a whole subculture with rich traditions and countless toasts. The greatest compliment an American can receive after a night of serious vodka drinking from Slavs is, "We didn't know an American could drink like that," meaning like a Slav. That is a rare compliment, indeed.

Homeless Slavs, gathering in tiny apartment courtyards after sunset and drinking vodka into the early hours, often amusingly insist that drinking without toasts is anti-intellectual; they will also tell you that happiness is the sound of two vodka bottles clinking in a bag as they carry them to an evening with their friends.

Slavs also like to peddle the myth that "only alcoholics drink alone." However, this national wisdom is just a slick justification for serious group drinking among veteran-bottle drainers.

Downtrodden, impoverished Slavs often extinguish their sorrows with vodka rather than resort to public protest. This is rooted in their keen appreciation of the futility of trying to battle a totally corrupt and unresponsive political system. To keep the natives subdued, authorities have, since Soviet times and with few exceptions, kept the price of vodka very low, thus, consciously contributing to their population's high alcoholism rate: the cost of a liter of average vodka in Ukraine in 2012 was a little more than five dollars. Significantly, Ukraine had the highest rate of teen alcoholism in the whole of Europe in 2012.

Slavic woman often bemoan the fact that their men know no limit when it comes to drinking vodka. This tragic fact is captured in the Slavic saying: "One shot of vodka transforms you into a new person. However, the problem is that that person also wants a drink and this goes on and on."

But sooner rather than later, the heavy drinking of Slavic men catches up with them. Generally, by the age of 45, veteran-vodka drinkers in Ukraine, and Russia especially, receive a serious wake-up call. Heart problems begin to surface and a weeklong stay in a hospital is common. Often the ill Slav will quit drinking vodka and shift to beer. His drinking buddies, however, typically continue their heavy drinking routine until it is their turn to be hospitalized. Often they exclaim, "Life is very hard, but fortunately short."

It's very easy for a foreigner, living and working among average Russians and Ukrainians, to become an alcoholic. Their culture of social drinking is deeply rooted and inescapable, and well illustrated by the following anecdote: A Russian man in his early 20s brings his foreign fiancé to meet extended family members who have gathered in his granny's rural village. They sit down at the festive dinner table and as the first toast is about to be made, with glasses of vodka and champagne raised, the fiancé exclaims, "Sorry but I don't drink." The elderly women present giggle heartily and in unison say, "Don't worry dear. We'll teach you!"

Welcome to Russia and Ukraine! And be prepared to be an organ donor.

My Friend Kolya

> *"An old friend is better than two new friends."*
> -a Slavic saying

My friend Kolya lives in Kyiv and is in his mid-40s. He would say that fate brought us together. I met Kolya in the fall of 2003 when he was a gypsy cab driver working at a stand not far from my apartment building. I had a serious knee injury which prevented me from descending into the depths of the metro system, my usual means of transportation, and needed a ride to a Ukrainian hospital.

Taxi drivers in Russia and Ukraine are a special breed. Typically they are very tough, shady characters and often former convicts; worse yet, many are former corrupt policemen. Most, regardless of age, are confirmed bachelors who guard their independence, prefer working nights despite obvious danger, and enjoy meeting and driving "working girls" around the city. However, Kolya was different in many respects. He clearly enjoyed mingling with these low-life cab drivers and was accepted as one of them, but he was also a dedicated family man.

A short while after meeting Kolya, I again found him at his cab stand. I explained that I would be making about nine more visits to the hospital in the next few weeks for outpatient therapy and asked if he would like to drive me. Given that the taxi business was extremely slow at the time, Kolya jumped at the opportunity. During those long rides in heavy traffic to the hospital we had ample opportunity to chat and get to know one another better. Laughter quickly united us and it soon became apparent that we are both addicted to humor.

After my visits to the hospital ended, I kept in regular contact with Kolya and occasionally used his services. Often, when I did not even need a taxi, I would stop by his stand whenever he was in a long queue, sit with him and chat. With time, I met his teenage daughter, wife and mother. The four of them, three generations, live in a 30 square meter, Soviet-built apartment identical to mine and about the size of an average American living room. The fact that Kolya can cope successfully with this difficult living arrangement greatly distinguishes him from his cab driver friends. He also has an adult son from his first marriage and stays in close contact with him.

Kolya has worked as a cab driver for most of his adult life and, in recent years, as a driver for a foreign business in Kyiv. After compulsory military service he worked for a Ukrainian printing press for 10 years and then briefly as a driver in Germany, his only exposure to the West. Kolya has spent half his life under Soviet rule and half under an independent Ukraine. This makes him a very interesting and valuable source of perspective and insights into Soviet and post-Soviet Ukrainian life.

Kolya is very fortunate to live and work in the capital Kyiv, where there are many more employment opportunities, and to earn $300 a month. Most Ukrainians, even in Kyiv, earn far less. Kolya tries to supplement his monthly income whenever possible, often moonlighting as a gypsy cab driver on weekends. His family survives only by pooling his wife's modest income and his mother's monthly pension of less than $100 with his earnings.

Before long my relationship with Kolya moved in the direction of a budding friendship. He would occasionally visit me after work on Fridays for drinks, appetizers and long hours of conversation about everything and nothing, as Slavs like to say. This emerging tradition was reinforced by several day trips we took to visit his relatives in the northern city of Chernihiv, and even one to Chornobyl in 2006 on the 20th anniversary of the world's worst civilian nuclear accident.

They say that the three great loves of Slavic men are nature, women and vodka. With the high alcoholism in Ukraine and especially Russia, vodka seems to top this list. But there is unquestionably a fourth love, cars. During Soviet times, owning a car was a dream for most natives. In the post-Soviet era, this dream has become more attainable.

Still, Kolya has never been able to afford a new car. His most recently purchased car, only his second, is about 10 years old and is kept in immaculate condition. Kolya loves his car and spends Sunday afternoons ritualistically cleaning and maintaining it, along with cab driver friends who do the same. Used car owners, such as Kolya, as a rule also need to be car mechanics as their cars are their livelihood.

Slavs say an evening of very heavy drinking, more than a liter of vodka between two men, bonds a friendship like nothing else and gives them something to recall together for a very long time. They also say bring a camera along because you may not remember much the next day. Kolya and I have shared such an experience on more than one occasion. But January 21, 2007 is a day etched in our shared history. Somehow we consumed two liters of vodka over the course of seven hours of sitting at my tiny kitchen table, talking and eating appetizers and survived to tell about it; did I mention that I hate the taste of straight vodka? We always laugh when we recall this foolish milestone in our history, wonder how we survived, and often mark the date by having a drink or two, or three together.

These days Kolya and I may meet only once a month, primarily because of his busy work and family life, but when we do we'll easily spend an entire evening together around a tiny kitchen table on a weekend night drinking, eating and lost in endless soulful conversation. He'll typically bring me up to date on his family, tell me secrets about his recent womanizing and his closest male friends' activities, and we'll talk about current politics in Ukraine and America. I also share news about my family and stories about life in America.

Then there was the bonding time when Kolya invited me a couple of years ago to go on a so-called fishing trip (the first of many) with two of his closest friends—another milestone in our relationship. It was an unusually warm September Sunday and Slavs were out in droves taking advantage of this unexpected last blast of summer-like weather. We spent what seemed like an eternity stuffing Kolya's car with fishing gear, portable chairs, a grill, alcohol, and food before we finally hit the road.

We sat in near bumper-to-bumper traffic for an hour and a half before we reached what Kolya described as a choice fishing district just outside of Kyiv. We finally drove onto an incredibly bumpy dirt road in a heavily wooded area along a river and searched long and hard for a free stretch of river bank. Everywhere we looked there were small groups of wild Slavs drinking, dancing to loud car music and barbecuing kebabs.

We eventually found an unoccupied spot that required us to leave our car a good distance away and climb over logs and many empty beer and vodka bottles to reach the river bank. We made several trips with our gear and supplies, collected wood and soon had a fire going.

It quickly became apparent to all of us that this area had a serious mosquito problem. To put it mildly, we could not have found a more mosquito-infested area if we had searched all week. Nevertheless, no one even entertained the thought of abandoning this choice area. To add insult to injury, this wooded area had signs posted on several trees alerting visitors to beware of ticks, a serious problem in Russian and Ukrainian forests.

We remained in this location on a river bank for about five hours, drinking vodka and beer, and eating kabab. Eventually I gave up swatting the mosquitoes which were starving and merciless. Only one member of our group actually sunk a fishing line into the water and retrieved a few minnow-sized fish. After we left this scene, we returned to Kyiv where we bought another bottle of vodka and had a few more drinks in a parking lot. Fortunately, we had a designated driver in the form of Kolya's son, our only fisherman.

The next morning I awoke to terrible itching. I examined the insoles of both feet and my ankles and found dozens of bite marks. Apparently, all the vodka I had consumed the previous day had anesthetized me to any pain from the bites, including during my sleep. Eventually after a week of no visible improvement in the region, I decided to visit a Ukrainian doctor. I was relieved to find that I didn't have tick bites and surprised to learn that no one else in our group suffered similarly.

When I told Kolya about my condition he said that the mosquitoes probably never tasted an American before, and he entertained me with an amusing fish story. He said a while back he went on a similar fishing trip with several friends. As usual, they drank, enjoyed nature and caught no fish. One of the group feared returning to his authoritarian wife, with no fish and reeking of alcohol.

To avoid a scene at his home, another member of the group suggested they stop at a large supermarket in Kyiv that had a live fish tank. The worried man thought he was safe when he proudly presented the big fish to his wife. She looked at it and then shouted angrily, "What kind of idiot do you take me for?" That type of fish lives only in sea water and not Kyiv's rivers!" Apparently the woman's father was an avid fisherman and she really knew her fish. Kolya now keeps a booklet in his car's glove box identifying fish types and their habitat.

Kolya has taught me many valuable lessons about life in Ukraine and Russia, and has helped me shatter some common myths and illusions.

For example, I've learned that average Ukrainians and Russians generally live for today. Their political and economic system is totally corrupt with no chance whatsoever for achieving any kind of American Dream. Pensions for citizens with 30 and 40 years of work typically are little more than $100 a month. Despite all of his hard work, Kolya has no security for the future. If his health seriously fails or his automobile dies he will be out of a job or worse. He and his family can save little from their meager earnings for a rainy day.

Given this harsh reality, Slavs like Kolya rely upon a network of loyal friends to survive, especially in emergency situations. For example, when a friend with little or no money is hospitalized and medications must be purchased, friends unhesitatingly pool scarce money and come to the rescue. This also holds true for funerals.

Kolya has had close friends die before 40 and others suffer heart attacks because of a lifestyle of poor diet and excessive smoking and drinking.

Over my many years in Russia and Ukraine I've learned that the word "friend" for Slavs implies a very close, loyal and long-standing relationship. And that we Americans use the word friend glibly and too generously when we really mean an "acquaintance." A classic illustration is a visit President George Bush Jr. made to Moscow. There he once made the conspicuous mistake of referring to Vladimir Putin in a joint press conference as "my friend Vladimir." Slavs viewed this as nonsense and an insincere effort by President Bush to endear himself to the Russian leader.

I've also learned that Ukrainians and Russians are very generous people with an ingrained tradition of gift giving. Ukrainians have a saying, "Guests never come empty-handed." Whenever Kolya visits me for an evening he always comes with drink, food and more, even though I've warned him repeatedly not to bring anything. Moreover, whenever I depart for the U.S. Kolya and his wife always force me to accept food for the road and a few gifts. "This is our tradition," they insist.

Kolya clearly is a good friend of mine, actually my best friend in Ukraine. He's a very decent and trustworthy person, who I know I can turn to in any emergency and who has never taken advantage of me. Our eight years together is a relatively short basis for a Slavic friendship. I know I have a long way to go before I can become an old friend of Kolya's. His old and closest friends are a handful of loyal men he has known and kept in almost daily contact with for more than 20 years. This is a Slavic fact of life.

Americans, through no fault of their own, generally don't have the very close and deep friendships that Slavs commonly have. Unlike Slavs, Americans often are highly mobile and many necessarily move every four or five years because of employment opportunities Consequently, Americans tend to form superficial friendships marked by surface friendliness.

Finally, I've learned that Russia and Ukraine are drinking cultures where it's not permitted to turn down a drink with a Slavic friend. As Slavs fondly say, "It's a sin not to drink with a friend." Consequently, there's no need to carry an organ donor card here. Most Slavic men are organ donors every day.

Slavic Faux VIPs & Elite

"You can dress a monkey in an expensive suit and tie but it will always still be a monkey."
                                                            -a Slavic saying

I first began to place the subject of Russia and Ukraine's so-called VIPs and elite under my microscope of critical analysis in the early 1990s in Moscow and Kyiv. While sitting in the new, modestly-priced cafes that were springing up in these capitals and having an evening drink, I began to notice an interesting phenomenon. These small cafés had about a third of their customer space, a corner with about a dozen small tables on average, roped off with a VIP sign in big letters on each table. Naturally this caught my eye and curiosity. My first thought was: What was I, an impecunious American, doing in a café frequented by Russian VIPs? And secondly: What kind of VIPs come to this mediocre, non-descript kind of café?

Often I would spend a couple of late evening hours with a Slavic friend in such a simple café and we would both wait with great anticipation to see who would be seated in the VIP section. We made numerous visits over several weeks to several of these so-called VIP cafes but never did see anyone sitting in the special sections.

However, we did see many dyed-blonde, Slavic Barbie-wannabes sitting in our plebian section and ranting out loud that it was unfair for them not to be seated in the VIP section. I found this quite humorous because there was absolutely no difference between the two sections apart from the cord that roped off the "special section" and the VIP signs on the tables; I even mused about bringing my own VIP sign and placing it on my working-class table. As the evening progressed and a few more customers took tables in our section, the buzz in the room clearly was about the VIP section.

With more similar scenes in other modest cafes in Moscow, and Kyiv as well, I eventually realized that these so-called VIP sections were created to be a magnet to attract the Slavic "newly rich" and their families and friends to these new, very plain cafes. However, the owners of these new establishments soon learned that it would take more than VIP signs and a roped-off section to bring in some of the filthy newly rich. They were throwing their looted wealth around at the numerous flashy and pretentiously decadent casinos in Moscow and Kyiv.

With this early introduction to the world of Slavic so-called VIPs and elite, I began to study the phenomenon more closely and to gather my observations. This is what I've found.

It's important first to recall that the French term elite, which came into popular usage at the start of the 20th century, referred to the best members of society, a select group with the highest psychological, social and moral qualities, and finest professional education, and comprising roughly 10 percent of any given country's population. Very Important Persons, VIPs, typically include exceptional statesmen, very accomplished cultural and art-world figures, and leading moral-spiritual voices in a given society. Moreover, they often enjoy international recognition.

Russia, and Ukraine especially, do not have an elite and VIPs in the classic sense. They have sovok relics, mostly former Communist Party functionaries, their family and friends. Today's Russian and Ukrainian faux elite-VIPs are for the most part their respective country's top looters of national wealth—energy, metallurgy and agribusinesses, notably—and experts at criminal-business schemes. They are the ones who knew best how to steal the state's wealth when the Soviet Union collapsed, and quickly learned how to register their businesses offshore to avoid paying taxes.

Russia and Ukraine's elite-VIPs, in fact, are simply their newly rich. Most grew up in small towns and even villages without indoor plumbing, and not long ago were riding tractors, horses, buses and the metro. This group includes not only family, but godparents, in-laws, and friends who need to show off their mansions, planes, prestige cars, designer clothes, and jewelry in order to advertise their new-found wealth, status, and importance. These Slavic clans have more in common with African tribalism than any classic concept of real elites.

As a group, they are desperate to conceal their mediocrity and criminality by buying symbols of respectability, sophistication and prestige. In Ukraine, for example, they reportedly buy seats in Parliament for $300 million or more; voters there choose an entire party list of candidates rather than candidates individually. Moreover, it is no secret to Ukrainians that their 450-member parliament is a closed club of businessmen and criminals—more than 300 millionaires and a handful of billionaires—who are guaranteed immunity from criminal prosecution.

To gain status, they also buy Ph.D. degrees, as well as national awards which were very prestigious during Soviet times. According to Ukrainian journalists, today there is an actual price list for the dozens of government awards sold privately.

A decade ago these newly rich Russians and Ukrainians were identified by driving around in their black Mercedes. In more recent years they have added more exotic and extravagant vehicles to their stable: Bentleys, Porsches, Jaguars and a fleet of huge gas-guzzling SUVs, which are apparently only available in black and only with blacked-out windows. This beloved "gangster-style" look to the luxury cars of the newly rich undermines their effort to add sophistication and respectability to their public image.

When it comes to fashion, these newly rich Slavic men and women get a big thumbs down from independent fashion critics. Many of the men wear shiny suits (apparently this helps conceal their big beer and sausage bellies) and unbelievably pointed shoes (shoes which many foreigners call clown shoes). They often have European shoulder bags (called purses in America), smoke Slim cigarettes, which only make them look fatter, and spend a great deal of time publicly admiring their enormous black luxury SUVs.

The wives and mistresses of these newly rich Slavic men have come a long way since their days chasing pigs on Soviet collective farms. They and their daughters spend small fortunes these days trying to achieve what they call an "absolute model look," but their appearance and dress typically reflects poor taste more than any sophistication and elegance; it occasionally reminds me of the saying "putting lipstick on a pig."

Their elite duds continue to feature essentials: stilettos, leather, mini-skirts and, of course, furs. These women bring to mind the popular Slavic saying, "You can take a person out of a village, but not the village out of the person." Desperate to appear exclusive, cheeky and radical, the wives and mistresses of Ukraine's newly rich flock to Kyiv's pretentious annual "Fashion Week" celebration. This is a chance for them to attend private parties and show off their designer brands and latest jewelry and pretend to have fun.

It's hardly breaking news that Ukrainian fashion, strictly speaking, does not exist. An owner of a Ukrainian boutique and a fashion critic provided the following insights following Kyiv Fashion Week 2010. She said the Ukrainian fashion scene is a pretend world with faux VIPs in attendance, "People whose appearance screams bad taste. It's all about being seen with no real fashion content. Ukrainian designers don't create, they imitate."

The Ukrainian and Russian VIP pop scene is hardly any better. It's dominated by groups of three or four scantily-clad, Barbie-esque, mediocre singers. And it's surprising just how quickly one tires of looking at these indistinguishable young women in underwear or mini-skirts gyrating their torsos on TV with insipid lyrics and large fans to simulate wind-blown hair.

But one cannot really appreciate Slavic VIPs, "Very Important Plunderers" of national wealth, without a few typical Ukrainian examples.

Viktor Pinchuk is the son-in-law of ex–Ukrainian President Leonid Kuchma and was worth $3.1 billion in 2010. He gained most of his fortune by looting the country's very rich metallurgy sector during the 1990s when Kuchma headed a mafia-like state. In an effort to cover his shady criminal past and build a respectable image, Pinchuk has purchased more than half a dozen

TV stations and sponsored occasional charitable events. He's also opened a modern art gallery and hosts extravagant international conferences in order to rub elbows with international dignitaries and celebrities, real VIP and elite. Despite Pinchuk's determined efforts to dramatically improve his image, average Ukrainians have a keen sense of historic memory and see him as one of the biggest looters of their nation's wealth.

Ex-President Viktor Yushchenko presided over Ukraine's democratic Orange Revolution of 2004 but ultimately failed to deliver its promises. In his national addresses, he often stressed family values, patriotism, and the need for a moral-spiritual revival in Ukraine; and decried corruption and the lavish lifestyle of the country's oligarchs. Interestingly, during 2005, his 19-year-old son, Andriy, was often seen spending huge amounts of money at exclusive clubs in Kyiv, such as Decadence and Fellini. He also received a lot of media attention for driving a BMW M6 costing 133,000 euros. So much for family values.

However, without a doubt the prize for insatiable and conspicuous greed among Ukraine's faux-VIP-elite must go to 42-year-old Irena Kilchytska. Until early 2010, she was deputy to 58-year-old Kyiv mayor, Leonid Chernoversky; his net worth in 2010 was $776 million. Kilchytska, a single mother with two very young children, is rumored to have been the married mayor's mistress for many years. Significantly, nothing in her professional background qualified to her to obtain even a low-level job in the mayor's office, let alone that of deputy mayor.

But it is Kilchytska's shamelessly extravagant and conspicuous lifestyle on a very modest Ukrainian civil servant's salary that continues to receive national media attention. Apparently she sees herself as a real VIP and behaves accordingly. She is famous for her taste in expensive cars and designer clothes. In 2009, she sold her Hummer and added a Mercedes Benz GL, worth at least 100,000 euros, to her Bentley and Porsche collection.

Kilchytska prefers designer clothes from Chanel, Dior, Ferre and Dolce & Gabbana and owns more than a dozen Hermes bags which cost $10,000 to $15,000 apiece. However, she really outdid herself and demonstrated her "more money than brains" personality when she arrived at a recent fashion show with her 2-year-old daughter sporting a Louis Vuitton bag. She did this at a time when the average monthly pension in Ukraine was just over a $100, and the average salary only about $250 per month. Similar examples of Russian politicians and their families flaunting ill-gotten riches could easily be cited.

A VIP-elite in a classic sense obviously does not exist in Russia and even less so in Ukraine. Instead you have clans of "newly rich" obsessed with extreme materialism and leading morally bankrupt lives. These status and prestige junkies fill the ranks of government and keep their totally corrupt, self-serving political system closed to any serious reformers. Tragically for the future of their countries, they are also ingraining these same immoral values and sense of false entitlement in their children and grandchildren.

Nearly twenty years have passed since those days when I first spotted VIP signs and sections in low-budget cafes in Moscow and Kyiv. Much has changed during that time. Those cafes have long since been replaced with gaudy, ridiculously-priced VIP restaurants daily serving the likes of Irena Kilchytska. One seasoned Ukrainian observer of the Russian and Ukrainian faux VIP-elite scene summarized this phenomenon quite graphically for me. He said, "These wannabe VIP-elite, former country bumpkins, are all so full of it. They all need an enema badly." *No comment.*

Slavic Fashion Police

> *"You never get a second chance to make a first impression."*
> —W. Triesthof

> *"Don't be deceived by first impressions."*
> — H. Jackson Brown, Jr.

Any American living among the locals in Russia or Ukraine and communicating openly with them will soon realize that there exists a Slavic fashion police. Slavic women living in Moscow and Kyiv, the "big apple" of these respective countries, can be very critical when it comes to other people's dress. This is clearly a post-Soviet phenomenon.

During the Soviet era, with only slight exaggeration, clothes and shoes were brown or grey in color. And who can forget Soviet standard-issue eyeglasses with lenses the size of beverage coasters? Somebody with a sense of humor, no doubt, designed them.

One American TV commercial which was popular during the Cold War mocked Soviet fashion mercilessly. It depicted a beefy Russian collective farm worker clad in overalls, a kerchief covering her hair and armed with a huge flashlight, prancing down a catwalk as an announcer called out "daywear." A minute later she returned wearing the identical outfit but with the flashlight turned on, and the announcer declares "evening wear." Indeed, a lack of closet space was never a problem during the Soviet era.

To be fair, many Soviet mothers only had two outfits to wear, but both were elegant and often complemented by tasteful scarves. Moreover, they devoted a great deal of time and effort to their personal appearance and achieved a manicured look before leaving home. Many proudly told foreigners that they dressed for work as though they were going to a party.

The collapse of the Soviet Union in 1991 changed Slavic dress dramatically. At first Slavs flocked ravenously to the large outdoor markets flooded with clothing and accessories from China. Two decades later, Slavs have the latest Western fashions readily available in posh stores in their major cities. All that's lacking for average citizens is the money to purchase these luxuries. Closet space is still not a problem.

Despite limited financial resources, Slavic women continue to follow a daily "dress-to-impress" lifestyle. They put on layers of make-up, dress in revealing tight clothing and like to show off their cleavage even in professional office settings. Office dress codes generally don't exist.

Not surprisingly, these Slavic women can be very judgmental when it comes to other people's dress. The very casual dress of American students and academics living and working in Moscow and Kyiv, for example, is often the topic of private criticism and ridicule even by their Slavic counterparts. Slavs tend to view visiting Americans as poorly and slovenly dressed and greatly at odds with their TV stereotype of Americans as being very rich and smartly dressed.

I recall a very candid conversation about American dress I had in 2004 with two Russian women in their early 30s, staff members with an American-Russian scholarly exchange program. Over the previous decade they had seen hundreds of American graduate students and teachers come through their year-long program. During a casual dinner conversation the two asked me, "Do Americans, especially women, ever check a mirror in the morning before they step out of the house?" They also suggested that American women should not be afraid to run a comb through their hair in the morning or even visit a hair salon.

Interestingly, if you enter a typical tiny Slavic apartment, the first thing you'll always notice just beyond the door is a mirror. Unlike Americans, Slavs always check themselves in the mirror before leaving the house and they are obsessive about lint removal, clean shoes and having a manicured look. Not surprisingly, locals flock to, and spend considerable time in front of, the large mirrors installed near cloakrooms in Slavic museums, theaters and cinemas.

A Ukrainian academic in her late 40s who worked at Kyiv State University told me the following story in 2008. A small group of American college students came to tour the university that same year. They were so shabbily dressed by Ukrainian standards that a few of the faculty joked that a collection should be taken up for them.

But what do we see when we place the dress of young Slavic women in 2011 under the microscope of critical analysis? The stated goal of many of these women is what they term an "absolute model look." In fact, the majority of young Slavic women in big cities seem to dress in a typically uniform manner, which lacks personal style and is boring, pretentious and often simply in bad taste: badly-dyed and unwashed-blonde hair, skin-tight designer jeans, black-leather or vinyl-form-fitting, waist-length jackets, stiletto high heel shoes or boots, and huge faux-designer bags slung over their shoulders like AK47 machine guns. Although this femme fatale outfit turns many male heads, especially those of visiting middle-aged foreign men, it can hardly be described as glamorous, let alone elegant, fashion. It's more of a Barbie doll meets hooker look; a porno-glamour or "plastic-fantastic" style.

Even more disturbing is the fact that many older Slavic women who work in prestigious professions subscribe to a very revealing and provocative style of dress. The attitude of a Russian lawyer in her mid-30s who wears mini-skirts in the workplace is typical of many older Slavic women. During a 2009 interview she said, "Just because I'm a lawyer, does not mean that I have to stop being a woman."

Perhaps, but the view of a Ukrainian man in his late 20s living and working in Germany since 2005 is also interesting. He grew up in Kyiv and vacations there each year to spend time with family still living there. During 2010 he phoned a Ukrainian radio talk show on the topic of female dress and asked, "Why do all young women in Kyiv dress like our German prostitutes?"

Much of the dress of young women in Kyiv and Moscow, notably, is the product of shopping at open-air markets, where much of the clothing and accessories are glitzy, cheap-looking, brand-name knockoffs from China. But just ride the Moscow or Kyiv metro weekday mornings at 6 A.M. and you will see how real Slavs dress. Many young and middle-aged Russian and Ukrainian women and men in 2012 dress worse than in Soviet times. And with average monthly wages just over $200, this is not at all surprising.

Americans are criticized for their alleged glaring violations of Slavic dress standards, but where are the Slavic fashion police when Slavs commit blatant violations?

Shoes are an important part of non-verbal communication for Slavs and an important indicator of social status and where a person comes from. Interestingly, many Ukrainian men working in business and government, including the police and army, have for at least the past five years had a love affair with extremely pointed dress shoes that extend one's foot by a good two inches. I think Freud would have a few insightful comments about men who appreciate an additional two-inch extension. Americans probably wouldn't be caught dead in this style.

A Ukrainian fashion critic appearing on a Kyiv radio talk show during late 2010 was asked about this lingering phenomenon in men's shoes. She chuckled and provided the following theory. She said she's mystified that men in Ukraine actually wear these shoes and believes that crates full of them were dropped in Ukraine and that men just fell in love with them. She finds them dreadful looking.

Another one of my favorite Slavic fashion statements involves summer wear for adult Slavic men, namely men in shorts with dress shoes and black ankle-high socks. Where are the Slavic fashion police when you really need them?

Believe it or not, fashion in Russia and Ukraine also extends to the plastic shopping bags natives use to carry anything and everything, including children's school books. Typically these bags have colorful, sexy pictures or prestige names such as Hugo Boss and Mango. They come in a variety of colors, sizes, and quality and make a fashion statement. I once heard a young Slavic women compliment another women on the "classy" plastic shopping bag she had.

However, I'll never forget one of the most egregious Slavic female fashion violations I've ever seen. A few years ago on a crowded Moscow subway in summer I spotted a considerably overweight 30-ish Russian woman in black, velvety fitness slacks standing facing the doors with her back to me. On her big bottom in white 4-inch letters was the word "Godsend." For a moment I was breathless. Clearly, this was a brand name and the woman probably did not even know what it meant in English. My immediate reaction was, "Take me now Lord, I've seen everything."

But I hadn't. When I heard that Ukraine's new president had joined the Slavic fashion police during October 2010 by issuing the first ever dress code for his country's civil servants, I almost dropped my spoon in my borscht. You see the president's inner circle, and their enormous sexy staff, includes some of the most flagrant violators of civilized dress norms. The Kafkaesque, stated purpose of the lengthy dress code was to secure "citizen's trust in the state service," which, incidentally, is totally corrupt.

A few highlights from the code's recommendations for how civil servants should dress are instructive. Men are simply told that they should own three suits and wear a clean shirt to work every day—easy. Women, on the other hand, should appear "business-like" but they must also look "feminine, stylish, elegant and have individual charm"—doesn't sound too business-like to me.

The regulations also point out the physiological differences between men and women's sense of smell: The document notes, "Women might get irritated when sensing a bad smell on a distance over half a meter," adding that bad odors can cause group conflict.

But my favorite new dress code rule is the following: "See-through dresses and blouses which make underwear visible" are now on a no-no list. *Oh, no!*

Orthopedic Consequences of Slavic Foot Candy

"When your feet hurt, you hurt all over."
-Socrates

Many foreign men visiting downtown Moscow and Kyiv describe Slavic eye candy on parade, a chauvinistic reference to the many attractive young Slavic women who intentionally frequent cafes and bars where foreign men are known to congregate. Indeed, there are many attractive young and not-so-young women to be found there. But there is another kind of conspicuous candy on parade in these capitals and other cities of Russia and Ukraine, respectively, that deserves attention: foot candy.

Many Slavic girls from about age 13 fall madly in love with high-heeled shoes. Young Slavic women gaze wantonly at these, especially the Italian brands, in the windows of countless boutiques in downtown Moscow and Kyiv with the same burning desire little girls exhibit in candy shops. Interestingly, I've been told by more than one Slavic woman that when a teenager gets her first pair of high-heels there's a longstanding ritual they often practice. They go to a local park with giggling girlfriends and fling their flat shoes far away to mark their new life with glamorous, sexy high-heeled shoes. And from that point on their addiction to the "heeling power" of high-heels grows each passing year and with each new style.

In downtown Kyiv and Moscow, one frequently hears the clickety-clack of countless high-heels as young and not-so-young women run to catch buses, walk through metro passages and shopping malls, and especially in the stairwells of Soviet-era apartment buildings without elevators. In Kyiv, you will see them scale the city's cobblestone streets in spike heels in record time. And the clickety-clack sound of their heels proudly announces to the world, and especially men, that they have arrived and special notice needs to be taken of them.

Foot candy, like chocolate, comes in a wide assortment. Each year brings many jaw-dropping and constantly changing styles, colors and even materials, along with classic spike and stiletto heels. Italian brand high-heels especially make Slavic girls swoon.

High-heels, or "hello-sailor" shoes as they've been fondly called in the U.S., first became popular in America in the 1930s. Originally they were worn only on special occasions. Today, however, they are daily wear globally. In Kyiv, for example, I am no longer surprised when I see a young worker with high-heels stocking the dairy case at my local supermarket, a female doctor or dentist wearing them during working hours, and throngs of university girls on their way to class.

But for everything in life you need to pay, sooner or later, as the saying goes. Big Slavic girls need to learn what little girls are typically taught, namely that too much candy is dangerous to your health. And here I'm not talking about excessive sweets causing obesity and diabetes. I'm talking about their addiction to high-heeled shoes and the magnetic power they hold over many men, local and foreign.

Believe it or not, St. Petersburg, Russia holds an annual sprint in high heels event with heels no less than 9 cm. (about 3 1/2 in.). The winner receives 50,000 rubles (about $1,400 in 2011);

other contestants receive injuries, grazes and bruises. Moreover, the main street is lined with many adolescent girls who look up to these role models and hope to one day be in their shoes. And there are similar races annually in New York City and Paris.

Young women often talk about the "heeling-power" of wearing high-heels daily: their ability to make them feel special, glamorous and sexy. Most, however, are unaware of the serious orthopedic consequences of wearing high heels, or they are in denial.

Our feet, in fact, are slaves of the body, tortured and ignored daily until irreversible problems often result. Each one is made up of 26 major bones, 33 joints, 107 ligaments, and 19 muscles and tendons. In the authoritative words of Leonardo Da Vinci, each one is "a masterpiece of engineering and a work of art." But wearing high-heels brings a woman's entire body weight crushing down on the base of her foot rather than upon its 26 major bones evenly.

The medical evidence is abundant and clear. Eighty percent of women who wear high heels have foot problems. Furthermore, prolonged daily use of high heels can damage leg muscles and cause arthritis around the knees, thighs, pelvis, and even spine. Very common complications include swelling in the legs that can cause inflammation, thumbnail problems, broken bones, various problems of the front of the leg, metatarsalgia, neuroma, and tightening and shortening of the tendons. Sounds sexy and glamorous?

A word of advice to foreign men addicted to Slavic women who wear high-heels. As the saying goes, "For everything in life you need to pay, sooner or later." Look down the road 20 years and consider the orthopedic consequences of this sexy, almost daily, footwear for many women. In many cases today's images of stiletto and spike high-heeled vixens, with time, will be replaced by limping and moaning older women with heavy Slavic accents. Sounds sexy and glamorous?

Many young Slavic women, no doubt, tell themselves "I'll just wear them until I catch that special man, a rich Slav or even a poor foreigner, who can get me out of this insane asylum," as one woman described the living conditions in today's Russia to me. However, many women are simply addicted to high-heels and it's an addiction that only gets a wakeup call when one's health suffers dramatically, and then the damage is typically irreversible.

Interestingly, according to Italian researchers (as reported in the British Daily Mail), this addiction also has a physical underpinning. In late 2008, they reported that women wearing a 2-inch heel and holding the foot at a 15-degree angle increase the electrical activity to their pelvic muscles that play a vital role in sexual performance and satisfaction. Question: Is permanent knee osteoarthritis and/or tendon damage worth a little more buzz in your pelvic region?

Tendon problems, in particular, are no fun. Trust me. During the 2010 Washington, D.C. major snowstorm—likely to be one of the greatest of the century—I ruptured my left arm's bicep tendon, leaving my bicep unconnected to my tendon and floating. Several screws in my arm and a shortened tendon later, I underwent a six week recovery, including therapy. My weightlifting and heavy exerting days with my left arm (they were few and far between) are over and, yes, I am left-handed. The good news is that I obviously don't need to carry my full body weight on my repaired arm. The bad news, however, is that damaged Achilles' tendons and damage to knees, spine and feet routinely follow dedicated years of wearing high-heeled shoes.

For Slavic and other women still unwilling to curb their high-heeled ways, let me leave you with the following image. An American podiatric surgeon (British Daily Mail, September 2008) highlighted the irreversible damage to the leg tendons of women who wore high-heels over many years. Prolonged wear tightened and shortened the tendons of these women and eventually made it impossible for them to put their feet back in flat shoes. As a result, many 70-year-old women are forced to hobble around in high heels because it's too painful, and dangerous to their tendons, to put their feet back in flat shoes. *Sounds sexy and glamorous?*

A Proud Tradition of Stealing & Cheating

> *"Only a fool does not steal if there is no chance of getting caught."*
> —a Slavic saying

Slavs unquestionably have a proud tradition of stealing and cheating. If you're a foreigner, just ask any Slav. They'll instinctively deny it and get very offended. No one likes it when a foreigner criticizes their country or political system regardless of how much they may agree. But privately the same offended Slav will laugh with a fellow countryman and express surprise that "the foreigner understands our life." Stealing and cheating are learned, ingrained and widely shared social norms in Slavic society. Slavs like to call them survival mechanisms.

Transparency International also understands Slavic life. Ukraine and Russia, no doubt, have had to work overtime to earn a high corruption rating from this respected international monitor:

in 2011 Ukraine came in an impressive 152 with only 31 countries found to be more corrupt; Russia didn't perform too shabbily either coming in at 143. As Slavs are fond of saying, "Corruption is the lubricant that keeps life moving smoothly in Russia and Ukraine."

This Slavic culture of stealing and cheating has deep Soviet roots and has received a big boost thanks to the wild capitalism and extreme materialism of the post-Soviet era. The collapse of the Soviet Union in 1991 let the genie out of the bottle and there is no sign of him returning soon. It's no secret that Russia and Ukraine have been sliding into increasing lawlessness, aggressiveness and immorality for the past two decades.

During the Soviet era most citizens lived with constant shortages of food, clothing and decent shelter. Waiting in long queues, and collecting and hoarding available food and household items became a national sport. To cope with this shortage economy and make life more tolerable, Slavs increasingly embraced a noble, national tradition called "bringing home."

Depending upon their place of employment, workers would bring home meat from their meatpacking factory, bricks from their plant to use to build a tiny summer cottage, or skim gasoline from their place of employment. They would use these personally or barter them for other goods and services.

Children especially would often anxiously await their father's return from work and ask, "Dad, what did you bring home today?" Often the prize would be several belts of sausages liberated from a meatpacking plant and concealed under a coat. Interestingly, disabled persons were looked down upon during Soviet times because they had no jobs and were not in a position to bring anything home and help their family.

Fast forward 20 years and this deeply rooted tradition of bringing home, or stealing as it is more commonly known, continues (meat, bricks, gasoline, and much more) and has been taken to new heights with the collapse of the Soviet Union. The most blatant example is Russia and Ukraine's "newly rich." Politicians in both countries used the period of post-Soviet chaos to enrich themselves, family, and friends by carving up and grabbing their country's wealth, factories, agribusiness and natural resources, instead of passing laws and major reforms to improve the lives of average citizens. Slavs call this massive theft of state property "grabitization," and the newly rich who landed well after the collapse of the Soviet Union, "parachutists." And they see their respective parliaments today as consisting mostly of kleptocrats.

The unethical and immoral conduct of top Russian and Ukrainian officials does not fool average citizens. Ukrainian pensioners, for example, are very savvy when it comes to politics. One told me, "Europe does not want Ukraine because the country's rich steal, and Ukraine's rich don't want to be in Europe because they can't steal there. They are happy to steal unrestricted at home."

Russian and Ukrainian college-age students also are no fools. They are acutely aware that their political systems are totally corrupt and closed, and avoid them like the plague. They have a "live-for-today, and you don't get rich by hard work" attitude. They know the best jobs are obtained through personal connections, and that skills and diplomas play a secondary role at best. It's no secret that today's newly rich earned their millions and billions through illegal or shady deals and not through hard work. Consequently, they spend most of their time with friends, computers, DVDs, music, and even drugs.

A prime example of this culture of stealing and cheating is tax evasion, a Slavic national sport fueled in part by a draconian tax code. The newly rich and average citizens partake in various schemes to avoid paying taxes resulting in a shadow economy of more than 50 percent. Accountants typically keep two sets of books to significantly reduce tax and pension fund payments. Moreover, most employers pay workers half or more of their monthly wage unofficially "in envelopes" to evade taxes. Significantly, if a Slav is found guilty of not paying taxes, it is not viewed negatively by fellow citizens as in the U.S.

Petty theft, not surprisingly, remains a major problem in Russia and Ukraine. I continue to be amazed by the heavy physical security, a show of force, to be found even in supermarkets, bookstores and shoe stores, not to mention every store in any Slavic mall. In addition to video camera surveillance, Slavic businesses all employ strategically placed security employees to serve as a visible reminder to shoppers that, "We know Slavs like to steal but don't try it here!"

Student cheating and faculty bribe-taking is another important and thriving dimension of this Slavic culture of stealing and cheating. In recent years I've had many opportunities to speak to Russian and Ukrainian university students and answer their curious questions about American higher education. In return they've provided me with insights into their student life and classroom practices. When asked why students routinely collaborate during exams, copy students' homework, plagiarize, buy research papers and dissertations, and pay teachers for good grades, the reaction is always the same: a smile, laughter, never a denial, and an "everybody does it, it's no big deal" defense.

Surprisingly, I've received the same, simple defense to this question from researchers in their 30s and 40s working at respected institutes of the Russian and Ukrainian Academy of Sciences: "You don't understand, everybody here does it, it's the system." This laid back, very tolerant Slavic attitude toward cheating and stealing is reinforced every time I exit a downtown Moscow or Kyiv metro station and am handed several fliers telling me where I can buy university diplomas, dissertations and research papers.

It is also very evident in a park just across the road from Kyiv State University during exam season. The area is often generously littered with discarded student cheat sheets, undeniable evidence of a proud tradition of cheating and littering. In fairness to the students, I must say that the crib sheets I've examined all displayed excellent penmanship, an essential quality, of course, if they are to be legible during an exam.

In examining Russian and Ukrainian higher education one reaches the inescapable conclusion that it breeds not only unethical and dishonest practices, but also instills a deep cynicism and disrespect in young minds toward the authority figures who should be their role models. Students quickly learn that the laws in Russia and Ukraine have no meaning and that only a person with money has rights.

The more time I spend in Russia and Ukraine the easier it is to see the logic behind this culture of stealing and cheating and the profound differences between Slavic and American systems. In Russia and Ukraine you've always had cradle to grave (hospital-to-cemetery) institutional corruption and bribe-taking, bad in Soviet times and much worse today. This system and its social norms are learned early, ingrained, and shared widely. In Russia and Ukraine, people expect something extra (bribes) from clients in addition to their wage to provide basic services, otherwise you'll be in a long queue and waiting a long time.

The U.S., in contrast, emphasizes ethical and professional behavior and tries to instill, ingrain and promote these values. In the U.S. and West, people do their jobs because they're supposed to. To survive and succeed, however, Slavs must learn to adjust and adapt to their corrupt institutions and closed, totally corrupt political system, in particular. Americans, on the other hand, seek to change and correct their system which they see as open and malleable.

At the core of this culture of stealing and cheating are rotten role models, shameless materialism at the very pinnacle of power, and even sex used commonly as a currency to advance in higher education and the business world. This is even more conspicuous in Ukraine than in rootin-tootin Putin's Russia.

Sex is a very common currency, indeed, in Slavic business, politics and higher education. A poll conducted by a Ukrainian talk radio station in 2009 found that 92 percent of Ukrainian woman polled said they would sleep with a boss at work to keep their job or advance. One Ukrainian acquaintance said this attitude is painfully obvious. He said one simply needs to look at the women who are hired and how they dress for work. "Many look like they should be working in a massage parlor."

Ukraine's president and speaker of parliament provide glaring examples of unethical and immoral behavior and terrible role models for the young. Both have been publicly exposed as corrupt but this hasn't hurt their careers in the slightest. President Viktor Yanukovych is a twice-imprisoned felon who had his criminal record conveniently wiped clean, and it is no secret that he bought his advanced university degree. He is also responsible for stealing and distributing much of the country's wealth to his oligarch supporters and friends.

Volodymyr Lytvyn, the speaker of Ukraine's parliament, has been implicated, but never punished, for helping to organize the murder of a leading journalist critical of ex-President Leonid Kuchma. Lytvyn was also caught-red-handed plagiarizing an entire lengthy article on democratization by a distinguished American scholar; he had a translated version brazenly published under his own name and ignored the mild criticism that followed. Indeed,

"Ukraine gives corruption a bad name," as one international corruption monitor observed during 2010.

But can Slavs live honestly, pay taxes and not "bring home?" Indeed, they can and do when they reach America, Canada and many other Western countries. There they encounter governments and systems that place the public interest above private interests and are accountable to citizens. There they routinely live within the law, offer no bribes, drink less, and show respect to others.

Interestingly, today there is one thing that most Slavs in Russia and Ukraine don't want "to bring home"—themselves! This is especially the case with young Slavs who have managed to study in the U.S. for a year or more. I've had an opportunity to debrief several of these students who have had an opportunity to study in American colleges.

The picture they paint is refreshing and very similar. They emphasize that, unlike Slavic teachers who look down upon students, their American teachers were engaging, encouraged student interaction and were very interested in the views and experiences of all of their students. They were also very impressed to find that American teachers were available and accessible outside of class; and that American education focuses on practical application of knowledge, in contrast to their Slavic system's obsession with theory. In the words of one student, "They treated us like human beings, as equals." A mother of one of these students candidly admitted to me that many of the female students cried when they had to return to Ukraine, and a few even remained in the U.S. illegally.

What did these young Slavic students miss most when they were studying in the U.S.? One said she craved and even dreamt about her mother's *borscht*, a very tasty Ukrainian stew. She said, "The American diet is very heavy and difficult on our digestive tract." At times she also missed being with students who had the same Slavic mentality, and knew, for example, "What it means to wash your clothes in a bathtub and not have a clothes dryer."

American students (and parents) take notice. You don't know how good you have it!

Your American Cash Is No Good

> *"Money can't buy you happiness but it does bring you a more pleasant form of misery."*
>
> -Spike Milligan

It was summer 2002, a decade after the collapse of the Soviet Union, and I was preparing to visit Moscow yet again. Russia and Ukraine were still essentially cash-only countries. This meant I would have to have to pay for my rented apartment in dollars.

During many previous visits to Moscow I learned that dollars, and foreign currency in general, were carefully examined at the countless currency exchange kiosks on virtually every city block, and for good reason. Counterfeit currency had flooded the former Soviet Union since its collapse. And so I prepared appropriately for my return to Russia. Keenly aware that worn and marked dollars were unwelcome at most Russian currency exchange points, I explained the problem to my Washington federal credit union and soon picked up $2,500 in fairly new one hundred dollar bills.

A few days after arriving in Moscow, I set out to exchange some dollars for rubles. I went to a kiosk just across the road from the apartment I rented and gave the young lady within the tiny booth a hundred dollar bill, which she quickly returned. She said, "We don't accept these types." Puzzled, I asked her why? She pointed to two tiny words, barely perceptible, scribbled along the left edge of the face of the bill and the center of the note where Franklin's face had been folded.

Naively, I told her that this bill was perfectly acceptable in the U.S. She made a sour face, gave me a look as though I had escaped from an insane asylum and said, "You are no longer in America, you are in Russia!"

I hurried to another nearby money-exchange kiosk and received the same reply. I was in a state of disbelief. Determined to have my money accepted, I went to a proper bank an hour away in the center of Moscow and confidently presented the bill at the money exchange window. The teller gave me a scrutinizing look and said, "Our clients who buy dollars do not accept these kinds of bills."

My blood was boiling and I almost said that this bill is not intended for a currency collector but for practical use; fortunately I didn't. However, I did tell her that most of the rubles I receive in exchange points are very old, often falling apart and even taped together. She was not at all impressed but did say that for a seven percent commission I could exchange the bill on the second floor of their bank. I deliberated for a minute about the ridiculous charge and then made my way upstairs. What had started as an effort to make a quick morning transaction was now eating up my entire morning.

When I reached the bank's second floor, which had more security than Fort Knox, I was told that I would need to produce my passport as identification. I rarely carry it with me, fearing that if it's lost or stolen I'll be marooned in Russia for an inhumane period, and asked if a photocopy of it along with an international driver's license would suffice. The answer was a glib no.

Despondent, I considered drinking some alcohol but it wasn't quite noon yet. Instead, I retreated to my flat where I sat for a few minutes collecting myself and wondering what the gods had in store for me next. I then pulled three crisp new hundred dollar bills out from my remaining supply and returned to the first currency exchange kiosk that had rejected my money earlier that day.

Smugly I submitted all three bills to the same young lady who rejected me earlier. She looked at me suspiciously and then placed the bills under her ultraviolet light. To my astonishment, she said all three bills were unacceptable because they showed spots under the light. I wanted to question her credentials knowing that most of the young women operating these kiosks receive only a few hours of on-the-job training. Instead, I silently cursed my federal credit union. I was beginning to feel as though I was in a Mr. Bean-like comedy situation.

But I didn't give up. I then went to a currency exchange kiosk in my nearby Soviet-style grocery store and boldly walked up to the women within. I took a deep breath, presented the three one-hundred dollar bills, said a silent prayer, and turned my head away in fear. Seconds later the women was counting out rubles for me, old ones, some falling apart and even some taped together. For a split second I was tempted to tell her that the old rubles were unacceptable but then I regained my senses.

I left the shop feeling exhilarated. Oddly enough, I felt as though I had pulled a fast one even though I knew the dollar bills were good. Still I was happy that the women in the last currency exchange booth did not use her ultraviolet light.

A day later I examined my remaining hundred dollar bills. To my utter shock, I discovered that most of the bills were worn at the center and five were older vintage bills with very small pictures of the president. I had a sinking feeling in my throat and almost went into shock. I sensed this spelled more trouble. After some serious brainstorming, I decided I would slip these bills to the babushka landlady who was renting her flat to me, and keep my fingers crossed.

Slavic Bureaucracy & the 7 Circles of Hell

> *"...the most basic, most rudimentary spiritual need of the Russian people is the need for suffering, ever-present and unquenchable, everywhere and in everything."*
> -Fyodor Dostoevsky

If hell does exist, Slavs destined there need not worry. Repeated encounters with Russian and Ukrainian bureaucracies, and their so-called "public servants," will provide them with good coping skills.

Upon arriving, Satan will expose them to the horrors of hell. Slavs, no doubt, will calmly observe the circles of hell and then respond, "That's nothing! We had to go through periodic residence registration, new vehicle registrations, efforts to register a small business and don't even get us started about dealing with our Tax Police. Seven circles of hell, child's play! We had far more circles of hell in Russia and Ukraine."

Stunned, Satan will turn to the group of Slavs and say, "With your qualifications, how would you like to be tour guides in hell?"

As a foreigner living and working in Russia and Ukraine for a good bit of 20 years, I've experienced hell on earth in dealing with various Slavic bureaucratic offices. Fortunately, I've had only a fraction of the nightmarish encounters average Slavs are forced to endure in their lifetime.

Let me walk you through some of the bureaucratic hell of Ukrainian and Russian daily life.

Residence registration: To remain in Ukraine longer than the 90 day visa-free period that citizens of North America and the European Union enjoy, it is necessary to go through additional residence registration and to have a visa. I went through this process once, and once was enough. It was unbelievably complicated, time-consuming and frustrating:

1. Obtain a stamped document from the *ZHEK* (local residential utilities office for my apartment building) confirming my place of residence. My "neighborhood" ZHEK unlike most, unfortunately, was located an hour and 40 minutes away (metro and walking) and had visitor's hours only on Wednesday evenings. I waited half an hour to meet with the passport control person there, presented my passport and other needed documents, received the stamped document and made an appointment to meet her a few days later at my district's central police station to continue the process.

2. Met my ZHEK's passport control person at my district police station (an hour from my apartment) as agreed. She introduced me to the director of residence registration there, who took my passport and other required documents and directed me to another office in the building.

3. Waited in line outside the designated office for more than half an hour. Went in, received and filled out several required forms, received four fees to pay at a *Sberbank* (state bank) and was told to return after seven days with receipts from the bank.

4. Went to a Sberbank near my apartment, waited more than half an hour in line, submitted the bills and received receipts.

5. Returned to the designated office of my district police station after seven days with receipts for the paid fees. To my surprise, I was told that one of the four required fees was not registered as paid and that I would need to return to a Sberbank and remake this payment and obtain an additional receipt.

6. As luck would have it, electric power in this entire district was out that morning because a major accident downed a power line, and the nearby Sberbank was left in the dark. Rather than return to the police station another day, I flagged a car (people's cab service). I told the driver my situation and negotiated a price for him to take me to a Sberbank in a district with electric power and then back to the police station.

7. We drove a few miles looking for working traffic lights as an indicator that there was electric power in another district. Found a district with power and a Sberbank. I re-accomplished the needed payment and received a new receipt. We drove back to the police station.

8. Presented the additional receipt to the designated office and was told to go the director's office to pick up my passport with newly registered residence.

9. Waited in line for a short while outside the director's office. He told me to go down the hall and pick up my passport at another office.

10. Knocked on that office door and opened it to find a group of three workers chatting and having tea. Told them I needed to pick up my passport which I had been told was ready. They told me to wait outside the door. I waited nearly 30 minutes before I knocked again. They told me to continue waiting.

11. Instead returned to the director's office and told him I couldn't get my passport. He marched out of his office, into the designated office and seconds later handed me my passport.

12. Mission accomplished.

To avoid repeating this circle of hell, the next time my residence needed to be registered I decided not to repeat this process and instead took my chances at the airport's passport control before leaving Ukraine. I ended up having to pay a fine which I negotiated down to $80 from $100. Trust me, it was worth every penny.

According to official regulations, a fine for failure to register residence cannot be paid more than once without risking deportation. Consequently, I now go to the extreme of leaving Ukraine just before my 90 day visa-free period ends in order to avoid the nightmare of periodic-residence registration. Extreme? Perhaps, but it helps me retain my sanity.

Registration of a small business: Prior to the collapse of the Soviet Union in 1991, the Soviet republics of Ukraine and Georgia had virtually identical bureaucratic systems, both mired in red tape. Twenty years later, Georgia has successfully attacked corruption and introduced a transparent and accountable bureaucracy. As a result small businesses are thriving there, unlike those in Ukraine. There it typically takes a month to run around collecting documents and greasing palms to even have a chance to register a small business. In Georgia it takes just a few hours and a visit to a single office. Ukraine and Russia are countries of document mania, and each document has a fee and each transaction requires going to many offices to pay a fee and get another document with a fresh ink stamp.

Registration of a newly purchased car: One of the most corrupt divisions of Russia and Ukraine's bureaucracy is their auto division. It is not at all uncommon to spend weeks trying to register a newly purchased, used car. Yasha Levine, in a recent Internet article titled "Zen and the Art of Volga Ownership," describes how he spent 60 days and went through 36 steps trying to register a late-model Russian car he bought. In the process he spent an entire week waiting in Sberbank lines to pay fees, collected a pile of required documents after greasing more than a few palms, spent an afternoon at a notary public's office correcting a single letter in one of the documents, and even had to give a Russian traffic cop a bottle of American whiskey for assistance in registering his car. *Welcome to Russia and Ukraine!*

Could things possibly be any worse? Yes, indeed. Ukraine, following the election of a new president in February 2010, now has a Tax Police that makes America's IRS look like Mother Teresa. The newly beefed up Tax Police has armed goon squads dressed in ski masks and flak jackets. Their motto should be, "We're coming to you!"

Under the pretext of court-sanctioned tax inspections, they raided an agricultural enterprise in September 2010 and fired rubber bullets wildly into a crowd of workers, injuring six individuals. Days later they raided a business in the city of Kherson, beating up a mayoral candidate who ended up in hospital. It seems that Ukraine's Tax Police is once again being used politically to take control of enterprises and settle business disputes, rather than merely collect taxes.

Ukraine and Russia's bureaucracies are not "user friendly," to put it mildly. Clients typically wait in tiny, packed, airless rooms with only one small window open. Moreover, if you ask a worker a basic question they will not provide the needed information, saying they would then have to answer everyone. Citizens in need of basic services routinely receive abuse and disrespect from their so-called public servants.

Dealing with Slavic bureaucracies doubtless drives many of the locals to heavy alcohol consumption. It's a tortuous experience you wouldn't wish on your worst enemy. Going through it even once makes a visit to an American DMV office seem like going to Club Med.

ГРОШОВІ ПЕРЕКАЗИ
fastest money transfers in the world

Western Union Slavic-Style

> *"The fastest way to send money—worldwide."*
> -Western Union's trademark

During 2007 I attempted to live on an average Ukrainian's monthly salary of $200 (about $250 in 2012). My experiment failed after less than two months. Despite subsisting largely on a pensioner's diet of tea, cabbage salad, sardines, apples, oatmeal and other delicacies, I almost went broke. A few emergencies arose and, as a result, I had spent most of the money I had budgeted for a four-month stay.

It was time to call the U.S. and arrange for a quick and easy Western Union money transfer. I already had planned where I would first spend some of this incoming cash. For some time I had been walking past Kyiv's TGIF ("Thank Goodness It's Friday") restaurant, an identical replica of the ones found in many American malls, on my way to an Internet café. I decided that this would be my first stop after receiving my money transfer and an opportunity to once again experience what meat tastes like.

TGIF's outdoor advert of "American size portions and friendly service," fighting words for most Slavic restaurants in the city's center, naturally caught my eye. However, I had more compelling reasons for this selection. I wanted to see the young Ukrainian staff, graduates of boot-camp training in American smiles and friendly small talk, in action. I also wanted an opportunity to inspect their public restroom (I presumed they had one) and compare it to Ukraine and Russia's best, McDonald's, and see if it offered their happy customers the luxury of toilet seats.

I anxiously scouted the city center the day before the money transfer was to arrive and found two banks with Western Union signs. I decided to go to one early the next morning just before it opened. After a short wait, I entered the bank and learned that they only send money via Western Union. Disappointed, I went on to the second bank and after a short wait there learned that the computer that handles their transfers was down and they had no idea when it would be up and running again.

Desperate, I then went to the city center in search of the main Western Union office. A little more than an hour later I found it and felt great relief after the hectic start to the morning. When I entered I was delighted to see that only two customers were ahead of me and three young female staff members were behind the service counter. But more than an hour later I was not so glad. The two customers ahead of me were still there, both were filling out additional forms and one of them was still waiting for a family member to bring a required document. Moreover, I learned that two of the women behind the counter were not authorized to do Western Union transactions. Meanwhile, more Ukrainian Western Union customers were queuing impatiently behind me.

Another 45 minutes passed and it was finally my turn. Instead of a quick check of my passport, I was given two very detailed forms to fill out. I completed them and waited for the young lady to finish with a customer before returning to me. She reviewed the forms, took them to an administrator in another office and returned to tell me I had been given the wrong forms to fill out. Feeling guilty she filled out most of the new forms for me while I waited. At this point I was feeling faint, due to a combination of a lack of any ventilation in the steamy room and my low blood sugar. But then I recalled the smiling and cheerful staff waiting for me at TGIF and this gave me new strength.

With the necessary forms completed, I handed my passport

over to the young lady as documentation. Almost finished I thought. Wrong! She then asked me if I had any documents (the favorite word of bureaucrats in a country afflicted with document mania) showing where I live in Kyiv. I did not and, exasperated, I questioned the need for such a document. She politely told me it was their office policy. I then asked to speak with the office administrator. The young women went to a different office and returned 15 minutes later with good news. She said this requirement would be waived in my case. I thanked her but was really thinking "next speed reverse."

To add insult to injury, she politely asked if I would take a few minutes to fill out a customer-service questionnaire. I told her I would do it after I received my money. At this point, I expected this young lady to return with my cash. Instead, she returned with six copies of some forms for me to sign. I signed without even reading them because I just wanted to get out of there.

"Now can I have my money?" I beseeched. Instead, I was given several of the forms and told I needed to go to their cashier. The cashier was concealed out of sight in a small kiosk with a sliding tray for documents and cash. Unfortunately, this kiosk also served as a hard currency exchange point and the room had more than half a dozen customers waiting. A half hour later it was finally my turn. I presented the Western Union forms and my passport. In return I was given four copies of a form to sign before receiving my cash.

Nearly five hours after visiting the first Western Union authorized bank I had completed my Western Union money transfer. One thing for certain, I signed more forms that day than are probably required to adopt a child in America. And who gets all of these duplicate copies? Where do they go in this country which is recognized internationally as totally corrupt? Little wonder that this country of less than 46 million people has one million bookeeper-accountants.

In the end I never did go to TGIF's after getting my cash that day, or any day thereafter. I decided it was too cheerful and comfortable for me. As Slavic fatalists would say, it was not meant to be.

In Defense of Ronald McDonald

"Going to McDonald's to eat a salad is like going to a brothel for a hug."

                                                         -unknown author

The Golden Arches are the international symbol of McDonald's, America's hamburger giant. They are well known to young and old alike, and symbolize the gateway to McDonald's "happy meals" and much more. By 2010 its tentacles had spread to over 32,000 locations in over 110 countries.

Second only to the Golden Arches symbol is Ronald McDonald, the clown mascot and patron saint of this fast food chain and hero of many tiny and not-so-tiny children who visit McDonald's. A hamburger-happy clown, Ronald first emerged on American television in 1963 as an inhabitant of a fantasy world called McDonaldland. Today the life-size statues of the clown found at many Russian and Ukrainian outlets allow families to take memorable photos.

Since erecting the first Golden Arch in San Bernardino, California in 1940, the food giant has also had great success in the former Soviet Union. McDonald's first opened in Russia in Moscow's Pushkin Square in January 1990, setting an opening-day record. Lenin, lying in his dusty mausoleum in the Kremlin, could only envy the 30,000 Russian customers who lined up for hours that day to honor Ronald McDonald and his tasty burgers, in contrast to the meager turnout he receives on most days.

In recent years Ronald McDonald has been given a big, black eye by American critics of the fast food industry. The 2004 film *Super Size Me* provided a damning indictment of McDonald's and presented cogent medical evidence demonstrating that steady consumption of McDonald's fast food is hazardous to your health and a major contributor to the epidemic of obesity in America.

Let me set the record straight. I fully agree with the findings in *Super Size Me* and I never eat at McDonald's when in America. However, I do appreciate the easy availability of McDonald's when driving across the U.S. and frequently stop for a coffee and restroom break when making long road trips.

In nearly 20 years of living in Russia and Ukraine intermittently, I have only visited McDonald's on a handful of occasions. These visits were requested by Slavic friends and my participation was limited to coffee. However, I must admit that on more than one occasion, when feeling deeply depressed in the Slavic kingdom, I've been tempted to get a big Mac and more, but have somehow resisted the temptation.

It's no secret that McDonald's is extremely popular in Russia and Ukraine, with new outlets emerging rapidly. In downtown Kyiv, for example, there are four McDonald's in less than a half-mile area. But there is another side to the overseas Ronald McDonald and Golden Arches that is only dimly perceived, if at all, by Americans. For average Ukrainian and Russian citizens who make $200–$300 per month (in 2012), trips by family members to the Golden Arches are not cheap and yet are frequently made. What best explains this practice?

In traditionally non-service and weak work-ethic countries such as Ukraine and Russia, McDonald's is truly an oasis in the desert. Most importantly, it is an easily accessible piece of America for natives who very likely will never be able to visit the U.S. It's a slice of America, complete with a relaxed atmosphere, a squeaky clean and cheerfully colored environment, quick smiling service and tasty food—features alien to a Slavic non-service culture.

Significantly, in these countries McDonald's provides locals with something sorely lacking 20 years after independence, namely a safe, casual meeting place for teens. The sad fact is that political leaders in each of these countries are callously indifferent and have made no systematic effort to provide clubs for their youth which keep them safe from the growing drug epidemic. McDonald's provides this.

Given the go-slow culture in Russia and Ukraine, teens and grownups tend to stay at McDonald's much longer than Americans who eat and run, and the corporation has made this cultural adjustment. Stated differently, Slavic loitering is acceptable and even encouraged at McDonald's.

Another major contribution of McDonald's overseas is that compared to most of the unregulated fast food available there, there is little chance that McDonald's food will immediately poison you. As the film *Super Size Me* demonstrates, the McDonald's menu requires frequent visits over a protracted period of time to have a serious negative impact on one's health.

Ukraine is a good example of poor, and often no, inspection of public eateries. In September 2009 it set a new record for public food poisoning across the country. The casualties included more than 30 high school students in the city of Kremenchuk; 192 children hospitalized in Dzhankoi; more than two dozen soldiers in Bila Tserkva and the poisoning of nearly the entire staff of the First Specialized Presidential Regiment in Kyiv. Shortly thereafter, customers of the Celentano pizzeria in Mykolayiv were hospitalized and 22 people in the Lviv and Volyn oblasts. The situation in Russia is similar.

Another major contribution of McDonald's in Russia and Ukraine over its many years of service is to instill an American work and service ethic in a new generation of young Slavs less infected by the lingering Soviet mentality. I had an opportunity to speak to female college-age McDonald's employees enjoying a conspicuous cigarette break outside an entrance in downtown Moscow. Both had been working there for nearly a year and said they enjoyed the cheerful environment very much. Interestingly, they said their training included learning to smile at customers and to be cheerful. Both noted that learning to smile frequently was at first somewhat painful, but eventually their facial muscles adjusted.

Slavs often remark that only clowns smile at strangers and that smiling for no reason is insincere and stupid. Both girls agreed that working in a family-oriented American restaurant where customers are conspicuously happy does lift their spirits. They did stress, however, that their work is very intensive and demanding and, thus, a very atypical regime for most Slavic jobs.

Americans typically are unaware of Ronald McDonald's greatest contribution to Russia, Ukraine and many other countries. Slavs, however, are keenly aware. Ask any Slav familiar with McDonald's what immediately comes to mind when he hears the word McDonald's and virtually all will respond resoundingly: free, clean, sit down (versus squat) toilets with seats! In short, civilized toilets thanks to McDonald's. And many Slavs unabashedly enter McDonald's simply to use the toilet, knowing that they will never be reproached for this by this American institution.

Viewed in this light Ronald McDonald is, indeed, an unsung American hero abroad, especially after a decade of America getting a black eye overseas for foreign policy reasons. The fact is that every time Ukrainians and Russians, young and old, visit a McDonald's they consciously or subconsciously register a vote of confidence, with their feet and meager incomes, in America's culture of friendliness and service. Objectively speaking, Americans can be proud of the sorely needed family institution McDonald's brings to Russia, Ukraine, and many other developing countries.

Food politics aside, I think that the U.S. State Department should erect a large monument to Ronald McDonald and recognize him as a distinguished American diplomat and an exceptional ambassador of goodwill in the former Soviet Union and many other developing countries, especially at a time when the U.S. is heavily criticized for military activity abroad. Criticized to no end in the U.S. by various groups for good nutritional reasons, one fact is unmistakable: The constantly spreading Golden Arches of McDonald's have long since replaced the remaining monuments of Vladimir Lenin in any meaningful sense to many young and old Russians and Ukrainians.

Swimming with Slavs

> *"We live but once, life is short"*
> -a popular Slavic saying

Over the past 20 years I've spent my share of sizzling summers in Moscow. For a few years, just after Vladimir Putin came to power, I was even lucky enough to rent a flat just across the Moscow river from Gorky Park. Early each morning I would walk the banks of this river to get a breath of fresh air and some exercise before the city filled with the fumes of bumper-to-bumper traffic.

I enjoyed crossing the ornate pedestrian bridge to the Gorky Park side of the river and often chatted with fisherman who frequented that bank. I recall vividly one conversation I had with a veteran, Russian fisherman. I asked him about the quality of the water and whether he could eat the fish he caught. He said he never ate them and once even saw a two-headed duck floating in the river. I took this as his exaggerated way of making a point. After this conversation, I no longer dipped my feet into the Moscow river to cool off on unbearably hot days.

Temperatures in Kyiv (frequently called the Miami of the former Soviet Union by Muscovites) often reach a sultry 95 degrees in summer. Although one of Europe's greenest cities, in recent years it has become more of an asphalt jungle, with bumper-to-bumper traffic weekdays. Thus, when Ukrainian friends suggested one sizzling weekend in 2009 that we cool off at a Dnipro river beach in Hydropark in the heart of Kyiv I unhesitatingly agreed.

Two Ukrainian couples, a 10-year-old daughter and I piled into a compact Ukrainian-made car fit for 4 passengers and made our way to Hydropark on the left bank of the Dnipro river. But first we spent almost 2 hours buying all of the essentials that normally sustain a small group of festive Ukrainians for a 5–6 hour outing: beer, vodka (just in case), soft drinks, water, sausage, cheese, vegetables, fruit and more.

We arrived at Hydropark, a beach and amusement complex, located not far from the heart of Kyiv. I had visited the park's rides before, but never the beach. Katya, Sasha's 10-year-old daughter, eagerly led the way to the beach from the parking lot. A short while later she exclaimed, "Mama, we're here and it's not even crowded!"

Indeed, it wasn't crowded but the scene I saw left me breathless. Several dozen mostly middle-aged men and women were either entering or leaving the water, others were actively exercising and they were all nude. My heart sank. When it comes to men's beach apparel, I'm a typically prudish American: Of course, I've worked hard over the years to successfully overcome this prudishness when it comes to women's beach wear. Moreover, I had prepared myself psychologically to deal with the typical men's Speedo monopoly at a Slavic beach, but nothing prepared me for these locals showing their "junk" in public.

Had Katya been my 10-year-old daughter, I would have immediately covered her eyes with my two hands, but she seemed oblivious to the entire spectacle. I, on the other hand, must have turned beet red at the realization that we were going to a nude beach. More disturbing still, a scared special part of my male anatomy immediately seemed to retract many inches (here I'm being generous) like a frightened turtle withdrawing into its shell.

A few minutes later my Ukrainian friends, and Katya, broke into non-stop laughter. Sasha explained that the group decided to play a cruel, carefully orchestrated joke on their American friend. Keenly aware that Americans are stereotypically prudish compared to Slavs and Europeans, in general, they devised this prank. And to add insult to injury, they even enlisted the active participation of Katya, quite a convincing little actress.

Rather than go directly to the large Speedo beach, our true destination, our group went out of its way a bit to expose me to a small stretch of nude beach near Hydropark's pedestrian bridge, which existed even during Soviet times. They said the detour was well worth the additional 15 minutes. I said nothing. I was still recovering from the shock.

Not surprisingly, the Speedo beach was packed bumper-to-bumper with people. No American beaches, including Florida's South Beach, prepared me for this experience. The egregious violation of personal space, from an American perspective, on Slavic streets, stores and transport becomes almost child's play when an average American experiences a grossly overcrowded Slavic beach.

Although Ukrainian men come in all sizes (many with huge beer bellies after age 30) it seems that their European-style swimsuits (Speedos for Americans) all come in one size, tiny. The women, young and old, also were displaying their wares for all to see. I, on the other hand, represented the U.S.A. proudly in my modest swim trunks.

Apart from occasionally having body limbs of strangers touch me while I rested on the sand of the crowded beach, cigarette ash cascade down upon me from smokers stretching their legs, and the frequent sight of male and female middle-aged groins hovering over me, the day was quite refreshing. After an hour of unforgettable people watching, and being assured that the water quality was safe, I joined my friends and the masses in the cool waters of the Dnipro river, Ukraine's major river.

I also observed the age-old Slavic tradition of intoxicated young men diving into the waters from a nearby bridge. This brought to mind the fact that Russian men typically drown at a rate more than five times that of Americans. It seems that alcoholics are not only poor drivers but also poor swimmers.

All in all it seemed like a very pleasant Slavic-style day until a week later when I heard a very authoritative and independent report about the quality of water in Dnipro and Ukraine's other water outlets. Anatoliy Yatsyk, the former deputy head of Ukraine's Environmental Ministry had some very alarming news. He said that all of the banks of the enormous Dnipro river which slices Ukraine in half, and all of Kyiv's 400 or so lakes and ponds, are contaminated and unsuitable for swimming and recreation. He also stressed that he would never swim in any of Kyiv's water.

This former high government official noted that Kyiv's fish are always sick and that swimming in these waters could make your fingers peel. The waters are contaminated by animal or human waste and can cause not only chronic diarrhea but also cholera, leptospirosis (a disease spread by rats in public water pools which can lead to jaundice), meningitis, and kidney failure. Significantly, during June 2011 Ukrainian officials in the southeastern port city of Mariupol, located on the coast of the Azov Sea, reported more than a dozen citizens infected with cholera as a result of eating fish caught in the area.

The Dnipro river is also contaminated by more than 1,500 factories. Collectively they dump tens of thousands of tons of petrochemicals, nitrogen and nitrates into the Dnipro yearly. Yatsyk also stressed that one must never forget about Chornobyl, located just 60 miles north of Kyiv. Since the world's worst civilian nuclear disaster there in 1986, 90 million tons of radioactive waste is silted in the Dnipro reservoir.

The Dnipro river, in short, is wastewater, which cannot be adequately purified for over 60 percent of Ukraine's population, over 30 million people who nonetheless continue to use it at home. To add insult to injury, erosion of the Dnipro's river banks has already affected several nearby cemeteries dating back to the early 20th century, sending bones into the water.

Ukraine's environmental activists battle daily with their population's denial and indifference to the country's unabating environmental catastrophe. The fundamental problem as they see it is media inattention and government neglect and indifference. Consequently, Ukrainians live in the dark ages and know nothing about what they eat and drink, and about the quality of the water they bathe in.

After some very disquieting scientific reports, I didn't return to join the masses bathing in the Dnipro's refreshingly cool waters. Instead, I waited anxiously for days to see if my fingers would peel and for visible signs of disease. I also told my friends about the very contaminated state of Dnipro and Kyiv's lakes and ponds.

My friends, including little Katya, all scoffed and snickered at the findings of environmental activists, and responded with two popular Ukrainian sayings: "What is good for a Slav is death for a German," and "We live but once, life is short." My friends had survived Chornobyl and now they should worry about a beach where they have been bathing all their lives? To fear this, in their opinion, was absurd.

Ukraine's Ticking-Time Bomb

"What is the difference between Chornobyl and Kyiv? No difference—60 miles!"
                                    -Ukrainian black humor

The world has heard about Chornobyl, Ukraine, the 1986 scene of the world's worst civilian nuclear disaster. But Ukraine today faces another ticking-time bomb, a deepening systemic crisis with catastrophic implications for every dimension of its citizens' lives. Russia faces similar horrors.

A quarter of a century has passed since Chornobyl captured international attention. Living in Kyiv just 60 miles south of Chornobyl, I am acutely aware of the fact that Chornobyl continues to leak radioactive material. Moreover, it was only in 2010 that an American company, with international funding, finally began to construct a confinement shelter over the ruins of the Chornobyl nuclear plant. The effort is expected to take at least five years and last 100 years. Until the work is completed, 5 million residents in the region must live with the risk of leaking radioactive material.

But Chornobyl is just the tip of the iceberg. Ukraine faces

a profound systemic crisis with multiple interconnected and seemingly intractable crises: health, housing, demography, and environment. A country the size of Texas with a 2012 population of less than 46 million, Ukraine once held the proud reputation of being the "breadbasket" of Europe. Amazingly, it has more than 20 percent of the world's most fertile soil, called chornozem. Sadly, the country's "newly rich" post-Soviet leaders, and their families and friends, grabbed and divided the country's immense metal and chemical resources for quick profits and refuse to invest in Ukraine's immense agricultural potential.

Ukraine's medical system, which was greatly neglected in Soviet times, has continued to collapse over the past 20 years. Existing facilities are falling apart and not easily accessible for disabled persons. Several years ago I underwent 10 weeks of therapy for a knee injury at Kyiv's very large Pimonenko health clinic. I recall vividly the dozen very disabled-unfriendly, crumbling stairs leading to the only entrance, the surly nurses in high heels, and the sole dirty, unlit men's toilet in the basement of this four-floor facility.

Conditions in Ukrainian hospitals are truly decrepit. Little wonder that the political elite and their families leave the country for medical care. I've visited a few Ukrainian friends in hospitals over the years and the conditions are shockingly third or even fourth world. Patients are required to bring all of their food, medicines and linens, and to make cash contributions—bribes, strictly speaking—to doctors who, in all fairness, receive a meager official wage from the state for their intensive work.

Ukraine's health crisis also includes multiple epidemics: the greatest and fastest growing AIDS, STDs, and tuberculosis in the whole of Europe and Russia, and the highest teenage alcoholism in the whole of Europe. Once called the breadbasket of Europe, Ukraine today is the "bridebasket" (for foreign men) and Europe's sex tourism capital. There are more than a few conspicuous "working girls" living in my apartment building and countless other apartment buildings in Kyiv.

Housing is another major dimension of the country's growing systemic crisis. The crumbling exteriors of the country's mostly Soviet-built apartment buildings are a real eyesore, but the real danger lies within. The infrastructure of these buildings and their deteriorating gas lines, in particular, are a ticking-time bomb.

Each year in Ukraine and Russia, especially in winter months, numerous gas explosions occur which can destroy an entire five-story apartment building. Virtually no effort is made by the state to see that these buildings are safely maintained.

I live in one of these collapsing and potentially explosive five-story buildings in Kyiv. Each time there is a reported gas explosion in one of them, I give serious thought to what I would do if my building was next on the list. At one time I thought of packing a small overnight bag with my valuables and essential documents and having it ready just in case. But what if the bag should blow up? Instead, I now make sure that I go to bed in a full set of pajamas. I don't want to be embarrassed when I get outside and meet any surviving neighbors.

The quality of water reaching a majority of Ukrainian homes, including my Kyiv apartment, is another reflection of the country's seemingly intractable systemic crisis. All of Ukraine's water outlets are contaminated with human and animal waste and many with radioactive waste from Chornobyl. Dnipro, the country's largest river which cuts it in half, is "wastewater" because the treatment stations cannot adequately purify it. I often think that American tap water would be a dream come true for Ukrainians and Russians.

Ukraine also faces a very serious demographic crisis. Since 1993 its population has dropped from 52 million to less than 46 million (2012) due to a growing death rate and lower life expectancy; given current trends, the population is estimated to drop to 39 million by 2025. On average, men in Ukraine live to 62 years of age, women to 73; in Russia, men on average only live to 59. The able-bodied male population in both countries is dying early due to alcohol abuse and smoking, both of which cause heart disease and cancer-related deaths.

Ukraine, according to UN studies, is undergoing a sharp worsening of all demographic processes: a low birth rate, a decrease in marriages and an increase in divorces, a decrease of average-life interval, a sudden increase in the death rate, and a strengthening of emigration. Since the collapse of the Soviet Union, 4 million poor Ukrainians (including 3 million illegals) have left their homeland to work mostly at menial, hard-labor jobs in Western Europe in order to send money home.

Finally, there is Ukraine's raging ecological catastrophe. In 2009

I visited Donetsk, a key industrial center and egregious polluter in eastern Ukraine, and had an opportunity to experience the putrid smoke that hangs over one of the country's largest cities. Factories owned by rich local business groups daily release toxic fumes into the air and toxic waste into rivers. As a result, the toxicity of city and rural water supplies, and the air and soil quality in Donetsk and numerous other Ukrainian cities, have reached critical levels.

To add insult to injury, trash is commonly burned commercially and by private citizens in small towns and villages throughout Ukraine. Moreover, there is the annual national ritual of burning leaves in the fall. Viewed in this light, it's not surprising that the World Health Organization estimated in 2010 that 155,000 Ukrainians die prematurely each year because of pollution.

Russia faces a similar systemic crisis with a long list of environmental horrors. For example, the Aral Sea, once the world's fourth largest inland sea, is disappearing. Over the past 50 years, it has lost more than two-thirds of its volume and all of its fisheries. The Chelyabinsk region in the Urals has been decimated by the twin horrors of industrial pollution and nuclear radiation, the result of decades of nuclear testing.

Ukraine's deepening systemic crisis, with its many dimensions, has deep roots. For decades Soviet leaders focused most of their resources on military buildup, while seriously neglecting the country's non-military infrastructure and well-being of their citizens. However, Ukraine's post-Soviet rulers have deliberately and unconscionably neglected this crisis for the past 20 years.

Ukraine's ruling classes live in a different world, a guarded community of riches and mansions, and foolishly believe they can insulate themselves and their families and friends from their country's growing systemic crisis. Their priorities are clear and their actions shamefully telling. They seek to build ever greater personal wealth while in office by violating the public trust placed in them.

Rather than budget significant funds annually to tackle Ukraine's multiple crises, they chose to devote $15 billion to prepare the country for the Eurocup 2012 soccer finals to be held in Ukraine and Poland: to modernize four airports, four stadiums, and to build hotels, elite resorts, and malls to welcome European soccer fans for three weeks.

But back to Chornobyl. In April 2006 on the 20th anniversary of this civilian nuclear disaster I decided to visit Chornobyl with my Ukrainian friend Kolya, a former cab driver in Kyiv with more than 20 years experience. Getting into the Chornobyl Exclusion Zone, as it's called, was a challenge. But Kolya resorted to *vranyo*, Russian and Ukrainian for a white lie, and it worked. He told the guards at the checkpoint that we had a relative in their cemetery and that we wanted to pay our respects.

Frankly, there wasn't much to see. Not surprisingly, it was a ghost town. There were many abandoned, burglarized apartment buildings, with overgrown courtyards and a few handfuls of villagers who maintained the grounds surrounding the town's small administrative center.

However, we did have an opportunity to speak to a few of these villagers while they were enjoying lunch outdoors on that warm day. They were very friendly and interested in our visit. We asked them if they had any worries regarding the reported continuing leaks of radiation. They laughed instinctively and said, "No, we take precautions daily to deal with the situation." When we asked for details, they said, "We drink vodka nightly as a prophylactic to fight radiation."

I then asked them why they chose to remain in Chornobyl, to live and work there. They explained that jobs are impossible to find elsewhere in the region and that Chornobyl has always been their home. They then asked, "Why do you stay in Kyiv, to live and work there? There's no difference, only 60 miles between us, and the air here in Chornobyl is much better. We don't have Kyiv's pollution from a million cars." We had no good reply.

Abraham Maslow in Moscow & Kyiv

> *"How do you make a Russian happy? Turn off his hot water for three weeks and then turn it back on."*
> —Russian anecdote

In Germany, October is a time to rejoice and partake in an age-old tradition called Oktoberfest. Many years ago in Munich, I had an opportunity to share in the celebration and watch the locals in action. Enormous tents with long communal tables were erected in a picturesque setting. The air was filled with the aroma of sizzling sausages, sauerkraut, potato salad, and overpowered with the smell of hops.

It's no mystery that Germans love their beer. During Oktoberfest celebrations, many men arrive armed with huge, ornate beer mugs to demonstrate they mean business. The many hours of serious drinking are punctuated with the sounds of raucous singing and dancing by grown men in funny shorts. It's a merry time for all until the alcohol really kicks in. Then it's time to run for the hills.

Those huge, ornate beer mugs sometimes become handy weapons. In Munich I observed more than a few Germans loose their festive spirit after consuming several gallons of beer. What surprised me the most was the use of their prize mugs to hammer fellow countrymen on the head. After just a few minutes of these non-festive activities, I concluded that these mugs are not only attractive, they're also unbreakable. I would advise foreigners planning to attend an Oktoberfest celebration for the first time to come equipped with a safety helmet just in case. Trust me, you'll be grateful you did.

Russian men are also known to get violent and even take an axe to their women when they have had too much to drink. Ukrainian men, however, behave differently. They tend to get sentimental when they've had too much, and either cry or sing their beloved national songs.

But Russians and Ukrainians experience a different kind of "October Fun" every year. With the arrival of chilly Octobers in Russia and Ukraine, public attention focuses sharply on the start of the heating season and the burning question: When will heat finally be delivered to our damp and chilly apartments? It's a theme that consumes locals during at least the first half of October. Municipal authorities in both Russia and Ukraine are required by law to provide heat to apartment building radiators immediately after three consecutive days of outdoor temperatures below 8 degrees Celsius (about 46 degrees Fahrenheit).

However, there always seem to be delays and excuses even in the capitals of Moscow and Kyiv. And so the locals spend several weeks sneezing, complaining, and trying to keep their very young children warm and healthy during this period. When heat is finally delivered, and often you need to take the word of authorities because your radiators feel tepid at best, Slavs rejoice. Moreover, if municipal authorities generously throw in a few hours of hot water along with the heat, the mood among Slavs is one of euphoria with young children exclaiming, "We have heat!" and near dancing in the streets.

Over the years I've learned to dread October in Moscow and Kyiv and the national ritual of waiting for heat to be delivered to crumbling Soviet-built apartment buildings. A very black mood inevitably descends on the locals for several weeks and colors virtually every conversation, including many on TV and radio shows. One especially cold early October in Moscow my thoughts turned to Abraham Maslow, a noted American psychologist. I was exposed to his theoretical work in college psychology classes but it never really resonated with me until I started living and working in Russia and Ukraine.

Maslow's most noted contribution is his easy to understand and insightful hierarchy or pyramid of five basic needs. His theory contends that humans must first meet their basic needs, namely physiological and then safety before they can move on to the next needs: love/belonging, esteem and finally actualization.

Sitting in a very cold Moscow or Kyiv flat and starring at peeling original Soviet wallpaper with roaches wondering when I'll finally turn off all the lights, any thoughts of love and self-actualization are fleeting. One misses terribly American creature comforts. Upon returning to the U.S. for a few months I always gaze lovingly at any thermostat I spot in homes and apartments and the miracle of central heating. I even dream about it occasionally when I'm away from the U.S.

And then there is the miracle of America's uncontaminated tap water delivered right to your home. What a luxury! You just turn it on and you have it to brush your teeth, wash your fruit, vegetables and dishes; and unlimited gallons of clean water to bathe in and even wash a family car or two.

In Russia and Ukraine the water situation is dramatically different. In Kyiv, for example, I am keenly aware that the water that reaches my apartment and at least 60 percent of the population of Ukraine (about 30 million people) is wastewater that has been inadequately purified because of poor equipment at treatment stations. I know this is true because it was reported not long ago by the former head of the country's Environmental Ministry, who can now speak candidly. The figure is actually much higher than 60 percent of the population because thousands of Ukrainian villages do not have indoor plumbing and rely on totally unpurified and unregulated water.

Foreigners living in third world countries like Ukraine and Russia are often advised simply to boil the water. I used to do this until I learned the true facts about water quality in Ukraine and Russia. Subsequently, the idea of making tea with boiled wastewater seemed very unappealing.

In Kyiv, I begin each morning by walking half a mile to a free clean-water pump (one of only three I've found in this entire capital) to collect at least four liters of water; city authorities periodically certify that the water is clean but my gastro-intestinal system often begs to differ. Living on a shoestring, I can't afford to buy that much bottled water daily; in Moscow I have no choice but to do so. Viewed in this light, coming home to American tap water and not having to carry it long distances is like being on a little vacation until I leave once again.

But October chill in Russia and Ukraine is just a preparation for what is to follow if you live in an average Soviet-built flat. Bone-chilling winds and freezing temperatures make themselves felt easily in these poorly insulated apartments with mostly cold radiators. Little wonder many people go to the extreme of turning on all four stovetop burners and even an oven with an open door to get relief (Slavs still pay a low flat rate for apartment gas, a Soviet legacy). Unfortunately, winter especially is a time for frequent gas explosions in these apartments with sorely neglected infrastructure.

I'll never forget my teeth-chattering winters in several, old-apartment buildings in Moscow. Eventually, I decided to wear a warm jacket, knit cap and even garden gloves whenever I would sit indoors, read and watch TV. One quickly realizes how difficult it is to sleep indoors when you can almost see your breath. To cope with this situation I would go to bed fully dressed in several layers, under a few blankets, often covering my head and not worrying that I might suffocate in my sleep.

Add to this picture of daily life the fact that the average monthly Ukrainian pension in 2012 was $110 and the average monthly wage, $250, and you'll understand why Ukrainians and Russians often tell foreigners emotionally, "We don't live, we survive." It's hard, indeed, to move up from the bottom of Maslow's hierarchy of needs, when all of your time and energy is focused on the need for food, health, shelter, and removal from danger. Many Americans are no strangers to these existential challenges. Here, however, it's the norm for most Slavs.

If indoor camping is your thing, you'll have a jolly time in wintry Russia and Ukraine. Just be sure to bring your sleeping bag, a well-insulated track suit, knit cap, and garden gloves. Oh, and be sure not to miss Slavic "October Fun."

Coldest Winter in 80 Years

> "If the thermometer had been an inch longer we'd have frozen to death."
>
> -Mark Twain

It's early December 2010 here in Kyiv and temperatures have been at or below -10 degrees Celsius (14 degrees Fahrenheit) for days. Mornings the streets are full of red-faced Slavs bracing themselves against the bitter cold as they trudge to work. In old Soviet-built apartment buildings like mine, the radiators are just warm enough to get you angry and there's nothing you can do about it.

I grew up in snow country, upstate New York near Lake Ontario. Winters were bitterly cold with heavy snowfall and our proximity to the lake ensured an extra dousing of the white stuff. Often we would shovel the family driveway two or three times in a single evening to make snow removal manageable the next morning. I can also remember earning substantial pocket money as a child by shoveling neighbors' driveways.

I'm no stranger to winter cold but I can honestly say that I've never experienced anything compared to Ukraine's winter of 2006, the coldest in 80 years. Temperatures there dropped to -30 Celsius (-22 Fahrenheit) and remained in that range for weeks.

Unless you've actually experienced it, it's hard to imagine how it feels to be outdoors for extended periods in these kinds of temperatures. Bone-chilling and teeth-chattering cold is a hackneyed cliché that doesn't do justice to the experience. You can no longer feel your face and nose, and the cold literally sucks the air out of your lungs. You quickly learn to wear a knit cap and breathe through a scarf wrapped tightly around your face, exposing only your eyes.

Even in Kyiv, the capital of Ukraine there is no real refuge on the streets from this kind of cold. The few grocery stores that remain open are not customer friendly and only distant metro stations provide a dose of warmth. The need to buy groceries and other essential supplies eventually drives you out into the frigid cold. I tried to continue my normal routine of filling plastic bottles with free, clean water (the tap water in Ukraine and Russia is lethal) from a rare city pump in a nearby park until I nearly got frostbite while filling the bottles.

The fear of frostbite in these conditions was very real. To alert citizens to the dangers authorities provided daily counts of frostbite cases among city workers responding to broken water mains and other emergencies. As a result of the bitter cold, the water main connecting our building burst and took nearly five days to repair. It required a lot of excavation and left our building without water. It also created a nearly impassable skating rink with small icebergs in the arc leading out of our apartment complex.

Cabin fever was my constant companion for weeks, along with great uncertainty about just how long these severe temperatures would last. At one point I caught myself thinking fondly about the enormous American malls that I've found refuge in during frigid months in upstate New York. I used to joke that they were havens for grey panthers, the conspicuous retirees who spend countless hours exercising by mall walking and chatting with friends in the foodcourt area.

The only heat provided in the old Soviet-built apartment buildings like mine came from radiators which city authorities turn on each year about mid-October. The two radiators in my one-room apartment were worthless. They were never more than lukewarm and located near several very large non-insulated windows which provided no defense against the bitter winds. Many elderly residents of my building, and throughout the country, often resorted to the desperate measure of igniting all four gas burners on their stoves for heat.

However, most of the Ukrainians in my eight-story building apparently had a different strategy to fight the cold. They resorted to electric-gobbling space heaters which immediately caused electric outages. Not surprisingly, our building's antiquated Soviet-electrical system could not handle this power surge and we soon lost all our electricity for several days before residents could be convinced to stop using these incendiary devices. Brief outages persisted throughout the winter.

With these electric outages we naturally lost use of the elevator and hallway lights in our eight-story building. As a result, residents would occasionally be stranded for several hours on the elevator which produced interesting scenarios. Living on the seventh floor I vividly recall the added burden of carrying groceries and liters of water in the dark when the elevator was out, and life with candle-light dinners for one.

I know I annoyed my Slavic neighbors during one of our electric outages when I played my battery-operated radio. I could hear a couple arguing through the thin wall adjoining our apartments, and saying that I must have electricity because they could hear my radio. Not having electricity and only a few candles gave me much time to reflect upon how exciting it must have been when people lived without electricity in America. I found myself concentrating on getting paperwork done before sunset and I even learned to enjoy Ukrainian talk-radio.

Could things possibly get any worse in this Slavic winter wonderland? Indeed, they could. To add insult to injury, a month before the arctic blast hit us I accepted an invitation from my Ukrainian friend Kolya, a former cab driver, to visit his relatives in a rural village three hours away from Kyiv. They were keen to see us and would have been very disappointed if we had failed to arrive as scheduled. This, and Kolya's confidence in his driving skills, prompted us to set out in dangerous weather.

I still recall sitting in the passenger's seat of Kolya's car near the heater and tapping my feet to keep the circulation going. The fear of our car breaking down on country roads far from any life form was never far from my mind. I soon realized why I saw no other cars on these country roads: A breakdown in this frost-bitten weather could easily mean the end for a car's passengers.

Upon reaching our destination, Kolya's aunt and uncle greeted me warmly just outside their door with a special traditional loaf of bread with a bit of salt on top of it, an age-old Slavic custom. Their village was very primitive and located a good distance from any paved road. The first sensation I had upon entering their humble home was a burst of heat. It lacked running water and gas heat but had a classic earthen stove in the kitchen crackling with wood and a traditional sleeping nook adjacent. The windows were carefully sealed with heavy plastic and this made the tiny dining area a bed of warmth. I was in heaven.

For the next 7 hours I sat with Kolya and his uncle at the small dining room table, learning the couple's fascinating history and having vodka toasts seemingly every 15 minutes. His aunt force-fed me non stop for the entire time and I eventually reached a point where I thought I was either going to deliver a baby or have appendicitis.

I also learned that the urge to use an outhouse quickly wanes when one is reminded it is more than -20 degrees Fahrenheit outside; furthermore, frostbite in private areas is not a fun condition. Their outhouse reminded me of the inside of a freezer that needed defrosting. However, its wooden seat did have a padded-knitted ring that I'm certain Kolya's very elderly aunt lovingly added for her foreign guest. A metal bucket was thoughtfully placed just inside the entrance to the house as a comfort station for any needy party in the middle of the night.

I finally had a good night's sleep induced, no doubt, in large measure by the two liters of vodka that the three of us drained. Kolya's aunt greeted us in the morning with a huge breakfast but first demanded that we each have a shot of her homemade moonshine, another Slavic custom, to cure us of any hangover. After our morning feast and more abdominal pain, I was more than ready to hit the road. However, Kolya's aunt insisted that I stay for a few more days, and Kolya looked at me as though he was seriously considering the proposition.

We finally reached a compromise. I promised I would return

soon and accepted a sack of potatoes, a half-dozen cabbages and a frozen slab of salo that weighed at least 20 lbs. and was the size of a small suitcase. Salo is often jokingly called Ukraine's talisman and is considered a delicacy, especially by working-class Ukrainians. This very generous but poor elderly couple repeatedly apologized to me for not having anything else to give their guest.

Ukraine's winter of 2009–2010 was no walk in the park either. It was marked by a record snowfall and the failure of Kyiv's mayor to adequately respond to it. And it was much more dangerous than the icicles and other ice formations which fell from the rooftops and gutters of tall city buildings and apartment houses onto passing pedestrians. That winter thousands of residents of Kyiv received serious injuries from slipping on icy, snow-covered sidewalks and streets; and most residential districts turned into skating rinks with iceberg-like formations.

According to Ukraine's Ministry of Health, 284 people died as a result of cold weather by the end of January 2010 alone, including 64 people who froze to death in their homes. Moreover, 4,259 people with frostbite asked for assistance during the same period, and 2,809 were hospitalized.

In reflecting upon the arctic conditions I experienced in Ukraine during 2006, I recalled the maxim, "You can't always change your situation, but you can always change your attitude." I asked my friend Kolya for a reaction and he almost dropped a spoon in his borscht. He said: "Whatever idiot said that must live in sunny Florida or California. Our severe cold is confining, exhausting, depressing and promotes alcoholism among Slavs."

All I know is that after I left a very kind, elderly Ukrainian couple in their simple village during the winter of 2006, I was very happy to return to my cold flat in Kyiv, with no force feeding, its indoor toilet, running water, and with a lifetime supply of salo!

World Smile Day 2010 in Kyiv

> *Only clowns and idiots smile for no reason."*
> —a Slavic saying

There is a question that continues to intrigue me: Why is it that Slavs, who firmly believe that laughter is the best medicine to deal with life's daily hardships and absurdities, generally view public smiling as suspicious, even offensive, activity? I set out in earnest on the 1st Friday of October 2010 in Kyiv to find a convincing answer to this phenomenon.

The day I chose was not just any other day. It was the 12th World Smile Day, a day rich in history. It began with Ukrainian TV and radio morning talk show hosts highlighting the holiday's history for their respective audiences and encouraging everyone to smile.

From these and other sources I learned the following about this hardly new celebration. Harvey Ball, an American commercial artist who created the Smiley Face in 1963, wanted to ensure that this internationally recognized symbol remained more than a commercial icon. To this end, he declared that the 1st Friday in October of each year, beginning in 1999, be devoted to World Smile Day.

Harvey Ball died in 2001, but his World Smile Day continues to be celebrated enthusiastically in his hometown of Worcester, Massachusetts, and many countries around the world. The official theme for this day remains constant: "Do an act of kindness. Help one person smile." Participants everywhere are encouraged to organize events and spread smiles and goodwill.

Aware that the Ukrainian mass media had publicized World Smile Day, I set out with high expectations. I decided to spend a good part of the day investigating how natives in Kyiv, a city that prides itself on being European and trendy, even if many West Europeans disagree, were marking this holiday. Specifically, I wanted to see whether there were any organized Smile Day events, any cheerful youngsters sporting smile buttons on lapels, and any noteworthy public smiling to be detected in the heart of the city, on public transport, in shops, and even in a public library.

I spent nearly two hours intermittently riding on various lines of Kyiv's subway system, during morning and afternoon peak and non-peak hours. The countless faces that I surveyed fell into three general categories: angry, suspicious and angrily suspicious. Upon closer inspection I could discern some more nuanced expressions among Slavic passengers: Why did you burn my house down? Why did you spit in my borsht? What's your problem? I'm wearing half of my wardrobe and my only pair of shoes and you want me to smile? Our medical system has been collapsing for the past 20 years and our free medical services are free from bribes only for the dead because they can no longer pay, and you want me to smile? The average pension in our country is $150 a month and our meat and dairy prices are higher than in America and Western Europe, and you want me to smile? I'm on my way to a tax audit. Our tax police beat citizens and even shoot them with rubber bullets and you want me to smile?

After two hours of metro rides all I found were countless "last look before we close the coffin" expressions on local passengers. I'm convinced the expressions on the faces of Slavs being transported by train to Stalin's Gulag of prison-labor camps could not have been more somber. Interestingly, during my two hours riding the metro, I observed that even the comedic antics of Mr. Bean displayed frequently in one-minute bites on the video screens in metro cars did not elicit a laugh or even a smile from passengers.

While standing on the crowded metro, I repeatedly heard Harvey Ball's words wringing in my ears: "Do an act of kindness. Help one person smile." I was very tempted to smile generously in the hope of infecting others. But then the fate of Tolstoy's Anna Karenina came to mind and a bone-chilling fear that the crowd might suddenly turn on me, and throw me beneath an oncoming train at the next station. And so, instead, I continued to smile on the inside.

Depressed, I walked Kyiv's busy downtown for over an hour passing thousands of Slavs only to find more doom and gloom and not a single World Smile Day event. In the interest of objective reporting, I should note that I did spot quite a few young Slavic women smiling. They were walking and lost in conversation on their cell phones. The few times that I tried to enter their personal space and return that smile I received a quick rebuff, and a "you're a dirty old man" look. I assure you I'm not a dirty old man, at least not at the time of this writing.

By late afternoon I found that the doom and gloom of the locals had seriously infected me. As a last hope I turned to the local library, a tiny, vintage Soviet-era building with a staff well beyond retirement age. I quietly approached two elderly, female librarians working behind a counter and politely asked one if any celebration of World Smile Day was planned at the library. The two both dropped their jaws and simultaneously said, "Are you joking?" I said I was very serious and received a look as though I had just escaped from an insane asylum.

I remained perplexed. It's a well-known fact that Slavs are not humorless, quite the contrary. They love jokes about sex, spouse relations, mothers-in-law, and politics. Moreover, humor has always been a tool of survival for Russians and Ukrainians and a means of protesting repression and hardships. Why then is public smiling not infectious here and instead viewed cautiously and even suspiciously?

I finally turned to Kolya, my Ukrainian friend of many years and a taxi driver of more than 20 years, for a possible answer. After more than two decades of driving the mean streets of Kyiv mostly in the late night hours, he was very streetwise and quite a philosopher. He provided me a crude but simple and convincing explanation for the absence of public, versus private, smiling. He said, "The vast majority of us live a shitty, impoverished life in a shitty country where our leaders care only about themselves, their families and friends."

I then asked Kolya for examples of when Slavs do smile. He smiled generously and said: "When our hated neighbor's house burns down, when his cow dies, or when he loses an eye." That day Kolya did what Harvey Ball had wished for: He made one person smile—me.

Slavic Humor

> "Why did God give mankind a sense of humor?
> So that men would not bite each other."
> —a Slavic saying

Slavs may not have a habit of wearing a smile in public, but there's no denying they have a profound sense of humor and love to laugh privately with close friends and family. Unlike Americans, they wear heavy protective armor for survival purposes outside of their apartments and small circle of friends and family. It's a "don't talk to strangers and don't smile at them" policy which makes more and more sense the longer a foreigner lives here. Moreover, it's an extension of a golden rule Americans drill into their little children.

A few years ago this rule was drilled into me in Moscow when a Russian friend invited me to his 50th birthday party, a major event to be celebrated at his home. After work on the festive day, we took the subway together to his old high-rise apartment building on the outskirts of the city. We got on the elevator there and made a stop before reaching his floor. A frail Russian man in his late 70s entered the elevator. I greeted him with the words "Good Day," but he said nothing and only looked at me quizzically like someone suffering from Alzheimer's.

My friend, however, immediately nudged me in the ribs with his elbow. After we got off on our floor, he took me aside and asked if I knew the elderly man. I told him I didn't and said I was just being polite. He then reproached me saying, "We don't make it a practice here in Russia to speak to strangers. It's not our way."

However, Slavic anecdotes "are their way" and they have a rich and therapeutic history. In harsh and absurd times, they have been a coping mechanism and an instrument of protest against repression. They mostly cover topics common to joke-telling worldwide: sex, spousal relations, mothers-in-law, politics, drinking, but also police, bureaucratic corruption and much more.

Unfortunately, many anecdotes are untranslatable because they require experiencing the absurd realities of daily life for average Slavs; others rely on wordplay and linguistic puns. Many, however, require no translation whatsoever. As a rule, the best anecdotes are very short dialogues or fictional stories with a punch line.

A taste of anecdotes popular with Russians, Ukrainians and citizens of other countries of the former Soviet Union follows (I've translated most of them from Russian and Ukrainian):

A Russian man regains consciousness in an ambulance and asks the doctor in attendance, "Where are we going?" The doctor replies, "To the morgue." "But I'm not dead yet," says the man. The doctor responds, "But we're not there yet."

After a night of passionate love making, a young Russian man turns to his new girlfriend at a tender moment and asks, "Am I your first lover dear?" She replies, "Yes, of course, but why do all men ask me that?"

The always tough Prime Minister Putin takes his babyfaced, handpicked President Medvedev to dinner and orders a steak. The waiter asks, "What about the vegetable?" Putin looks at Medevdev and says, "The vegetable will have steak, too."

A slit in the side of a woman's dress means "Maybe." In the back, "Follow me." In the front, "What are you waiting for?"

"You men are so rude! You need only sex! We women, however, need attention." Her boyfriend responds, *"Attention, we will now have sex!"*

A boy asks his father, *"Dad what's money?"* The father thinks a bit and says, *"Money, son, that's a fine car, cognac and beautiful women."* *"And when you don't have money?"* the boy asks. *"That's a bus, tea and your mother."*

A man complains to his neighbor: *"That darn polluted environment! Yesterday I opened a can of sardines and all of the fish were in oil and dead!"*

(Russian and Ukrainian traffic police are poorly paid and notorious for bribe-taking.) A Russian traffic cop flags a car with his baton. A man jumps out of the car and indignantly asks, *"Why did you stop me? I haven't done anything wrong."* The cop replies, *"Because you didn't do anything wrong, my children should go hungry?"*

What do Russian police and many young Slavic women have in common? They often mistake visiting foreign men for ATM machines.

A Russian woman and her young daughter go to their local police station. Crying, the woman says that her husband has disappeared. A policeman asks for a description. The woman says: *"He's very attractive, well-built, tall, hard-working, and not a womanizer."* The daughter listens and whispers to her mother, *"Mom, dad isn't like that at all."* The mother says, *"Quiet dear, maybe they'll find one that I like."*

"Your father is a doctor and your mother is a teacher. How is it that you became an elite prostitute?" *"I don't know, I guess I was just lucky."*

A sick man goes to a doctor. *"Help me doctor, I've been dreaming of roaches playing soccer for a month now and am exhausted."* The doctor says *"Here's some German medicine. Take it this evening and your problem will go away."* The man asks, *"Can I take it tomorrow? They're having a final match tonight."*

One microbe meets another one and says to him: "You look terrible. How do you feel?" "Don't come any closer," says the other. "I think I might have penicillin."

(Marshrutkas are public minibuses authorized to carry 20 passengers but often loaded with 50 and driven at break-neck speed by drivers who typically work 15 hours shifts.) A Russian priest and a driver of a marshrutka die and meet St. Peter at the pearly gates. He tells them he can only admit one of them and has chosen the marshrutka driver. The priest protests. St. Peter tells him, "When you gave your sermon the entire congregation slept, but when the marshrutka driver was at the wheel all of his passengers made the sign of the cross and prayed."

Do you want to press against flesh? To feel hot breathing? To sweat from exhaustion? To enter, withdraw, go back and forth? Do you really want this? Then what's the problem? Ride the subway in rush hour!

What is non-traditional sex for Russians? Sex without vodka.

Finally:

The best anecdote is our life.

And in closing a traditional Ukrainian parting wish:

"May the home campfire of laughter never die out."

Slavic Superstitions & My Tortured Childhood

"It is bad luck to be superstitious."
-Andrew W. Mathis

As luck would have it, the devil resides just behind my left shoulder. This was my mother's belief and it launched the start of my tortured childhood in upstate New York. One might think that, after coming to America at the age of 12 months on a slow boat full of refugees, displaced from their homeland by war and years in refugee camps in Germany, a relatively peaceful American childhood would await me. No such luck.

Growing up in a poor Ukrainian village, my parents never had the opportunity to pursue much formal education. As young children they were very fortunate to survive a great famine which killed millions of their fellow citizens. Luckily, they also survived World War II and the failed effort to repatriate them from a German refuge camp to Stalin's Soviet Union after the war ended. These formative experiences, and struggling in America after arriving penniless, required uncommon determination and persistence, a characteristic of many Slavic women. My mother would apply these very same, positive qualities to make my childhood a tortured experience.

Getting back to the devil behind my left shoulder, I had the great misfortune to be born left-handed to a very traditional Slavic mother who viewed this condition to be evil. Yes, this was an irrational superstition, but one which was deeply ingrained and widely shared in my parents' Slavic culture and which had serious implications for me.

Adopting a move right out of Soviet dictator Stalin's playbook, my mother tied my evil hand so that I would be forced to use my righteous one to write. In support of her campaign, she enrolled me in a Ukrainian Catholic grammar school where the nuns were known for concealing heavy wooden rulers up their sleeves. My mother did this not for religious instruction—we were after all Ukrainian Orthodox, not Catholic—but because she knew these Ukrainian nuns also viewed "lefties" as evil and would work diligently to make me right. They gave it a valiant try but eventually realized I was a hopeless cause.

My first year in school was tortuous. The nuns were merciless and my mother gave me no peace at home. I would come home from school and hide behind our sofa to quickly do my homework with my left hand before my mother returned from work. But my mother was very determined and persistent. For much of that school year she would sit with me at our dining room table and require me to do my homework with my right hand. However, by the end of that year she too realized that I was a hopeless cause. Thereafter, she would just look at me very disappointedly whenever I favored my left hand.

My mother did rejoice, however, when I was 11 years old and fell out of a tree and broke my left wrist; this also made my school's nuns very happy. For six weeks my arm was in a cast and I was forced to use my right hand to do my school work. But my mother's joy was short-lived. I quickly went back to my evil ways. As luck would have it, in college I broke my left thumb and once again my arm was in a cast. This made my mother a much happier person for about six weeks.

I recall an interesting superstition of my mother's that surfaced when I was only about four years old. It was so strange that it's still etched in my memory. One day my mother reprimanded me for walking around the house in one sock saying, "If you don't stop doing that, it will kill your mother!" She later expanded that to also include walking around the house in a single shoe.

I didn't really understand this superstition but I found it very useful. I remember for a while whenever I was very angry at my mother I would march around the house with only one shoe on, arms folded and a sour face. She never found this amusing.

While still in grammar school, my mother often told me to stop whistling in the house because it would bring bad luck, but she never provided a fuller explanation. Moreover, she would always scold me whenever I would place a loaf of bread on a table upside down or on its side, saying this was disrespectful. Even as a teenager I failed to see the logic in this.

And it was only after spending many years living and working among natives in Russia and Ukraine that I gained a deeper understanding of my mother, her superstitious ways, and learned many new Slavic superstitions.

The most important lesson I learned is that Slavic superstitions are a legacy dating back to Russia and Ukraine's ancient pagan culture. When Slavs finally embraced Christianity in the 10th century their prevailing pagan beliefs, for example, worship of fire, water, sun, were forced out of their faith but retained as superstitions.

Superstitions are deeply embedded in Slavic culture. They are things that people do or avoid doing daily simply out of fear that it might bring misfortune and bad luck. They are acquired early in childhood, held tenaciously throughout life, passed from generation to generation, and fiercely resist dispassionate examination in the light of contradictory evidence.

In Russia and Ukraine I met many older natives who said that it was very common for a parent to tie a child's left hand to encourage him to become right-handed. They say "misery loves company" but this news was little consolation. Interestingly, I learned that the Soviet system did not consider left-handedness to be evil—good news! The bad news is that they viewed it as "nonconformist behavior" which was very bad and not permitted—get a rope!

I also found a rhyme and reason for respecting bread and not placing a loaf upside down on a kitchen table. In Russia and

Ukraine bread is considered holy and there is actually an age-old cult of bread which is observed in Ukrainian customs and rituals. For example, during wedding ceremonies traditional bread called *Korovai* is served instead of a wedding cake. Moreover, Russian and Ukrainian hosts typically give foreign guests visiting their respective countries a special loaf of bread with a small thimble of salt implanted in it; a very symbolic tradition which dates back many centuries.

There is an added reason for my mother's respect of bread. As a child of 11, she barely managed to survive Ukraine's "Great Famine" of 1932–33, which claimed millions of lives.

The reason not to whistle indoors, I learned, was obvious: Any Slavic fool knows that by doing so you will whistle, or blow away, all your money. This leads to the most important reason why Slavs, and other cultures, cling to their superstitions: There may be some truth to the superstition, so why not go along with it, just in case? Why tempt fate?

Among my favorite Slavic superstitions learned overseas are the following. Many Russian and Ukrainian students never wash their hair before a big exam because they fear they will forget everything they know. Why risk it?

And let's not forget the Slavic superstition that a cat must enter (more accurately, be tossed) into a new apartment or house, otherwise death will take your grandmother. Question: What if your grandmother is already deceased. Can you skip the cat toss?

But let's get back to left-handed people and the devil who resides behind their left shoulder. I never had an opportunity to revisit the subject of left-handedness with my mother before she passed away in 2006. It was an old wound which I didn't want to reopen. However, I sometimes wonder how she would respond to the news that there are many very successful and talented left-handed people in the world. To name but a few: President Barack Obama, the three candidates in the 1992 U.S. Presidential election (Bill Clinton, George Bush Sr., and Ross Perot) actors Nicole Kidman and Morgan Freeman, singer Pink and comedian Jerry Seinfeld. Knowing my mother well, I think she would probably have the last word and say, "The devil was sleeping on the job."

Slavic Fear of Cold Drinks & Deadly Drafts

> *"What is good for a Russian is death for a German."*
> —a popular Slavic saying

I grew up in America with a stereotype of Russians, and Slavs in general, as a rugged and hearty bunch, unperturbed by bone-chilling Siberian winds and inclined to dip into icy waters on New Year's Day like polar bears. And what student of Russian history can forget the role of "General Winter" in ultimately defeating the mighty invading armies of Napoleon and Hitler.

But after living in Russia and Ukraine for a good bit of 20 years, I've come to seriously question this popular image. It's not a widely publicized fact, but Slavs do have a national fear of cold drinks and deadly drafts; a draft is a current of air in any enclosed space.

Make no mistake, Ukrainian and Russian supermarkets and small groceries do stock drinks in coolers. The only problem, based on my experience in many stores over many years, is that these coolers are kept on a setting of no more than 0.5 on a 4-point scale. This Slavic concept of a chilled drink differs from the United Kingdom, for example, where the setting on store coolers is probably between a generous 1 and 2.

It seems Slavic mothers have been insisting on room-temperature drinks for themselves and their children for generations. This habit was made clear to me several years ago when I visited the Moscow zoo with a Russian couple and their 9-year-old daughter.

It was a lovely warm day in May. However, the mother bundled the little girl up in a heavy coat and hat as though it was still winter. Not surprisingly, after an hour strolling around the zoo, the little girl overheated and asked for a drink. Her mother requested some bottled water at a nearby refreshment kiosk. After the attendant pulled one out of a cooler, the mother carefully inspected it and returned it saying that it was too cold. She then asked for one that was not yet in the cooler. I had a warm bottle from the cooler and can testify that it was not set higher than zero and one half. Surprisingly, the little girl scolded me for having a drink from the cooler.

Slavic mothers are overprotective of their young and make it a hobby to torment them daily. Typically, they constantly nag them about the need to protect against drafts, about their non-existent coughs, and proper level of dress for any given day. This behavior, not surprisingly, produces neuroses and guilt complexes when this code of behavior is violated. Slavic mothers can be real drama queens and are famous for insisting that their heart problems are caused by disobedient young and adult children, rather than by their artery-clogging diets.

And God forbid if young Slavic girls should sit on a cold marble staircase near a museum or other building. Not only do Slavic mothers and grandmothers find this inappropriate, they insist that this unhealthy behavior may even cause gynecological problems. I've witnessed this mother-daughter scene countless times.

Drafts are another Slavic national obsession. Opening a window and allowing a current of cool air to blow on Slavs, if it is less than 80 degrees Fahrenheit, is considered almost criminal behavior in Russia and Ukraine. I've risked doing this on unbearably crowded, airless buses on more than one occasion. Each time the reaction has been the same. In less than a minute a chorus of middle-aged

Slavic women, angry as wet hens, curses me and demands that I immediately close the window. Several of them then clutch their necks and simulate pain for the remainder of their ride. Funny how in America we often call these so-called drafts cool summer breezes when they enter our homes.

In defense of Slavs, it needs to be said that America is an ice-cube nation. Most Americans are addicted to ice in their soft drinks. Americans are programmed at a very young age to worship ice cubes and to believe it is not possible to have a soft drink without them. This social norm is reinforced throughout childhood and widely shared in adulthood. It's no mystery how we became addicted. Fast food restaurants and convenience stores, in particular, find it more profitable to fill a customer's cup up with frozen water than to add more of the desired drink.

I should note that I have never seen an ice cube during my many years of living and working in Russia and Ukraine. I'm sure I could see one tomorrow if I went to an expat bar or club, but I choose not to. Moreover, given contaminated tap water in these countries, any ice cubes in restaurant drinks should be viewed very suspiciously.

It's fun to watch Americans on trans-Atlantic flights when the beverage cart rolls down the aisle. They can be distinguished easily from most Europeans on board. They typically request ice for their soft drinks even though they are already chilled.

America, in my considered opinion, is sorely in need of ice cube consciousness-raising. Ice use has gotten terribly out of control in our culture and has restaurant and bar owners laughing all the way to the bank. I'm personally prepared to offer inexpensive group consciousness-raising seminars. Naturally, I'll include a 12-step program to wean Americans off ice cubes, and Ice-Cube Junkies Anonymous support groups to ensure that recovering ice addicts don't dip back into the ice tray.

Slavs simply cannot understand our national obsession with ice and very cold drinks. Amazingly, the same Slavs who fear cold drinks and deadly drafts apparently don't fear flying through car windshields when traveling at high speeds. This is evident in their stubborn national refusal to wear seat belts. Moscow and Kyiv cab drivers and private motorists have told me countless times, "It's not necessary here." And if you do insist on wearing a seat belt, drivers will consider it an insult to their driving skills.

On a more personal note, I'm embarrassed to say I conducted a cold drink and draft experiment on a Russian acquaintance who visited Washington, DC a few years ago. Oleg, a researcher from Moscow in his early 40s, was attending a Washington conference on globalization. In return for the kindness he showed me in Moscow, I offered to show him a few tourist sites after the conference ended.

It was a hot summer day and we stopped at a local 7/11 convenience store. Since this was Oleg's first visit to the U.S., I insisted on treating him to a very American drink, a Slurpee, a syrup-covered slushy ice drink. When I handed Oleg his 48-ounce drink he looked bewildered. Seconds later he made a thoughtful remark. He said "America truly is a superpower, not only in the size of its missiles but also in its Slurpee technology." I said this was nothing and told him that 7/11 advertises a 1.9 liter Slurpee and I would treat him to one during his next visit.

Oleg asked me how he should drink his Slurpee. I told him there is a special ritual Americans follow akin to the way Slavs drink vodka. I told him to suck as much of the Slurpee as possible in one try through his straw. Seconds later Oleg was clutching his forehead and in shock. He looked at me and desperately asked what was going on. I said *"Welcome to America! That's a brain freeze."* (For the inexperienced, this is the sharp shooting pain in your forehead that feels like it will never go away and always occurs when you rapidly suck a great amount of a frozen, slushy Slurpee through a straw.) Oleg was very worried that some permanent damage may have been caused by the Slurpee. However, I assured him that no more had been done than by all of his years of drinking vodka.

But I had an additional surprise for Oleg. Earlier I offered to provide him a ride to the airport. We went back to my house to pick up Oleg's suitcase. Shortly thereafter a car in front of my house beeped its horn several times. Oleg looked out the window and spotted a convertible with a man waving to him. He turned to me and said, "What is this? Do many Americans have these?" I told him it was my neighbor in his convertible and that he had kindly offered to take us to the airport after I told him I had a visitor from Moscow.

Oleg looked less than excited. He approached the car apprehensively, obviously looking for its top. At that moment it struck me that I had never seen a convertible in Russia or Ukraine in all my years there and for a good reason. These are countries where reckless, speeding drivers hide from pedestrians and the ideal car is a huge, black-luxury SUV with blacked-out windows. This was an alien vehicle for Oleg.

It was a warm summer day with the temperature reaching the mid-80s and no cold Siberian wind in sight. It was at least a 45-minute drive to the international airport on a major highway, but I'm sure it seemed much longer for Oleg. He probably got more wind (drafts) that day than during all of his days riding public transport in Moscow. By the time we arrived at the airport I noticed Oleg was clutching his neck a great deal. I asked him if he was alright. He said it was probably from the draft.

Slavs like to underscore their heartiness by often saying, "What is good for a Russian, is death for a German." However, what is good for a Russian apparently does not include brain freezes and rides in convertibles.

Moscow Summer 2011

> "...on balance life is suffering, and only the very young or foolish imagine otherwise."
> -George Orwell

Somehow I missed the fireball that plagued Moscow for weeks during the summer of 2010 and brought with it raging fires, thick toxic smoke and temperatures hovering around 104 degrees. I've spent many a summer suffering in Moscow over the past 20 years and it was a sad pleasure to watch Slavs melt on TV from the comfort of my A/C bubble in Washington, D.C.

I really don't know how I managed to miss out on Russia's hottest summer in one thousand years with my luck. Perhaps the gods were asleep at the controls. In any case, I wanted to give them another crack at making me suffer Slavic-style in Moscow especially in a sizzling summer. And so I left Kyiv in mid-June after three weeks of baking in 90-plus temperatures (good training I thought) and flew to Moscow but only for a few weeks. After all, I'm not a glutton for punishment.

I chose my June 12 departure date for Moscow carefully. Russia's 2010 summer inferno erupted on June 13 and I chose June 12 as my arrival date to tempt the gods. But this time I came prepared to handle any heat, or at least I thought so. Drawing on lessons learned over the past 20 years in Russia and Ukraine, I brought along two white, quick-dry athletic t-shirts. Many years ago in a very hot and humid Ukraine I learned not to wear dark t-shirts for a simple reason: A body releases considerable sweat after spending many hours in an asphalt jungle among the locals and, in my experience, often leaves record-breaking, embarrassing salt stains upon drying.

I also packed a fishnet, "wife-beater" tank top for use only in an extreme emergency situation, such as Moscow's 2010 summer; a small handheld battery-operated fan (U.S. Dollar-Store quality) to avoid fainting on overcrowded, poorly-ventilated metro trains should temperatures again climb over 100 degrees; and a pair of those Slavic lightweight thatched shoes with countless tiny holes that made me laugh heartily when I first spotted them years ago. After visiting many shoe stores in Kyiv, flooded with hooker-looking Slavic women fighting over the latest stiletto-heeled shoes, I finally managed to find a tan pair (thatched shoes not stilettos) rather than the abundant white ones which remind me of retirees in Miami Beach.

I was keenly aware that my stay in Moscow would be brief this time and I wanted to make the most of it. My objective was simple: To observe and be awash in a sea of Slavs and to test once again my weak American credentials for Slavic life. To this end, I designed an intensive exercise in largely non-verbal communication with Slavs from all walks of life. My daily regimen would include no less than five to six hours on foot away from my crumbling apartment on the impoverished edge of Moscow, a daunting challenge for any American addicted to his car culture; and at least two hours riding (actually standing on) many of Moscow's metro lines, with people packed like sardines during morning and afternoon rush hours and, of course, huddling and pressing at congested metro entrances and escalators. I decided to spend an additional three to four hours daily walking and observing Slavic life in central Moscow, and visiting many of the old, rundown neighborhoods and apartment buildings on its outskirts where I lived over the course of the last 20 years.

My second day in Moscow saw torrential rains and flash flooding throughout the city. I managed to join the rush-hour crowd at the metro that morning before the skies unleashed buckets of rain, but wasn't very lucky the rest of the day. In fact, it rained so heavily and continuously that café owners in downtown Moscow positioned staff strategically beneath their terraces' awnings with long brooms in order to release the gallons of water that quickly accumulated there.

I became an experienced puddle jumper that day and learned an important lesson. My lightweight Slavic thatched shoes with little holes were not water resistant; in fact, they welcomed water. Moreover, I was alarmed to learn that these countless holes ended about an inch above the shoes' instep. This curious design feature, along with my very soggy socks, ensured that my Slavic shoes retained a generous bed of water most of the day.

With only a carry-on-bag to take along on this trip, and size 12 shoes which take up nearly half of my suitcase, I never gave any serious thought to bringing a second pair of shoes. I had after all decided to go native. Now that I think about it, I can't ever recall seeing Slavs wear this type of shoe in rainy weather.

I found temporary refuge from the heavy rain that day by riding many metro lines, surveying districts outside several distant stations and stopping at McDonald's. In 20 years in Russia and Ukraine, I've probably entered McDonald's less than a handful of times and only for coffee. This trip it became an essential late morning stop to rest my weary feet, have a coffee and observe the endless stream of people who enter unabashedly simply to use Russia's best and, most importantly, free toilet.

After nearly two weeks of pounding Moscow's hard pavement and riding most of its metro lines, I was ready to draw a few important conclusions.

The Moscow metro is much more than one of the world's most efficient and architecturally stunning metro systems. It also offers more excitement than many American amusement park rides. The system has 11 lines, a total of 182 stations and only charges passengers a single fare of about one dollar.

My grey apartment building was appropriately located at the end of the grey line, the most exciting one in my opinion. It has the greatest number of stations, 25, and is the second longest line, 41 kilometers (about 25 miles). Each morning I would squeeze into an airless metro car, join huddled Russians, work up a good sweat, and zoom through 10 distant stations to reach the center of Moscow. I often would enjoy riding the grey line's entire stretch of 25 stations during non-peak hours.

I'm no newcomer to the Moscow metro system but never rode more than a stop or two on the grey line before. My first ride through 10 of its stations was breathtaking. The train rocketed through space with numerous sharp turns and made more noise than many amusement park rides I've been on. It immediately reminded me of my childhood and a favorite ride of mine in a park in upstate New York called the Bobsleds. The only real difference was that this raging train didn't do figure eights but did seem at times to jump off its track and bounce off of walls. I had the distinct impression that the conductor might be a 16-year-old high on adrenalin drinks.

In general, the Moscow metro is not only a joy ride but also a great boot camp for learning how to be a savvy metro rider in any country. My advice to foreign visitors riding it for the first time: Don't worry it won't crash or go off the rails even though it feels like it will; and the smell of burning brakes is normal.

After nearly two weeks, I also concluded that public toilets in Russia remain scarce, costly and nasty. In the 10 years since I first observed the monumental unveiling of portable, blue-plastic toilets (probably American made) outside Moscow's central metro stations, little has changed. In a few stations the number has gone from two to five, with one serving as an office, and perhaps sleeping quarters, for a Russian babushka. The unforgettable one I used outside of Lenin Library metro station, near the historic Old Arbat district, cost nearly a dollar (20 rubles) and didn't even include a clothespin for my nose. On the positive side, an elderly beggar strumming on a guitar just 10 feet away provided soothing music.

Here I must comment about the men's restroom at the McDonald's on the Old Arbat. It's a restroom to die for: Sparkling cappuccino-colored and tiled walls and floors, soft lighting, spacious stalls, limitless toilet paper (finally no hefty Russian babushka to wrestle for an extra square), running water and, most importantly, non-squat toilets equipped with toilet seats—in a word, heaven!

My first reaction upon finding this oasis in the Russian desert was to take a few photos, but two words quickly came to mind: arrest and scandal. Yes, taking photos in a men's room was not a good idea; bad things could happen. A few mental pictures would have to suffice.

During my stay in Moscow I also observed that Russian drivers behave no differently than their Slavic brothers in Kyiv. They stop very reluctantly, if at all, for pedestrians at crosswalks and only because they consider them to be a nuisance, much like potholes but bumpier and requiring hours of paperwork when hit. Clearly the weapons of choice on Moscow streets today are the black prestige-class Audis belonging to the filthy rich Russians who've stolen the country's assets since the collapse of the U.S.S.R. and pay virtually no taxes. Moreover, they seem determined to imitate the rocketing driving habits displayed by James Bond in the recent film Casino Royale, despite lacking his skills.

Each day I returned to my depressing apartment building battered, weak and dispirited. A voice in my head would echo the common Slavic saying, "Life is very hard, but fortunately short." I obeyed the voice and to cope with Slavic life after returning home each day (a 30-minute walk from the metro), I immediately retreated to my tiny but generously littered courtyard and rewarded myself with a chilled pint-size bottle of local beer and a small American "Gold & Mild" cigar (a ritual I never practice in the U.S.). An hour or so later I would soak my weak American feet as a reward for their prolonged and tortuous exposure to a non-car culture. This modest indulgence gave me the will to live and carry on my five to six hour, daily pounding of Moscow streets and metro riding the very next day.

In many respects, Moscow was a sentimental journey, old neighborhoods and apartment buildings, and one that left me with several burning existential questions: Will glamorous Moscow ever move beyond the few seedy portable public toilets outside central metro stations as long McDonald's graciously provides natives with free, clean toilets? Can a middle-aged American living in Moscow on a shoestring ever cope successfully with the trivial, daily challenges of living in a Slavic non-car culture without daily resorting to alcohol and tobacco? And finally, will I ever be able to wear thatched Slavic shoes again following my disturbing experience in Moscow?

There was no baking heat during my stay in Moscow, but I returned to a deathly heat wave sweeping across the U.S. Temperatures on the East Coast topped 100 degrees, with Washington Dulles airport registering a record-breaking 105 degrees and Newark, New Jersey, 108 degrees on July 22.

At the risk of sounding un-American, I returned home only to find that my body had grown unaccustomed to, and even uncomfortable in, America's ever present air-conditioning. Stepping into a large supermarket from 90-plus degree temperatures was like entering a massive refrigerator, a shocking experience. I often longed for a warm sweater. Even my American A/C bubble at home seemed alien. Apparently I've lived and worked in poorly-ventilated Russia and Ukraine far too long.

Clearly, the gods had awakened and now were having a bit of fun at my expense. It was a sad pleasure, indeed, to leave Moscow and return to my life in an A/C bubble, American car-culture and spacious, sanitary, free public restrooms.

The Cab Driver from Hell

> "One must choose in life between boredom and suffering."
>
> -Madame de Stael

I had not been in Moscow for several years for a simple reason. All of the essential ingredients to make an American like me suffer were readily available in its Slavic neighbor Ukraine, plus a 90 day visa-free regime, guaranteed non-service in the country's "service sector," motorists who view pedestrians as a nuisance and demand the right of way even on sidewalks, and stampeding hordes of Slavs on Kyiv's streets and in its metro and supermarkets.

Why, then, did I choose to leave Kyiv and return to Russia during June 2011, especially given its tough and costly visa procedure for foreigners? I wanted to end my gathering of cross-cultural observations about the differences between Slavs and Americans where it all began 20 years ago, Moscow. Toward this end, I booked a cheap apartment for my two-week stay in a working-class district on the outskirts of Moscow. All I really needed to know about this apartment was that it was located conveniently between two metro stops, and no more than a 30-minute drive from the airport on virtually traffic-free weekend mornings.

My flight from Kyiv, where I had spent the previous three months, arrived in Moscow as scheduled Sunday morning. I chose this arrival time carefully to avoid Moscow's notorious weekday traffic jams that could make even a Mother Teresa curse like a sailor. I sidestepped the small group of cab drivers huddled outside the airport's exit, each with a sign asking the same fare of $60 (in rubles), and approached a cab driver dropping off a young woman. We quickly agreed on a fare of less than $50 in rubles, and I gave him the address of my apartment and the name of the two metro stations closest to it. He replied, "No problem."

My driver was a short, swarthy man in his 50s who hadn't found time to shave in a few days. His car was a street-weary, late model Mazda which contrasted sharply with Moscow's large fleet of GPS-equipped "New Yellow" cabs.

It was a pleasant sunny morning in the mid-80s and our ride began with the kind of small talk and search for common ground one often encounters in any cab ride. I told the driver I had just spent three months in Kyiv and was in Moscow for a short stay. This aroused his interest.

He said he too was from Ukraine, its southeastern city of Luhansk, and had been working as a cab driver in Moscow for the past 15 years. It was clear from his swarthy appearance that he was not an ethnic Ukrainian or Russian and I asked him about his roots. He said he was originally from Azerbaijan and that his son and other family members were also living and working in Moscow.

A proud Azeri, my driver lectured me for several minutes on his country's rich history, ancient culture, and favorable climate and location on the Caspian Sea. A strategic crossroads between East and West, Azerbaijan was a Soviet republic until the collapse of the U.S.S.R. in late 1991. Hard economic times had forced his family to relocate to Ukraine and finally Russia.

After about 15 minutes on the road his phone rang and he politely excused himself and said he would be speaking to his son in Azeri. Meanwhile I examined the well-worn interior of the vehicle and the back seat's roll-down windows which both curiously lacked handles. We continued our pleasant small talk and I learned that his son also drove a cab and had just woken from working an all-night shift.

About 30 minutes into our ride, as expected, we passed one of the two metro stations that bordered my apartment building. We were in a green district of Moscow with many blocks of crumbling, Soviet-built five-story apartment buildings that were bordered by several superhighways.

My Azeri cab driver drove through several of the residential neighborhoods in this district and searched intuitively for my street. While surveying each neighborhood a one-way street eventually forced him on to a stretch of highway for 10 minutes before he was able to circle back to another green neighborhood. This went on for 30 minutes and each neighborhood had more than a half dozen speed bumps to discourage highway commuters from taking shortcuts. At first these speed bumps were a minor annoyance.

My apartment building was located somewhere in the roughly one square mile area we were circling with repeated, long excursions on to a major highway. By now my driver was showing visible signs of frustration and I was losing any hope that he would find my building. I began to examine his cab more closely and noticed that it was equipped with a dispatcher radio which showed no sign of life and with several maps on the passenger seat in front of me.

After about an hour and 15 minutes my driver made a bold move, stopped and asked a local man standing near one of our two designated metro stations for directions. He returned visibly confident and drove quickly to another green neighborhood, flew over more speed bumps and then returned to the superhighway—deja vu. We spent yet another 10 minutes on this highway before we returned to the same green neighborhood and this time flew even faster over the speed bumps, past blocks of crumbling apartments and back on to the same highway.

By this time we were no longer speaking. My driver was mumbling in Azeri and no longer looked in his rear-view mirror to make eye contact with me. An hour and a half had now passed and our prospects for finding my apartment building had not improved at all.

Meanwhile the temperature outside was in the high 80s with a scorching sun. Moreover, during the second hour of our ride, my driver went from initially smoking a cigarette every 15 minutes to virtually chain-smoking. However, as a courtesy he opened his window while smoking and ran the air-conditioning which was out of Freon and blew only hot air. He clearly failed to grasp (or care) that his exhaled cigarette smoke simply jetted back to me with greater force and, with the car's locked back windows, turned me into a heavy, passive smoker.

To add insult to injury the three cups of coffee I drank since leaving Kyiv early that morning and arriving in Moscow were now begging for release. Believing I would reach my apartment in about 30 minutes after arriving at the airport, I violated a major lesson I learned in Russia and Ukraine over many years: Always use any available toilet before setting out even on a short trip.

In the interest of finding my apartment building in my lifetime and keeping my bladder from exploding, I made a simple request. I beseeched my driver to stop at one of the gas stations we circled several times in the last hour, ask for directions and allow me to make an urgent pit stop. He responded by ignoring me entirely and flying over the next set of speed bumps as though he was driving an American rental car. In an effort to get a breath of air, and avoid losing consciousness, I reached for a window handle only to recall that they had been mysteriously removed. I began to feel like a hostage in this vehicle and for a moment considered paying the driver the full fare simply to release me, but then I remembered my heavy suitcase and even heavier bladder and continued to sit passively.

Soon it would be two hours since we set off on what should have been a 30-minute ride to my destination. I could see no rhyme or reason in the behavior of this unorthodox cab driver. Given the set cab fare, it made no sense for him to burn expensive fuel and waste precious time rather than pull into a gas station for directions.

After two hours on the road, my driver made another stop. He glanced at his crumpled maps scornfully for a few seconds before tossing them on the floor and leaving to ask for more directions. When he returned we sped off to a green neighborhood we had entered multiple times but this time we found my street tucked away behind one that we flew past at least a half dozen times.

My Azeri driver pulled in front of my building, grabbed the fare out of my hand, and jumped out of the car as though it were on fire. He quickly opened the trunk and stood there but did not bother to remove my suitcase. I waited for an apology that never came and instead received only a nod and a disdainful expression. We parted with our eyes barely meeting and without a word.

He turned a 30-minute cab ride into a tortuous, speed-bump marathon, and I'm the bad guy? This was clearly the worst cab ride I've ever taken in Russia or Ukraine in the past 20 years and in my life, in general.

I recounted this ordeal to my Russian friend Sasha and his reaction was typically Slavic. He said, "Your experience was bad but not boring, and now you have something you'll always remember." I was speechless.

I'm certain my cab driver from hell spent the rest of that day cursing me and, no doubt, will always remember me as the fare from hell.

You Know You Are in Russia or Ukraine If

1. If every meal begins with frying onions.

2. If a meal is not complete without mayonnaise.

3. If American-style ketchup is an exotic sauce for pasta instead of a simple condiment.

4. If salo is an aphrodisiac for Russian and Ukrainian men, in particular.

5. If in the mob of people waiting to get through international passport control after arriving in Moscow or Kyiv, there's a Slavic family with a half-dozen members who break up and go into six different lines in order to find the quickest one and then

regroup when they have.

6. If after you clear international customs and enter the greeting area, a mob of "sharks," gypsy cabdrivers, attacks you and follows you around the airport even after you've told them you don't need a cab.

7. If police and young women in spike heels mistake foreign men for ATM machines.

8. If the same women also mistake foreign men for transportation out of the country.

9. If traffic police would rather have motorists commit violations in order to extract bribes.

10. If people are more afraid of police than criminals.

11. If cleaning up after your dog in public is something only Americans do.

12. If trash bin fires in city centers started by burning cigarettes are a common sight that alarms no one.

13. If downtown Moscow and Kyiv smell like big ashtrays.

14. If A.M. Ale is a Slavic national breakfast drink.

15. If going fishing means that three or four men gather, barbecue kebab, and drink vodka and beer in a mosquito-infested forest near a river bank.

16. If drinking vodka with Slavic friends means mandatory toasts every five minutes and inevitable "time travel" (blacking out).

17. If children routinely go to the corner kiosk early in the morning to buy beer for their hungover fathers.

18. If you have to wait for your communal apartment building's plumber to sober up before he can come over and take care of a problem.

19. If a perfect stranger comes up to you on the street during daylight hours and asks if you'd like to share a bottle of vodka with him.

20. If cars are sold with blacked-out windows as a standard feature.

21. If staying in a single lane is an alien concept for motorists.

22. If drivers consider pedestrians a nuisance like potholes but bumpier.

23. If cab drivers and friends tell you that you don't need to use your seat belt, and doing so is viewed as an insult to their driving skills.

24. If pedestrians take a deep breath and cross their fingers before trying to negotiate a cross walk with a green light.

25. If a courteous Slavic driver is one who blows his horn to warn other drivers before routinely running red lights.

26. If personal space in public settings is an alien concept.

27. If fatalism becomes a glib excuse for Slavs not getting things done—"it was not meant to be."

28. If work is a place to drink endless cups of tea, recover from heavy drinking and a hectic life, and plan your after-work activities.

29. If after a week of official May holidays, Ukrainians and Russians return to work to talk about their plans for a summer vacation.

30. If Christmas and New Year come twice a year, new and old calendar celebrations.

31. If supermarkets look more like high security facilities and liquor stores than food markets.

32. If young supermarket workers stock shelves wearing high-heels, skin-tight jeans and visible thongs.

33. If shoppers' carts in your supermarket are filled mostly with alcohol, cakes, chocolates and fatty sausage.

34. If customers in your supermarket pull their shopping carts instead of pushing them.

35. If supermarket cashiers greet you with a "Why did you burn my house down?" expression.

36. If supermarket cashiers always ask you for correct change.

37. If middle-aged Slavic women curse at you for opening a window on a crowded, stuffy bus.

38. If the secure-code lock to your apartment building's entrance has been broken for three or more years.

39. If you regularly find cigarette butts in your apartment building's mailbox.

40. If your apartment building has endless remont (remodeling of apartments) going on.

41. If your apartment building's water is periodically shut off unannounced just after you've put shampoo in your hair.

42. If your apartment neighbors regularly slam their apartment door to let you know they are leaving or arriving.

43. If there are no working lights in the stairwell of your apartment building and you need to carry a lighter with a built-in flashlight to look for muggers in the dark and find your apartment door's keyholes.

44. If female college students go to class at 9 A.M. dressed like hookers.

45. If young Slavic women go to mass Sunday mornings dressed like hookers.

46. If the sinking sidewalks remind you of a war-torn country.

47. If city manhole covers seem to be Slavic collectors' items.

48. If using a public squat toilet requires special yoga training and one hand to hold the broken door in order to prevent theft of your valuables.

Finally,

49. If you can see used condoms in your apartment building's outdoor recycling bin.

Things I Miss about America

1. The Walmart store greeter.

2. Friendly, smiling strangers.

3. Casually (i.e. slovenly) dressed Americans.

4. Hearing the words excuse me, pardon me, I'm sorry.

5. My car, though I would never dream of driving any car in Moscow or Kyiv.

A Weak American in Russia & Ukraine

6. SUVs without blacked-out windows that come in colors other than black, are not maximum size, have smaller than V-8 engines, and don't have maniacs driving them.

7. Drivers who use turn signals.

8. Non-white, non-European people.

9. Temperatures in Fahrenheit.

10. People who don't constantly violate your personal space on city sidewalks and in stores.

11. The TV shows Cops and America's Most Wanted.

12. Seinfeld reruns and the TV show Curb Your Enthusiasm.

13. Central Heating.

14. Uncontaminated tap water.

15. Neighbors who don't scream while beating and stabbing one another.

16. Supermarket checkout clerks who don't greet you with a "Why did you burn my house down?" expression.

17. Supermarket checkout clerks who don't always ask you for exact change.

18. Government staff in public service offices that don't treat you like you just walked into their living room unannounced.

19. American high capacity, quick-wash machines versus washing clothes in Slavic bathtubs.

20. American clothes dryers versus Slavic balcony and bathroom drying.

21. Very orderly and efficient U.S. passport control lines and

service.

22. A largely non-smoking country.

23. American recycling versus widespread Slavic public littering.

24. Hot water for showers and dish washing.

25. Police who don't ask to check my documents simply to try to get a bribe.

26. Drivers who stop for pedestrians at crosswalks with lights.

27. Motorists who don't routinely drive on sidewalks.

28. IRS officers who don't fire rubber bullets at citizens as they do in Ukraine.

29. Supermarket shoppers who push their shopping carts rather than pull them through stores.

30. Not having to pay for supermarket items accidentally broken.

31. Public libraries with heating, A/C, water fountains, public toilets, and free Internet service.

32. Men who don't wear super-pointy, extended-tip dress shoes that could easily kill roaches in tight corners.

33. Men who don't walk around everywhere with "man purses" or, as they call them in Europe, "European shoulder bags."

34. Young women who don't wear skin-tight jeans, waist-length black-leather jackets, stiletto heels, heavy make-up and smoke Slim cigarettes.

35. The freedom not to clean my shoes and check my clothes for lint every time I leave home.

36. Not having my dinner plate continuously loaded with food by the hostess when I'm invited to a friend's home for dinner.

37. Not being told "wash your hands, the city is dirty" every time I visit someone's apartment.

38. Government offices that don't routinely extract bribes for public services.

39. Manhole covers.

And finally I miss:

40. Jerry Springer and Judge Judy TV shows.

Things I'll Miss If I Leave Ukraine & Russia

1. Freshly and generously littered apartment hallways and courtyards.

2. Sounds of drunken Slavic neighbors screaming, beating and stabbing one another.

3. Halls of apartment buildings where late night drinking and smoking is a noisy native tradition.

4. Contaminated tap water.

5. Men unabashedly spitting and blowing their nose contents on to city sidewalks.

6. The crumbling exterior and interior hallway walls of Soviet-built apartment buildings.

7. Swimming in contaminated rivers.

8. Sprinting across pedestrian crosswalks to avoid death daily.

9. The ability of Slavs to litter and jaywalk in front of local police.

10. The countless smokers in non-smoking areas of street underpasses and outside entrances to the metro, including police.

11. Massive gas explosions in winter in crumbling Soviet-built apartment buildings.

12. The chronic absence of hot water and ability to take a cold shower only on most days.

13. The search for hypodermic needles and medicines at Slavic drugstores to bring to hospitals for treatments.

14. Hot water service being turned off summers for up to a month in Kyiv and Moscow to allegedly clean city water pipes.

15. My Slavic friends' wives and mothers feeding me as a sign of respect and affection until I almost burst.

16. Police, especially in Russia, who stop you to check your documents and hold you in conversation until you offer them a bribe—they call it a fine.

17. Frequent, lengthy unannounced disruptions of apartment electric and water service because someone in my building suddenly decided to remodel a flat.

18. Urinals that are a whole in the ground in public restrooms.

19. Bloodless, mute cashiers in supermarkets.

20. Countless mandatory handshakes upon meeting Slavic acquaintances and upon departing.

21. Deep, ankle-twisting holes on city sidewalks and public parks.

22. Slavic punctuality (add at least one hour).

23. Constant violations of one's personal space by Slavs on city sidewalks.

24. Natives running into you bodily and with shopping carts at supermarkets.

25. Supermarket cashiers' constant demand for change from customers.

26. Chronic urinators in apartment building's hallways.

27. Chronic door-slammers in apartment buildings.

28. Clickety-clack sound of the stiletto heels of the working girls in my apartment building descending rapidly down the stairs as though the building is on fire.

29. Endless *remont* (i.e. remodeling) of flats, accompanied with vibrating walls, in any Slavic apartment building you may ever live in.

30. Heavy smokers who leave their apartment door ajar while smoking in an effort to keep their flat virtually smoke-free.

31. Enormous icicles and sheets of ice falling on pedestrians in winter from city buildings.

32. Enormous prestige SUVs and other cars parked on city sidewalks which make it almost impossible for pedestrians to pass.

33. Motorists who routinely drive on city sidewalks inches behind pedestrians and honk angrily for them to move out of their way.

34. Low-capacity washing machines that run for more than two hours.

35. Hanging wet wash to dry on a small balcony in winter.

36. Washing and wringing out jeans by hand in a bathtub.

37. Slavic police and young women who mistake foreign men for ATM machines.

38. Slavic females in stiletto heels who routinely walk on ice and race down subway escalators.

39. Obligatory toasts with vodka every five minutes when drinking with Slavic friends.

40. The mandatory requirement that hands be washed thoroughly after returning home from the "dirty city".

41. The mob of sharks (i.e. alleged gypsy-cab drivers) who descend on arriving foreigners at Moscow and Kyiv international airports and refuse to take no for an answer.

42. Slavic fear of deadly drafts (i.e. fresh air blowing directly on you from an open window in temperatures below 80 degrees Fahrenheit).

43. City bus drivers who crack their window open while smoking on no-smoking buses as a courtesy to their passengers.

44. Elderly, female attendants in public restrooms who routinely decide to mop the floor around my feet while I'm standing at a urinal.

45. Aggressive Slavs who step on the back of my shoes without saying, "Excuse me" while I'm walking on city streets.

46. Not wearing a seatbelt because if I do it will insult the Slavic driver—as they like to say, "It's not necessary here."

And finally:

47. Public toilets where you have to squat.

A Lecture for Foreign Men Seeking Slavic Brides

> *"There's no fool, like an old fool."*
> -a common saying

It's my great pleasure to be here before you today to share my experience and insights into this topic of great importance to each of you. It's been a long time since I've been asked to give a lecture. I was a college teacher for many years and I can tell you that the test of a real college professor is his ability to speak on any topic for an hour and say nothing.

I assure you I've passed that test more than once. However, today I plan to break from that hallowed tradition and during the next hour provide you with some seasoned observations based on my many years of living and working in Russia and Ukraine among the natives, and hopefully provide you with some practical and useful information and suggestions to aid you in finding a special Slavic bride.

It is indeed a pleasure for me to speak before this distinguished group. Yes, I said it, distinguished. You are, in my opinion, distinguished by your courage, boldness and adventurous nature. All of these are essential requirements for any man even considering the challenge you are planning to undertake.

Getting up and moving away from your computer screen, with its hundreds of profiles of attractive Slavic women, and your dreams of finding a Slavic partner and possibly even a soul mate, to even the first decisive steps, real action, is, indeed, very bold and adventurous. Two sayings come to mind. One is, "If you don't do anything, you'll never make any mistakes." Perhaps, but much that is special and precious in life may pass you by.

The other saying is one that I find more appealing, namely, "Opportunities are transient by nature, here today, gone tomorrow." You are here today because you see an important opportunity in your life. The crucial question is, will you go forward and try to seize this opportunity, or will you do nothing and perhaps regret it for the rest of your life? The decision obviously is a very difficult one and potentially one that will dramatically change your life. But if you do decide to go ahead you must do so very intelligently, cautiously, with a keen knowledge of many pitfalls ahead and, most importantly, with a strategy and game plan to avoid them and reach your goal. Make no mistake, it's a very tall order but it is achievable. There are success stories.

By now many of you, no doubt, are already thinking, "This guy has already passed the college professor's test that he opened his presentation with, the ability to speak at length and say very little." But I assure you I'm just getting warmed up. The real meat of my presentation begins now.

Today I'd like to do four things: First, to share with you a typical horror story that many foreign men have experienced after bringing a Slavic bride home to the U.S., Canada or the UK; secondly, to temper this horror story with a positive story of an American-Slavic marriage; third, to draw some useful lessons from these two cases and list some important red flags and green lights you will likely face in your quest; and lastly, to offer you my personal suggestions for achieving success in your search for that special Slavic partner.

Let's get started. *Case number one* is a typical horror story. Steve is a middle class American in his early 40s, raised and still living in Lansing, Michigan, and a home owner. He had several serious relationships in his life but they did not lead to marriage. Steve started to explore online dating and was quickly drawn to the many beauties he found on Slavic bride sites. He contacted several and eventually established a serious online relationship with Natasha, a 24-year-old Moscow beauty with limited English-speaking ability. After two-months of very romantic emails from Natasha, Steve boarded a plane for Russia.

In Moscow, Steve wined and dined Natasha and treated her to a shopping spree at exclusive boutiques. Steve was intoxicated with Natasha's model-like looks and after a few intimate nights together she convinced him that she loved him like no other man she had ever known. Fearful that this love of his life might slip away, Steve decided to marry Natasha immediately in Moscow.

When Natasha arrived in the U.S., she seemed to be a different person entirely. She resisted Steve's romantic advances, saying she was tired or didn't feel well. She made impossible, extravagant demands: designer clothes, expensive jewelry and a fancy car. In addition, she made hundreds of dollars' worth of monthly phone calls to Russia. To add insult to injury, she began to spend a great deal of time with Russians closer to her age that she met in Lansing. Soon arguments over money and lifestyle erupted nightly in their home.

Natasha, upon advice from her new Russian female friends, filed false domestic violence charges against Steve, had him jailed and even obtained a restraining order requiring him to move into an apartment. Escalating legal fees further drained Steve's limited savings. In the end, he was devastated and scarred for life by this experience.

At this point, I'd like to offer you a short break. This will allow some of you, who may have had a change of heart about seeking a Slavic bride after hearing Steve's story, to exit gracefully, go to the nearest bar, have a drink, and thank your lucky stars that you are not Steve.

Case number two is our positive story. Jack is a working-class American in his late 40s living in Syracuse, New York. He's divorced and has two adult children. He dreams of finding a woman who is more traditional and feminine than many American women with whom to share his life. Like Steve, he surfs the Internet and is attracted to Larissa, an alluring 29-year-old unmarried Ukrainian woman in Kyiv with limited English skills. After receiving dozens of romantic emails, Jack boards a plane and soon meets Larissa. They wine and dine and shop but he feels no chemistry between them.

Depressed and quickly running out of money, Jack thinks about returning home. Instead, he decides to contact a Ukrainian bride agency and spend a few more days in Ukraine. He reviews many profiles of potential brides and is attracted to Irina, a good-looking, never married 36-year-old nurse with limited English-speaking ability who lives in a small town outside of Kyiv.

Jack travels to Irina's town. They meet and she immediately introduces him to her large, extended family and prepares a special meal for him and all her relatives. Jack decides to spend an additional week in Ukraine getting to know Irina and her family. Most of their time together is spent sightseeing, strolling and talking. Jack and Irina find that they share many mutual interests and have a lot of chemistry. Before returning home, he tells her that he would like her to visit the U.S.

Irina soon receives a fiancé visa and stays with Jack for a month. He goes to great effort to show her his city and introduces her to his children and friends. Irina returns home but they remain in almost daily contact and in a year's time they marry.

Irina, with her provincial roots, is very satisfied with life in Syracuse, and after significant additional training becomes a certified nurse in America. Jack and Irina spend a great deal of time with Jack's friends, and he gladly takes Irina to meet and associate with Ukrainians at the local Ukrainian Orthodox church. Irina proudly contributes to the family's finances with her job as a nurse, which she loves, and Jack is grateful. The two are very happy together.

What useful lessons can we draw from these two cases? Steve was very naïve and no match for a cunning, young pro-dater like Natasha. He found the nectar of the young berry (Natasha was almost half his age) intoxicating and irresistible. Steve acted impulsively and did not take time to learn if Natasha's outer beauty was matched by any inner beauty. He did not investigate whether they had any common interests. He naively assumed that their "days of wine and roses" would continue in America and that Natasha would be a loving, doting wife.

Natasha had a very different game plan and didn't lose any time putting it into play once in America. She was a very experienced pro-dater and probably manipulated other foreign men in Moscow. They say women marry for one of two reasons, love or money. Natasha, and young women like her, demonstrate that there is a third reason, a green card and a ticket off the sinking ship and insane asylum many call Russia, or Ukraine.

Jack from Syracuse had a dramatically different experience than Steve. It seems he initially ran into a pro-dater in the big city of Kyiv, 29-year-old Larissa, who he treated to a shopping spree. However, he was not intoxicated by the nectar of the young berry, 20 years his junior. He soberly and quickly realized this was not a match. To his credit he regrouped while still in Ukraine and found a more fitting match: Irina, an attractive, slightly older (than Larissa) and very hardworking woman in a humanitarian profession, with provincial roots.

Jack took time to carefully explore Irina's interests, living conditions and to meet her family. After determining there was great personal compatibility, in addition to physical attraction, the two went through an extended courtship period before finally getting married. Once in America, both Jack and Irina made a concerted effort to embrace each other's culture and old and new friends.

The following red flags should be deal-breakers for you in a relationship with a potential Slavic bride: She insists on taking you only to expat hangouts, bars, cafes, clubs; she makes excuses why she can't show you where she lives and why you can't meet her family; she does not really know you at all but insists that she loves you like no man she has ever known, even though you are twice her age; there's no sign of her outer beauty being matched by inner beauty; she has little desire to talk about anything; she is overly emotional, easily angered, drinks and smokes; the two of you can't seem to hang out without spending lots of money; and she pressures you into marriage with sexual favors and promises of much more to come.

When you run into the following *green lights* you may have found a "Slavic keeper": She is well-rounded, informed and has much life experience; the two of you can joke and laugh together; you can hang out together without spending money; you both enjoy many common things and have mutual dreams; she has a strong desire to talk to you despite her limited English-language ability.

I also have a few personal suggestions in addition to these general red flags and green lights along the road to finding a Slavic bride.

Never forget the profound words of that legal eagle Judge Judy, "Beauty fades, stupid is forever." Don't get blinded by a person's outer beauty. That obviously has an expiration date. Take time to make sure that there is also inner beauty. Don't rush into any lasting relationship. If there is true love, it will withstand the test of time.

Don't put all of your eggs in one basket. Don't make the fatal mistake of becoming infatuated with one woman you don't really know, and blinded by what you think is love. Follow the example of sincere Slavic women: Be pragmatic, results-oriented, compare and really get to know a handful of different candidates and evaluate them using profile factors such as our red flags and green lights.

We men are very primitive. They say we fall in love with our eyes. In Russia and Ukraine, you will find a lot of eye candy on the streets: Slavic women are not prudish. They generally take great care of their appearance and dress to impress, often wearing tight and revealing clothing. A small amount of young eye candy is OK, but don't overdo it and don't bring any back to the U.S. You'll regret it, Steve did.

Next, I suggest you spend five minutes looking closely at yourself in a mirror and then imagine what your ideal Slavic bride will look like beside you. Will she pass the "out in daylight with you" test? Or will she look like your daughter, or even granddaughter? Similarly, will she pass the "evil eye from American (or Slavic) women your age" test when they see you together in public? Trust me, these are very important tests. You don't need a big generation gap with your partner, in addition to unavoidable cultural and language gaps in your relation.

When you do go to Ukraine or Russia and finally find the woman you consider to be a good match and future partner, proceed very cautiously. Take a few weeks to investigate the living conditions of your potential bride, insist on meeting her immediate and extended family (your future family), and spend at least several evenings with them. If they invite you to stay with them, and Slavs always will, do so even though the conditions will be cramped and very modest.

Live in her world as it will give you real expectations about whether she'll likely be happy in yours. If she doesn't want you to meet her family and insists that you stay at a hotel and meet only at expat hangouts, take this as a big red flag and move on. Remember this is the most important decision of your life. Too much is at stake.

I'd like to offer one more very important suggestion. In considering potential Slavic brides don't dismiss a woman with a small child. There are compelling reasons why this can be the best option. Any Slavic bride coming to the U.S. and torn away from her country and support group of family and close friends will be isolated, lonely and depressed for at least her first few months and probably much longer. It will also be difficult for her to adjust to America's alien culture and traditions and learn or improve her limited English-language ability. All of this will test and strain your relationship even under the best of circumstances.

A small child will provide a sturdy bridge between you and your Slavic bride. The child will be a source of boundless love and daily joy for the two of you. It will lift your partner out of her occasional dark moods with a child's natural excitement about American life. The two will learn American ways and the English language together, and will be very thankful for the secure, loving life you've provided them.

Slavic women are generally very tough and loyal. They have to be to survive in their jungle. If you do find a good match, she can be one of the best life partners you can imagine.

Because you've been such a good audience, I want to leave you with two sayings that Russians and Ukrainians are very fond of. One is, "Those who don't take risks will never drink champagne." The second one is, "We live but once, life is short." I think their meaning is obvious.

Finally, the most important advice I can give you. If you run into any problems at all while you are in Russia or Ukraine and see the police nearby, do what all Slavs do: Run as fast as possible in the opposite direction!

I wish all of you the very best of health, much happiness and success achieving all things most important to you.

Coming Home from the Insane Asylum

"*To discover America, you must leave America.*"
  -an expat axiom

"*The road too is a university.*"
  -age old wisdom

The word *durdom* is Russian and Ukrainian slang for insane asylum and, literally, means home for idiots. This word was embedded deeply in my mind by a grocery store clerk in Kyiv more than a decade ago during a conversation I had in a tiny corner-convenience store. I had spoken to the shopkeeper, a Ukrainian woman in her early 40s, on a few previous occasions, but this time it was different. Aware that I was an American she asked me, "What are you doing living in this durdom? Ukrainians are trying heroically to leave their impoverished, hopeless existence in this totally corrupt country, and you willingly came here to live?"

Clearly this was an occasion simply to listen to the woman's lament about a life of endless hardship. Nothing I could say at that moment would be appropriate, nor would it likely be heard, and so I listened. She recounted how she had to leave her husband and two school-age children in western Ukraine to come to the distant capital to work in this small grocery store because jobs back home were unavailable. In Kyiv, she worked 12-hour days, received a meager wage, and slept on a cot in the back room of this tiny grocery store of less than 30 square meters (the size of an average American living room). Once a month she would board a bus for a day-long journey home to spend a few days with her family.

Moreover, she is not alone. Thousands of her sisters from western Ukraine are also working in Kyiv at various exhausting jobs. She ended her story of personal hardship with these selfless words: "This is my life and I am fortunate I have this opportunity to help my family survive."

I left feeling badly for this woman but at the same time inspired by her perseverance and determination not to be defeated by a system which cares more about personal interests than the public interest. I was also haunted by the unanswered question, "What am I doing in this durdom?" I had no glib, convincing answer. I would need to think about this long and hard.

What have I discovered by leaving America and living and working in Russia and Ukraine?

America is much more than a cozy nest of creature comforts and surface politeness. It is also about genuine civility and a relaxed atmosphere that impresses even West European visitors. More importantly, America is about the rule of law, democratic elections, responsible government and an impartial court system. It's about not living in totally corrupt post-Soviet systems where bribes are the lubricant of life and insatiable greed is a pervasive characteristic of political life. And it's about not having to run in the opposite direction when you see the corrupt local police approaching.

Contrary to the belief of many Americans, the American Dream is still alive and well. Skeptics need only to live and work in a third world country like Russia or Ukraine to appreciate this. Its meaning has unquestionably changed with time and it's not just a dream of obtaining prestige cars, stately homes and high wages. It's about equal access to a level playing field where one has the opportunity to bring prosperity to oneself.

Significantly, it remains the sturdy national ideal which underpins our nation and continues to draw immigrants to our borders and shores. Sadly, there is no American Dream potential for Slavs in their countries. Their national wisdom dictates that success depends upon fate, not effort, and upon bribery, favoritism, and sex as currency in all of society's institutions.

I've also learned that living and working in Russia and Ukraine, with their unabashedly corrupt political and business elite, has made me an even more patriotic American, one proud of our political leaders when they aggressively advance the public interest. Interestingly, I've discovered that the old redneck slogan, "America, love it or leave it" is very shortsighted. In fact, by leaving America I've grown to love it more than I could ever imagine.

A great philosopher once said, "The unexamined life is not worth living." Semi-sober Slavs often echo their national wisdom, "The less you know, the sounder you sleep." Both views, no doubt, contain kernels of truth. I've examined my life so many times that I believe it's threadbare and dangerous to examine it any further.

What have I learned about my life over the past 20 years in the "university of the road?"

I've learned that true happiness is not possible without gratitude and that we all have many things to be grateful for. I, for example, thank my lucky stars that I had a tough and persistent Slavic mother who managed to get our family to America when other Ukrainian refugees in Germany were repatriated to Stalin's Soviet Union after World War II.

I've also grasped that happiness is both short-term and long-term. Material things, cars, jewelry, electronic gadgets, can make us very happy, but only for a short time. However, long-term happiness is about the things you can't put in a shopping cart. It's about family, friendships, helping the less fortunate and about realizing your dream in life, being all you can be.

My time in Russia and Ukraine, especially observing foreign men who visit, has made me keenly aware that men, indeed, are very primitive. They fall in "love" with their eyes and have very weak defenses against the Siren call and femme fatales waiting for them. And more often than not they mistake intoxication with a younger woman for love; they see what they want to see. But, most importantly, they fail to understand that true love is impossible without respect and this requires knowing a person well. Respect for a partner is what sustains a relationship when the honeymoon phase is over, when the children arrive, and when the relationship increasingly takes the form of genuine, caring attachment to one another.

With each passing year I've also become more aware that I have a golden parachute that separates me from Slavs, gives me a privileged status, and allows me to bail out of the region anytime, my U.S. passport. During times of my darkest despair in Russia and Ukraine, and there have been many, I always have my American passport waiting at home to cheer me up.

Many years ago the wonder of my U.S. passport was impressed upon me in Moscow by a young Russian woman, a staff member at an academic institute where I was conducting research. I had been coming to this institute for several summers and got to know the staff quite well. One day during a coffee break this young woman asked if she could see my passport. I found the request very odd but could think of no good reason to deny it.

After I handed it to her, she spent more time studying my passport's pages than they do typically at Russia's passport control upon arrival. She then cradled it to her chest like a little baby, smiled and gave it a long hug. For a brief moment I thought she might not give it back, she held it so lovingly. A picture is worth a thousand words, as they say. I still occasionally recall that event whenever I look at my American passport.

If anyone in America should ask me where I plan to vacation this year, I will answer unhesitatingly and categorically, "In America." And when they ask me where exactly, I'll say, "Anywhere in America." For me the entire country is vacationland, a big Disney World, where creature comforts and a relaxed atmosphere abound, and where a friendly smile awaits you even from a perfect stranger.

But I won't be away from my durdom in Ukraine and Russia for more than a few months. I simply can't. Despite the many miseries of daily life there, especially for a weak American, I still find it endlessly challenging and fascinating. "A boring life is not worth living," as Georgians like to say.

Moscow and Kyiv are cities I "love to hate," a feeling many New York City natives understand well. And so I'll continue to travel between these two worlds, one of enforced and accepted order and the other of accepted chaos, despite the constant need to adjust culturally to very stark differences. But I'll always have my golden parachute with me to brighten even my darkest day there.

A Russian friend who spent a few years studying in the U.S. once told me, after an evening of soulful conversation peppered with many shots of vodka, "Life in Russia and Ukraine is repugnant but never boring." His message was clear: Life in America in his experience was boring and often empty. His words struck home and, after dozens of cross-Atlantic flights over many years, made me realize that somewhere between repugnant and boring is where I feel most at home. I guess you could say I'm caught between two cultures.

"What no wife can ever understand is that a writer is working when he's staring out of the window."
-Burton Roscoe

About the Author

Walter Parchomenko, a distinguished college professor and civil servant in Washington, D.C. for more than 25 years, was born in a German refugee camp. He is the son of Ukrainian peasants, World War II refugees, deported from their war-torn Ukrainian village to forced labor in Germany. After a grueling crossing of the Atlantic in the storage of an ocean liner packed with Slavic refugees, he entered the U.S. (just 12 months old at the time) through Ellis Island's newly reopened reception center. Parchomenko grew up in snowy Rochester, New York and eventually fled his Slavic mother's strict regime, KGB-like Gulag to simultaneously work and attend graduate school in Washington. He directed a U.S. government, graduate school program in Russian and Eurasian Studies in Washington for 16 years. Over the past 20 years, he has spent a great deal of time living and working among the natives in Russia and Ukraine. Parchomenko's writings have appeared in the *New York Times, Wall Street Journal, Christian Science Monitor* and numerous other publications. A Georgetown University Ph.D., and Fulbright Scholar, he currently divides his time between Kyiv, Ukraine, and Washington, D.C. Readers' comments are welcome and may be sent to *wparkhom@verizon.net*.

Made in the USA
Charleston, SC
16 November 2013